THANK you!
Daniel

To Honk's Buddy, enjoy yourself,
And

First published in 2011 by Buckingham Book Publishing Ltd
Network House, 28 Ballmoor, Celtic Court, Buckingham MK18 1RQ, UK
www.chefmagazine.co.uk
© Buckingham Book Publishing Ltd

ISBN No: 978-1-908202-08-6

Printed in Singapore by Craft Print International Ltd.

Publisher: Peter Marshall
Managing Editor: Shirley Marshall
Editors: Sue Christelow, Katy Morris
Editorial Contributor: John Radford
Design Director: Philip Donnelly
Graphic Designer: Duncan Boddy
Photographers: Myburgh du Plessis, Ben Pollard
Gravetye Manor: Photography supplied

Recipe ingredients and finishing touches may vary slightly from picture shown.

Here we are only two years since the publication of the first-ever Relais & Châteaux cookbook, *A Taste of Relais & Châteaux*, bringing you a second edition of what proved to be a groundbreaker.

This new edition includes recipes from all the current UK and Ireland Relais & Châteaux chefs along with interesting information about their regions, the properties and the chefs themselves. All of these wonderful dishes created by the chefs are complemented once again by the stunning photography from Myburgh du Plessis.

There have been some changes along the way and we are delighted to welcome all the new properties to the family. Congratulations to Martin Burge of Whatley Manor who has become a Grand Chef since the publication of the first edition.

We hope you will enjoy looking through the pages and will be inspired to try making some of the recipes at home.

Good luck and enjoy!

Michel Roux

Created with the finest
ingredients available

RELAIS &
CHATEAUX®

A gourmet's paradise

RELAIS &
CHATEAUX®

ALL-CLAD ELEVATES TALENT

AS ALL-CLAD CELEBRATES ITS 40TH ANNIVERSARY THIS YEAR WE LOOK BACK AT ITS ORIGINS, ITS COMMITMENT TO TODAY'S CHEFS AND THE OUTSTANDING COOKWARE COLLECTIONS.

Born of the US steel age in 1967, Clad Metals found its roots in a small, metallurgical company that specialised in formulating bonded metals for a variety of industries. Company founder, John Ulam, realised the combination of dissimilar metals created composites that yielded superior results. He was awarded more than 50 US patents, specifically related to bonded metals. After years of perfecting his bonding process, Ulam established All-Clad Metalcrafters in 1971, and began producing professional-quality bonded cookware with extraordinary properties and exemplary cooking performance for working chefs and gourmet home cooks. Today, this revolutionary cookware is still made in Canonsburg, Pennsylvania, the same way it was four decades ago.

All-Clad is the only bonded cookware manufacturer to use American craftsmen and American-made metals to produce a complete line of superior bonded cookware. The secret to All-Clad's success is attention to detail: the ideal ratio of metal thicknesses, painstaking selection of the finest materials, stylish design, meticulous hand-finishing and rigorous inspection. The confidence and commitment in the product is unparalleled as All-Clad pans are warranted to last a lifetime, and stamped with the guarantee of excellence.

For more information about All-Clad visit www.All-Clad.co.uk

IN PARTNERSHIP WITH RELAIS & CHATEAUX

ALL-CLAD, THE COOKWARE CHOICE OF CHEFS WORLDWIDE, HAS PARTNERED WITH RELAIS & CHATEAUX TO PRODUCE EXCEPTIONAL DISHES THAT OFFER CUSTOMERS A UNIQUE CULINARY EXPERIENCE AT THEIR PRESTIGIOUS PROPERTIES.

All-Clad is proud to be associated with the 'Rising Chef Trophy' which reveals young talented chefs whose creativity, imagination and generous commitment will assure them to become the next generation of worldwide top chefs. Daniel Galmiche of The Vineyard at Stockcross, Rising Chef for 2011, reveals what this honour means for him.

"I think it is a reward that shows we have been recognised for the hard work, not only by me but all of my team. It also shows consistency and quality of what we are doing, I also think it fits the ethos of R&C as part of Club 5C." Club 5C is a privilege club for loyal guests giving them special advantages. Daniel describes his food as "... modern, classic with a Mediterranean touch. We work only with seasonal and British products; light colourful cooking." His All-Clad pans are an essential part of his cooking "... because they are the best! The heat distribution is very consistent across the pan, it is a very important tool for the chef. I couldn't cook without them! Because the heat distribution is consistent it allows the food to have the right texture and flavour. It makes sure the dish I am doing is perfect ...!"

All-Clad is passionate about passing on knowledge; for example, Grand Chef Martin Burge uses All-Clad for his masterclasses and is able to demonstrate the superiority of this cookware first-hand.

THE COLLECTIONS

STAINLESS® STEEL COLLECTION
The original bonded cookware

The Stainless Steel collection is All-Clad's best-selling cookware and the choice of professional and discriminating cooks across the world. This collection features several precisely formulated layers of unique stainless steel, pure aluminium and aluminium alloys, its bonded construction extends to the base and sides of each pan, ensuring unparalleled heat transfer with no hot spots. The whole exterior layer is magnetic stainless steel, making it the perfect partner for all induction cooking.

STAINLESS WITH D5 TECHNOLOGY COLLECTION™
The next generation of induction optimised stainless steel bonded cookware

This collection maintains the classic style of the original Stainless Steel collection, while introducing advanced performance and ergonomic enhancements. The patented design, made of five layers of different materials, ensures precision surface contact to optimise performance on the newest-technology induction cooker tops. The alternating layers of higher and lower conductive metals promote the lateral flow of cooking energy and eliminate hot spots. The patented stainless steel core significantly improves stability to prevent warping. This collection incorporates the stringent requirements of the world's most demanding professional chefs to produce consistently outstanding results.

COPPER-CORE® COLLECTION
The first induction copper cookware

This innovative copper cookware is perfectly suitable for induction cooking. Copper-Core® is the ultimate professional bonded cookware which has unparalleled conductivity and delivers an incredible cooking performance. At the heart of each piece is a pure, precisely milled, thick Copper-Core®, bonded between layers of selected alloys and metals, encased in durable stainless steel, making this range the perfect balance between the conductivity of copper and the ease of use of stainless steel. Each Copper-Core® pan features a unique incised band, designed to reveal the thick pure copper at its heart, and make this a stunning as well as a practical addition to the kitchen.

CONTENTS

■ RELAIS & CHATEAUX PROPERTIES   ■ GRANDS CHEFS RELAIS & CHATEAUX

LOCATIONS

■ RELAIS & CHATEAUX PROPERTIES   ■ GRANDS CHEFS RELAIS & CHATEAUX

1. LONDON

The Connaught
Le Gavroche

2. JERSEY

Longueville Manor

3. BERKSHIRE

The Waterside Inn
The Fat Duck
The Vineyard at Stockcross

4. DEVON

Gidleigh Park

5. DORSET

Summer Lodge Country House & Spa

6. HAMPSHIRE

Chewton Glen Hotel & Spa
Lime Wood Hotel & Restaurant

7. SUSSEX

Amberley Castle
Gravetye Manor

8. OXFORDSHIRE

Le Manoir aux Quat'Saisons

9. GLOUCESTERSHIRE

Lower Slaughter Manor

10. WILTSHIRE

Whatley Manor
Lucknam Park

11. SOMERSET

The Bath Priory Hotel
The Royal Crescent Hotel

12. WORCESTERSHIRE

Buckland Manor

13. WARWICKSHIRE

Mallory Court

14. RUTLAND

Hambleton Hall

15. CUMBRIA

Farlam Hall
Gilpin Lodge Country House
Sharrow Bay Country House

16. SCOTLAND

Airds Hotel
Restaurant Andrew Fairlie
Glenapp Castle
Greywalls Hotel & Chez Roux Restaurant
Inverlochy Castle
Isle of Eriska Hotel, Spa & Island
Kinloch House

17. WALES

Ynyshir Hall

18. IRELAND

Ballyfin
Cliff House Hotel
Marlfield House
Sheen Falls Lodge

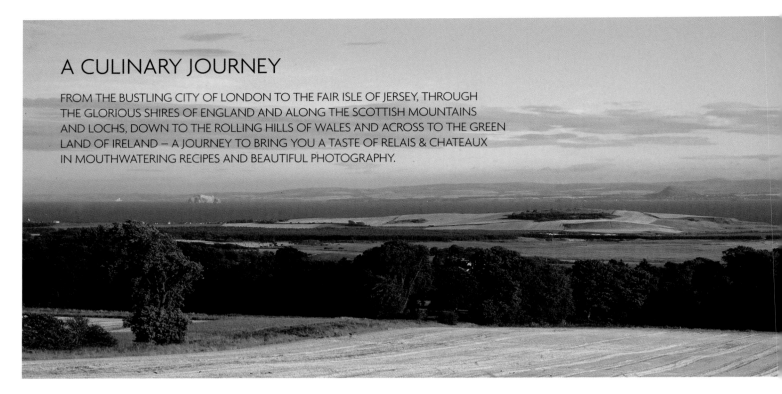

A CULINARY JOURNEY

FROM THE BUSTLING CITY OF LONDON TO THE FAIR ISLE OF JERSEY, THROUGH
THE GLORIOUS SHIRES OF ENGLAND AND ALONG THE SCOTTISH MOUNTAINS
AND LOCHS, DOWN TO THE ROLLING HILLS OF WALES AND ACROSS TO THE GREEN
LAND OF IRELAND – A JOURNEY TO BRING YOU A TASTE OF RELAIS & CHATEAUX
IN MOUTHWATERING RECIPES AND BEAUTIFUL PHOTOGRAPHY.

This culinary journey through the United Kingdom and Ireland begins in the capital city of England, London, a true gastronomic delight with its world-famous chefs and choice of eateries, whether they are offering simple fare or Michelin-starred cooking.

The journey finishes in the Emerald Isle, a land of beauty where the food is seasonal and true to its Irish roots. All 36 Relais & Châteaux properties in England, Wales, Scotland and Ireland have been visited to photograph their recipes for this cookbook, to capture these top chefs in their professional environments and to convey the beauty of the places and properties that are a part of the unique universe that is Relais & Châteaux. Join us as we recap this culinary journey so that you too can experience the Relais & Châteaux 'Route du Bonheur' of cooking.

In London both Relais & Châteaux properties are residence to Grands Chefs; this cookbook includes recipes from seven Grands Chefs in all, a quarter of all the chefs featured, masters of their craft who elevate fine dining to an art and turn each dish into a jewel. The Connaught is the latest addition to the UK Relais & Châteaux family and along with Le Gavroche gives you the opportunity to try French-inspired and classical cooking yet with modern influences.

On to Jersey, gem of the Channel Islands, for more French influence complemented by the freshest of seafood from the surrounding waters, the rich cream and butter from its famous cows and the Jersey Royal potatoes. Here the chef's involvement with the local farming and fishing communities ensures that he has a true understanding of where all of his ingredients have originated and this in turn

translates to the finest quality contemporary dishes on the plate.

Back to England and into Berkshire with two more Grands Chefs, both in Bray and both of whom hold three Michelin-stars. In one restaurant there is resolutely creative French cuisine and in the other unconventional dishes from the world's leading experimenter, despite their different styles each is outstandingly successful. Recipes from these chefs have the wow factor but for entirely different reasons! Over at Newbury more French influence is apparent with an emphasis on sourcing as much British produce as possible and sustainability to the fore – here you will find a stunning apple tarte tatin recipe 'deconstructed' for a modern approach.

The next port of call is Devon, where the chef serves distinctive and outstanding modern European cuisine utilising the finest local and regional produce. Try the wild salmon from the river Dart and seasonal pheasant partnered with pumpkin – an exquisite dish for the autumn and winter.

Nearby in Dorset the chef is also able to use a wide variety of locally sourced, fresh produce to create dishes which allow the flavours to speak for themselves. Whether it is crab from Portland or Exmoor venison this is "a gourmet's paradise".

In the beautiful area of the New Forest in Hampshire nestle two properties, fortunate to have an abundance of game on their doorstep from the forest as well as a wealth of seasonal berries. Here is a venison dish not paired with the usual chocolate but in this case with coffee for a modern touch.

Down in Sussex two more properties excel at modern British cuisine using locally sourced,

often organic, produce – rabbit, beetroot, native lobster, English red mullet, blackberries from the garden all appear here alongside a new version of banoffee pie – did you know it was invented in West Sussex?

Up to central England and Oxfordshire where one of the world's most famous chefs creates innovative food which is modern French but that draws its character from seasonal ingredients, often gathered from the magnificent organic vegetable garden in this stunning property's grounds.

Across to adjacent Gloucestershire where the chef has recently arrived from New York and brings with him many influences and exciting ideas for the delight of the Relais & Châteaux visitor.

Into Wiltshire and to the domain of two great chefs, one of whom is a newly created Grand Chef. Both look to the land nearby for seasonal vegetables and here you have a choice of two dishes using local venison.

Somerset in the south-west yields the delights of rabbit, Brixham turbot and fallow deer using only the best produce and suppliers available. Here one chef creates "food that is innovative without being gimmicky" and the other lets his Scottish roots show in his choice of dessert!

Entering next into the heart of England to find Cotswold lamb and wood pigeon on the menu in Worcestershire and a quail dish with celeriac and apple in Warwickshire. Rutland may be England's smallest county but fine dining is still to be found there with seasonal game and the use of herbs, salads and berries from the hotel's own gardens.

Somewhat further north the journey continues to Cumbria where three delightful

Hélène Darroze   Michel Roux Jr   Alain Roux   Martin Burge

Michael Caines   Raymond Blanc   Heston Blumenthal

properties hold court. In this county of plenty when it comes to food, it appears traditions have evolved from the land itself: farm-raised lambs for meat dishes, pigs for sausage and ham, and cattle for dairy products. The moors and mountains provide wild game such as duck and deer and the seas allow for herring, char, shrimp, trout and salmon. Indeed you will find recipes from this area for sea bass and organic sea trout as well as a wonderful cheeseboard 'soufflé style' using the local Stichelton cheese.

Crossing the border to Bonnie Scotland which has no less than seven properties offering the best of the Scottish larder, from its renowned beef, venison, lamb and game to salmon, trout and oysters. Here you can try dishes using Scottish crab, wild mushrooms foraged from the land and raspberries bursting with flavour.

Wales, land of song and food of note – this Relais & Châteaux chef is an avid forager of the local countryside – you will often find him in the hills collecting mushrooms and wild garlic or at the salt marshes gathering samphire.

And finally across the waters to the four properties in Ireland, where the chefs work with produce grown on Irish land, some in their own grounds and much that is fished from the Irish seas. Organic carrots, Irish farmhouse cheese, local lobster and seasonal game are all used to great effect, with many dishes having a traditional Irish background. For the ultimate indulgence why not finish the journey with a dessert at the heart of which is that old favourite, Irish coffee, but with a modern twist!

More than 100 recipes from 36 chefs to give you a taste of Relais & Châteaux United Kingdom and Ireland – may you have many pleasurable hours of cooking.

THE GRANDS CHEFS RELAIS & CHATEAUX

GRANDS CHEFS ARE ELECTED BY THE RELAIS & CHATEAUX BOARD OF DIRECTORS NOT ONLY FOR THEIR EXCEPTIONAL CUISINE AND SERVICE, BUT ALSO FOR THE QUALITY OF THE WELCOME AND THE HUMAN WARMTH AND PRESENCE THAT CAN BE FOUND IN ALL RELAIS & CHATEAUX PROPERTIES.

These chefs are the avant-garde of the finest hotel association in the world. One hundred and sixty chefs on five continents, monopolising the awards, acting as the foodie stars in their respective countries, but always the first to report for work in their own kitchen.

They like both tradition and modernity, and insist on the finest produce from around the world. They are to be found in cities like London, New York, Geneva, Sydney, Tokyo, Paris and Cape Town, but also in the country, such as in Great Milton or Chagford, wherever an ivy-covered inn, a country house in its park, or a seaside or riverbank resort conjure up peace and quiet.

They are legendary chefs. They are all shining examples to be emulated by generations of future chefs. In the UK we are fortunate indeed to have seven Grands Chefs: Alain Roux of The Waterside Inn, Michel Roux Jr of Le Gavroche, Heston Blumenthal of The Fat Duck, Michael Caines of Gidleigh Park, Raymond Blanc of Le Manoir aux Quat'Saisons, Martin Burge of Whatley Manor and Hélène Darroze of The Connaught.

THE ESSENCE OF ENGLAND

ENGLISH WINE HAS COME INTO ITS OWN AFTER 60 YEARS OF TOIL IN THE VINEYARDS, FIRST BY A FEW DIEHARD ENTHUSIASTS, THEN BY A GROWING NUMBER OF DIVERSIFYING FARMERS, AND NOW BY FULLY COMMERCIAL VINEYARDS WITH STATE-OF-THE-ART WINERIES.

It all started in the 1950s: English wine had more or less died out since the time of the mediæval monks, until a retired army officer called Sir Guy Salisbury-Jones planted an acre of Seyval Blanc at his home in Hambledon, Hampshire, making his first vintage in 1954. In the 1960s and 1970s it was essentially a hobby indulged in by people with the money and land for planting, and the patience to endure around seven terrible vintages per decade. For a brief period Renishaw Hall in north Derbyshire was the world's most northerly commercial vineyard, with two acres planted in a walled paddock, by the late Sir Reresby Sitwell. Famously he once told a guest: "I'll tell you how to enjoy my wine: first, you have a double whisky, then you have a glass of my wine, and then you have another double whisky." So, English wine was not to be taken too seriously at that time.

Gradually, however, growing grapes evolved from being a rural hobby into something more commercially viable. In the early 1980s Chilford Hall, then a mixed farm in Cambridgeshire (now a conference centre) had 22 acres of vines, and the

winemaker, Simon Alper, said that, even given the punitive bureaucracy and tax regimes associated with wine production, the vineyard earned a better profit per acre than his arable land. The 1980s, indeed, saw a big upsurge in investment, most particularly in 1984 when Adrian White, the founder of Biwater, bought the Denbies

estate in Dorking, Surrey and planted 250 acres of vines between 1986 and 1989. This was no rich man's plaything but a hard-headed business investment, and an act of faith in the future of English wine. It was then and is now, at 265 acres, England's largest vineyard.

There were similar, if smaller, developments in south Wales, the west country, Devon and Cornwall and especially the south east: Kent, Sussex and Hampshire, particularly along the south downs, where the south-facing chalk grassland was perfect for planting vines. Sparks began to fly in the late 1980s and early 1990s, when an American couple, Stuart and Sandy Moss bought Nyetimber Manor in West Sussex, and planted 50 acres, not of the grape varieties usual in England at that time, but Pinot Noir, Chardonnay and Meunier – the grapes used to make Champagne. Being American, they had no hang-ups about trying to compete with the Champenois and, indeed, imported Champagne technology and consultants to help them set up the business. To cut a long story short, the wine won the title of 'World's Best Sparkling Wine'

at the World Sparkling Wine Championships in Verona in 2010. Meanwhile, in East Sussex, Mike Roberts and his wife Chris planted 30 acres, again with Champagne varieties and Champagne consultancy. They now have contract growers supplying them as well, and their 2007 Grosvenor Blanc de Blancs won the sparkling wine trophy at the 2011 Decanter World Wine Awards. Growing grapes under contract has also given a boost to farmers in the area who have been feeling the pinch for many years. As in France, Spain and other European countries, this could turn out to be a real benefit for the future of farming. Meanwhile, the south downs is currently abuzz with new plantings – more than 500 acres are currently in progress – and it probably won't be long before English sparkling wine will be competing with the biggest and the best in world markets. Other sparkling wines to seek out include Chapel Down in Kent, Hush Heath in Berkshire, Camel Valley in Cornwall, Gusborne in Kent and Davenport in East Sussex.

Still wines are also winning medals: at the 2011 Decanter magazine awards more than 40 wines received an award. Names to look for include Ancre Hill in Monmouthshire, Astley in Worcestershire, Bolney in Sussex, Three Choirs in Gloucestershire, Brightwell in Oxfordshire, Furleigh in Dorset, Oatley in Somerset and Sharpham in Devon. They grow a wide range of grapes, but the one which seems to win most medals is the Bacchus, a cross between Sylvaner and Riesling, which ripens well in our climate and has a lovely, zesty, 'twangy' fruit and a crisp, fresh acidity. There are now more than 400 commercial vineyards in England, producing some two million bottles a year.

Climate change may have played a part in making England such a suitable place to grow grapes, but better vine clones and vineyard techniques have also helped, and for sparkling wines the *dosage* for the final fermentation in the bottle can turn a slightly under-ripe base-wine into a medal winner. Indeed, that's why Champagne was made to sparkle in the first place: in the 1690s it was too cold in that area to ripen grapes fully for still wines. It's rather appropriate that English sparkling wine is making itself known in the world: the technique for making wine sparkle was developed by an English doctor, Christopher Merret in 1662, 30 years before Dom Pérignon. There have been reports of cars with number-plates from Reims and Épernay having been seen scouring the chalk downs of southern England for possible sites for new plantings, so you know when you're getting something right.

For a complete list of medal-winning English and Welsh wines in the 2011 Decanter Awards, go to www.decanter.com/dwwa/2011 and search by location (i.e. UK). For the full range of English and Welsh vineyards and to find which is nearest to you, have a look at www.englishwineproducers.com – they have an interactive map and, for the record, Mount Pleasant Vineyard in Lancashire is now the most northerly in England, although there are non-commercial (so far!) vineyards in Scotland.

London

> *The most visited international city in the world. This unique capital city is known for its world-famous attractions – from Big Ben to Buckingham Palace, there are hundreds of sights on offer which top every tourist's must-see list.*

Whether visiting for retail therapy, a slice of history or culture, a taste of gourmet London, an undiscovered hidden gem or a one-of-a-kind entertainment or sporting event, there really is something for everyone. Only in London can you be inspired by more national museums and galleries than in any other capital city. Take in the bright lights of the theatre in London's West End – offering more theatrical performances than anywhere else in the world. Home to four World Heritage sites of Kew Gardens, Maritime Greenwich, The Tower of London and the Palace of Westminster, London effortlessly attracts people of all ages and interests. While you're there eat like a typical Englishman, with dishes such as sausage and mash, shepherd's pie and the great British Sunday roast. You could even visit the world-famous Billingsgate market where you will find the largest selection of fish in the UK.

Part of the fourth generation of a family of innkeepers, Hélène was born in a kitchen and grew up next to her grandfather's stove. After leaving school at 18, she studied at one of the big business schools. Hélène then joined Alain Ducasse at the Louis XV in Monaco to work in the office. She stayed there for three years, until Alain persuaded her to get in front of a cooker. He taught her always to look for quality when choosing ingredients, but also to be constantly rigorous and to combine it with honest cooking with real, authentic flavour.

Hélène then joined her father at his Relais & Châteaux in Villeneuve-de-Marsan, which gave her the chance to express what she felt instinctively. Five years later, Hélène opened her own restaurant in Paris. Hélène Darroze at The Connaught opened in 2008. Hélène cooks with ingredients from the south-west of France where she was born, which appeals to how she has always lived and to her emotions.

The Connaught

{ *Situated in Mayfair village, this London legend is one of the most distinguished addresses in the world. Following a recent restoration the hotel elegantly blends the old and new.*

With 120 rooms and suites, each served by the Connaught butlers, its two bars, Aman Spa, pool and a choice of restaurants, you are guaranteed a delightful stay. At the prestigious Hélène Darroze at the Connaught restaurant you are invited to discover a little piece of France through the gastronomic creations of Grand Chef Hélène Darroze.

Serves 4
Preparation time: 1½ hours
Cooking time: 45 minutes

Special equipment:
N/A

Planning ahead:
N/A

INGREDIENTS

scallop gnocchi:

150g	scallops, cleaned, meat only, beards and roe reserved for the cauliflower emulsion
5g	cornflour
1g	piment d'Espelette
1g	salt

cauliflower emulsion:

	beards and roe from the scallops
1	onion
2	Granny Smith apples, chopped
50g	parsley stalks, chopped
50g	celery, chopped
2	cloves garlic, chopped
½	stalk lemongrass, chopped
1 litre	water
1	cauliflower, broken into 2cm florets
	salt, to taste
1 litre	cooking cream
100g	butter
50ml	white wine

apple syrup:

250ml	apple juice (fresh) from about 6 apples

garnish:

4	queen/bay scallops in their shells
4	venus clams
100g	cucumber slices and balls
4	Fine de Claire oysters
12g	good quality caviar such as Sologne
100g	cauliflower florets
100g	Granny Smith apples, sliced into wedges
10g	fresh shoots eg. broccoli cress

CAVIAR, FINE DE CLAIRE OYSTER & BAY SCALLOPS WITH APPLE & CAULIFLOWER EMULSION
BY HELENE DARROZE

The combination caviar/oyster/cauliflower works so well that it is always with a deep pleasure I cook this recipe. This is a timeless dish, simple but elegant.

METHOD

scallop gnocchi:

Blend the scallop meat in a food processor for about 30 seconds to a purée. Add the cornflour and seasoning and mix for a further 30 seconds. Put into a piping bag and rest in a refrigerator for 1 hour. Prepare a pan of boiling seasoned water. Cut a hole in the piping bag and squeeze the 'gnocchi' mixture gently over the boiling water – it will come out like a sausage shape which you cut at 2cm intervals using kitchen scissors.

cauliflower emulsion:

Wash the beards and roe thoroughly, put in a saucepan with the roughly chopped onion, apple, parsley, celery, garlic and lemongrass. Cover with the water and wine then bring to the boil to make a light fragrant stock. Allow this stock to simmer for around 30 minutes then pass through a sieve. Meanwhile chop the cauliflower fairly finely. Season the stock with some salt and bring it to the boil. Cook the cauliflower in this for a few minutes until tender. Separately reduce the cream by half. Remove the cauliflower from the stock and purée the cauliflower and cream together. Finally mount with butter by whisking in cold small pieces.

apple syrup:

Pass the juice through a fine sieve. Place in a saucepan and reduce until a syrup consistency is achieved.

to serve:

First pan fry the scallops for a few seconds until only just cooked. Steam open the clams in a small pan with just a little water to help them open. Season the garnishes and place first the cucumber slices on a long plate. Drizzle some apple syrup over it with a spoon. Warm the gnocchi in some of the emulsion, adding the oysters at the very last second so that that they are only warm. Place the gnocchi on top of the cucumber and adorn each with caviar. Garnish with the oyster, add some cauliflower florets, sliced apple wedges, cucumber balls, one scallop and one clam. Finsh with the fresh shoots. Serve 100ml of the cauliflower emulsion separately and spoon some over the plate just before eating.

MILK-FED LAMB FROM THE PYRENEES, ROASTED SADDLE 'EN ROGNONNADE', GRILLED CHULETILLAS & 'CAILETTE' OF 'PIEDS DE PAQUET', FONDANT JAPANESE AUBERGINE, ROASTING JUS INFUSED WITH CARDAMOM & CONFIT CITRUS FROM MENTON

BY HELENE DARROZE

This is a very typical dish from the Basque country. I grew up with it: during the milk-fed lamb season it was in everybody's kitchen, my parents, my grand-parents, relatives and friends ...

Serves 4
Preparation time: 1 hour
Cooking time: 5 hours for the caillette,
                      20 minutes for the remainder

Special equipment:
N/A

Planning ahead:
The caillette needs to be started 1 day in advance.

INGREDIENTS

lamb saddle and chuletillas:

1	whole best end and saddle of milk-fed lamb (reserve the bones for the jus)
100g	bulgur (cracked) wheat
20g	parsley, finely chopped
salt and piment d'Espelette	

caillette:

2	pig's trotters
1	lamb shank
1	head garlic
100ml	Madeira
1 litre	chicken stock
1	bouquet garni
2	shallots, chopped
100g	back bacon, chopped
50g	chopped Andouille sausage
salt and piment d'Espelette	
1	dash Jerez vinegar
100g	crepinette (caul fat)

lamb jus:

lamb bones (from the milk-fed lamb)	
1	carrot, chopped
1	onion, chopped
100g	celery, chopped
1	garlic bulb
250ml	red wine
2 litres	lamb (or chicken) stock
zest of 1 lemon from Menton	
8	cardamom seeds

to serve:

1	Japanese aubergine
2-3	baby carrots
salt and piment d'Espelette	
20g	bulgur wheat (cooked)
fresh herbs eg. coriander, thyme or chervil	

METHOD

lamb saddle and chuletillas:

Remove the liver and the kidneys from the lamb. Cook the bulgur wheat in salted water for about 10 minutes. Purée 100g of the liver. Add the parsley and the bulgur wheat to it to make a farce for the rolls.

Split the rack and the saddle in two pieces. Remove the racks from the back bone and French the bones. It will be easiest to roast the racks whole. The saddle will form two 'rognonnades'. In French rognon means kidney, so rognonnade is when the saddles are rolled and cut so that the kidneys are visible. This is done by cutting away each half between the loin and the backbone to remove it from the saddle. Place each skin-side down on a chopping board. Next to the loin, place half of the farce mixture, then cut each kidney in half and place it on top. Roll each into two rolls and tie with butcher's string. Season with the piment d'Espelette.

caillette:

Brown the trotters, the lamb shank and the garlic in a deep pan. Deglaze with the Madeira. Add the stock and the bouquet garni and cook very slowly for about 5 hours until the meat is falling off the bone. While still hot, remove the meat and debone. Chop the meat and the skin very finely. Separately, sweat the shallot and bacon until soft. Add the chopped lamb, the trotter mixture and the Andouille sausage. Season well with salt, piment d'Espelette and Jerez vinegar. Rolls the mixture into small 'caillettes' (balls) and wrap each one with a single layer of crepinette.

lamb jus:

Make a jus by browning the bones and any trimmings in a heavy-based saucepan. Add the vegetables and the garlic. Deglaze with the red wine and add the stock. Bring to the boil and simmer. After 1 hour pass the resulting stock through a sieve and reduce until it reaches a sauce consistency. Infuse with the zest and cardamom.

to serve:

Roast the Japanese aubergine and carrots in a pan until they become soft, ensuring that they are well seasoned. Add the bulgur wheat and a spoon of the lamb jus to glaze. Roast the seasoned lamb rack and saddle in a heavy-based pan to get a golden colour. Place in an oven pre-heated to 190°C. The rack will take only about 4 minutes while the saddle will need 6-7 minutes. Rest the meat before carving. Each saddle should be cut to show the kidney which should still be pink. Cut the racks into 'chuletillas' or cutlets, leaving the bone attached. Serve on a large plate with the aubergine and carrots. Finish with lamb jus and garnish with some fresh herbs.

Serves 6
Preparation time: 1 hour 30 minutes
Cooking time: 1 hour

Special equipment:
Steamer, ice-cream machine, siphon.

Planning ahead:
The sorbet can be made in advance.

INGREDIENTS

pistachio biscuit:

150g	unsalted butter
125g	caster sugar
2	medium eggs
115g	T45 flour
1	pinch of salt of Guérande
4.5g	baking powder
55g	pistachio paste
25g	whole milk
0.1g	green pistachio colour

shortbread vergeoise:

100g	unsalted butter
45g	demerara sugar
100g	T45 flour
0.5g	fine salt

yoghurt sorbet:

52g	mineral water
43g	caster sugar
150g	Greek yoghurt
1.5g	lemon juice

grapefruit marmalade:

150g	supreme pink grapefruit
18g	caster sugar
2g	pectin NH

pistachio chantilly:

375g	whipping cream
30g	caster sugar
60g	pistachio paste

to serve:

24	pink grapefruit segments

PISTACHIO BISCUIT, PINK GRAPEFRUIT, GREEK YOGHURT SORBET
BY HELENE DARROZE & KIRK WHITTLE

For 8 years Kirk Whittle, my head pastry chef, has been creating the desserts for my menus. He has complete autonomy to elaborate all the sweet recipes in Paris and London. His original creations complete mine with style and flair. This dish is my favourite dessert.

METHOD

pistachio biscuit:
Combine all the ingredients respecting the order in a food processor. Grease a small (8cm long) rectangular mould. Pour the mixture in and close tight with a lid. Cook in a steamer for roughly 1 hour. When cold cut into 8 x 4.5cm rectangles.

shortbread vergeoise:
Whisk all the ingredients together in a food processor following the outlined order. Spread the mixture 0.5cm thick on a tray between two sheets of parchment paper. Roll out with a rolling pin. Cook in the oven at 160°C for 20 minutes. When cold cut into 8 x 4.5cm rectangles.

yoghurt sorbet:
Bring the water to boil with the sugar. Leave it to cool. Mix with the yoghurt and lemon juice. Put into an ice-cream machine and follow the manufacturer's instructions.

grapefruit marmalade:
Reduce the grapefruit segments by half in a pan. Mix together the sugar and pectin then add to the grapefruit. Bring to the boil again. Mix and leave to cool. Pour into a piping bag.

pistachio chantilly:
Gently heat 125g of cream and the sugar. Add the pistachio paste and mix until the mixture has melted. Deglaze with 250g of cream and cool it down. Pour into a siphon.

to serve:
Place a shortbread vergeoise rectangle on a serving plate. Pipe the grapefruit marmalade with the piping bag on top of the shortbread. Put the pistachio biscuit on top of the marmalade. Add four grapefruit segments on top of the pistachio biscuit. Finish with a yoghurt sorbet quenelle on top of the grapefruit segments. Serve the chantilly separately in a small ramekin.

Michel Roux Jr
Grand Chef Relais & Châteaux

A graduate of Le Gavroche, Michel Roux Jr was born into fine cuisine. He received his schooling in its kitchens, and is imbued with its unique atmosphere and style. He spent time working at Charcutier Mothu and La Boucherie Lamartine in Paris as well as a spell in Hong Kong, although perhaps the most predominant influence on his work is the two years he spent under Alain Chapel, a man heralded as one of the most notable chefs of his generation. With two Michelin stars to his name, Michel has exceeded his impressive pedigree with his own inspiring, independent style.

"Simply London's best. If the whole world is getting you down, grab your coat and make for Le Gavroche."

Le Gavroche

{ *Founded in 1967 by Albert and Michel Roux, Le Gavroche quickly became a benchmark for fine dining à la française in London's ever so exclusive Mayfair. To perpetuate the family tradition, Michel Roux Jr. took over in the kitchen in 1991.*

A new look, a fresh take, a new burst of creativity, combined with the incomparable recipes of his father and uncle — such as the Soufflé Suissesse — all further cemented the restaurant's international renown. A seasonal cuisine in which he doesn't hesitate to showcase the very best of French produce — Challans duck, lamb from the Pyrenees — and the finest vintages. A truly unique diner experience in London.

Serves 4
Preparation time: 20 minutes
Cooking time: 10 minutes

Special equipment:
N/A

Planning ahead:
N/A

INGREDIENTS

45g   butter
45g   plain flour
500ml   milk
5   egg yolks
salt and freshly ground white pepper
6   egg whites
600ml   double cream
200g   Gruyère or Emmental cheese, grated

SOUFFLE SUISSESSE
BY MICHEL ROUX JR

A timeless Gavroche classic: rich yet light, and definitely indulgent.

METHOD

Heat the oven to 200°C.

Melt the butter in a thick-based saucepan, whisk in the flour and cook, stirring continuously, for about 1 minute. Whisk in the milk and boil for 3 minutes, whisking all the time to prevent any lumps from forming. Beat in the yolks and remove from the heat; season with salt and pepper. Cover with a piece of buttered greaseproof paper to prevent a skin from forming.

Whisk the egg whites with a pinch of salt until they form firm, not stiff, peaks. Add a third of the egg whites to the yolk mixture and beat with a whisk until evenly mixed, then gently fold in the remaining egg whites. Spoon the mixture into four well-buttered 8cm diameter tartlet moulds and place in the oven for 3 minutes, until the tops begin to turn golden.

to serve:
Season the cream with a little salt, warm it gently and pour into a gratin dish.

Turn the soufflés out into the cream, sprinkle the grated cheese over the soufflés, then return to the oven for 5 minutes. Serve immediately.

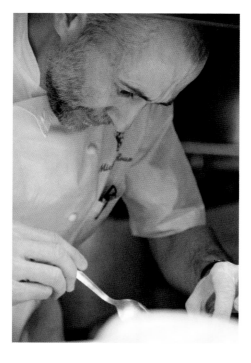

Serves 4
Preparation time: 10 minutes
Cooking time: N/A

Special equipment:
N/A

Planning ahead:
N/A

INGREDIENTS

2   cooked lobsters, 500-600g each
1   avocado, ripe but firm
1   mango, ripe but firm
2   spring onions, sliced
juice of 2 limes
peel of 1 lime, cut into thin strips and cooked in
a sugar syrup
12   basil leaves
4 tbsp   extra virgin olive oil
salt
green tabasco
endives leaves for serving (optional)

LOBSTER MANGO SALAD
BY MICHEL ROUX JR

A light summer salad that's bursting with flavour and colour.

METHOD

Cut the lobster tail meat into medallions and all the rest into dice. Peel the avocado and mango and dice the flesh. Add the spring onions, lime juice and peel, torn basil leaves, olive oil and seasoning. Toss very gently.

to serve:
Serve the salad in glass bowls or spoon into little endive leaves.

Serves 4
Preparation time: 45 minutes
Cooking time: 20 minutes

Special equipment:
N/A

Planning ahead:
N/A

INGREDIENTS

sea bass:

2	sea bass (600g each)
olive oil	
3	shallots, sliced
80g	button mushrooms, sliced
1 tbsp	white wine vinegar
100ml	dry white wine
400ml	veal stock (see below)
salt and pepper	
1 tbsp	butter

veal stock: (makes about 3.5 litres)

1.5kg	veal knuckle bones, chopped
1	calf's foot, split
1	large onion, roughly chopped
2	large carrots, roughly chopped
1	stick of celery, roughly chopped
5 litres	water
2	cloves of garlic
2	sprigs of thyme
½ tbsp	tomato purée

caramelised garlic:

8	small shallots
20	cloves of garlic
olive oil	

parsnip purée:

5	parsnips
120ml	milk
1 tbsp	butter
salt and pepper	

parsnip crisps:

1	parsnip
oil for deep-frying	

ROAST FILLET OF SEA BASS, PARSNIP PUREE & CARAMELISED GARLIC

BY MICHEL ROUX JR

METHOD

veal stock:

Roast the bones and calf's foot in a hot oven 220°C, turning occasionally until brown all over, then put them into a large saucepan.

Put the onion, carrots and celery into the roasting pan and roast until golden, turning frequently with a wooden spatula. Pour off any excess fat and put the roasted vegetables into the saucepan with the bones.

Put the roasting pan over high heat and add 500ml of the water to deglaze the pan; scrape the bottom with a wooden spatula to loosen all the caramelised sugars, then pour into the saucepan with the bones.

Add the remaining ingredients and bring to the boil. Skim off the scum and fat that come to the surface. Turn down the heat and simmer gently for 3½ hours, skimmimg occasionally. Pass through a fine sieve and leave to cool. This can be kept in the refrigerator for 8-10 days, or frozen.

sea bass:

Scale and fillet the sea bass, remove the pin bones using a pair of tweezers, rinse the fish and dry with kitchen towel. Score the skin of the fish several times with a sharp knife; this will help to prevent the fish from curling during cooking. Leave the bones (not the heads) to soak in cold water for the sauce.

Heat a little olive oil in a saucepan and cook the shallots for about 5 minutes, until golden and soft. Add the mushrooms and continue to cook for 10 minutes, stirring occasionally. Drain the fish bones, add to the pan and cook for 5-6 minutes. Add the vinegar and wine and let the wine come to the boil for 3 minutes, then add the stock, season lightly and simmer for 30 minutes, skimming at regular intervals. Pass through a fine sieve into a clean saucepan, bring back to the boil and whisk in the butter to thicken and gloss the sauce.

Heat a non-stick frying pan until smoking hot, add a few drops of olive oil, then add the fish, skin down, season with salt and pepper, and press the fish down with a palette knife if it begins to curl up. Once the skin is well browned, turn the fillets over and cook the other side; the whole process should not take more than 5-6 minutes, depending on the thickness of the fish.

caramelised garlic:

Peel the shallots and garlic. Blanch the shallots in boiling salted water for 10 minutes or until tender – cut them in half if large – then drain well. Put the garlic in a small saucepan of boiling salted water, bring to the boil for 2 minutes, then drain and change the water; repeat four times; drain well. Heat a little olive oil in a frying pan over medium heat, add the shallots and garlic and cook, shaking the pan so they don't stick, until caramelised.

parsnip purée:

Peel the parsnips and cut them into big chunks. Cook in boiling salted water until tender. Bring the milk to the boil and set aside. Drain the parsnips well, then put in a blender with the butter and some of the boiled milk and blend until totally smooth: the purée should be the consistency of double cream, so add more milk if necessary. Season and keep warm.

parsnip crisps:

Peel the parsnip and slice lengthways, using a mandolin to slice it as thinly as possible. Deep-fry in hot oil until crisp. Drain on kitchen towels to absorb any excess fat and set aside in a dry place.

to serve:

Spoon the parsnip purée on to warmed plates, make a hollow in the centre and fill with the caramelised garlic and shallots. Pour the sauce around the purée, place the fish on top and add a few parsnip crisps for decoration.

WILD DUCK WITH GIROLLE MUSHROOMS
BY MICHEL ROUX JR

Game should always be cooked on the bone and served with seasonal accompaniments.

Serves 2
Preparation time: 45 minutes
Cooking time: 30 minutes

Special equipment:
N/A

Planning ahead:
N/A

INGREDIENTS

1	wild mallard duck
80g	smoked duck breast
160g	girolle mushrooms, cleaned
2	shallots, peeled and chopped
1 tbsp	vegetable oil
1 tbsp	brandy
2 tbsp	Madeira
1 tbsp	chopped flat leaf parsley
2 dstsp	butter
salt, pepper	

METHOD

Trim and prepare the duck for roasting. Trim some of the fat off the smoked duck and cut into medium dice. Cut up the mushrooms if necessary. Take a cast-iron pan, small enough for the bird to fit in snugly, and heat up the oil until smoking. Place the seasoned duck in the pan and sear on all sides. Put in the oven at 200°C for 10 minutes. Then add 1 spoonful of butter and continue to cook for a further 10 minutes, turning and basting twice. Remove the duck and leave in a warm place to rest. Discard most of the fat, leaving a little for cooking the shallots.

sauce:

In the same pan, cook the shallots over a moderate heat for a few seconds. Add the mushrooms and continue to cook until they are soft and render some of their water. Pour in the brandy and Madeira, bring to the boil and fold in the rest of the butter, the smoked duck and parsley.

to serve:

Serve the sauce hot with the roasted duck.

Serves 6 – 8
Preparation time: 30 minutes
Cooking time: 20 minutes

Special equipment:
N/A

Planning ahead:
N/A

INGREDIENTS

cherries:

1 litre	Kriek beer (cherry-flavoured Belgian beer)
2	vanilla pods, split in half lengthways
1	stick of cinnamon
5	star anise
juice of 1 lemon and 1 orange	
½	zest of lemon, orange, and juice
½ tbsp	chopped ginger
300g	light brown sugar
1.5kg	cherries stoned
3 tbsp	kirsch liqueur

vanilla ice cream:

500ml	full-fat milk
2	vanilla pods, split
6	egg yolks
125g	caster sugar
1 tsp	vanilla essence

SPICED CHERRIES IN KRIEK BEER
BY MICHEL ROUX JR

Delicious even for the non-beer lovers.

METHOD

cherries:
Bring all the ingredients to the boil except for the cherries and Kirsch. Then add the cherries, cover and simmer for 2-3 minutes then leave to cool.

ice cream:
Bring the milk to the boil with the vanilla pods. Remove from the heat, cover and leave to infuse for 10 minutes.

Beat the egg yolks with the sugar until thick and creamy. Bring the milk back to the boil and pour on to the yolk mixture, whisking continuously. Pour the mixture back into the saucepan and cook over low heat, stirring continuously with a spatula, until the custard thickens slightly. Stir in the vanilla essence and pass through a fine sieve. Chill, then churn in an ice-cream machine until frozen.

to serve:
The cherries are delicious cold or warm but better if kept refrigerated for 24 hours. Add the Kirsch just before serving.

Jersey

Jersey – gem of the Channel Islands

Combining a beautiful coastline with sandy beaches, rugged cliffs and tiny harbours with tranquil countryside, green lanes and a bustling but unspoiled capital, the island of Jersey delights both its residents and visitors alike. Just 12 miles from France, there is a mix of Norman-French and English traditions, making the island truly cosmopolitan, which is reflected as much in the street and village names as it is in the island cuisine. The surrounding sea provides the freshest of seafood, while Jersey is rightly celebrated for the rich cream and butter from its famous cows as it is for Jersey Royal potatoes, vegetables and flowers. The history of the island dating back to prehistoric times is well documented, with the Occupation of the island during WWII remembered. The island's advantageous tax regime has seen Jersey become a major financial centre, with many international names having premises in St Helier. But far from being merely a corporate centre, the lively capital is very much the social and cultural heartbeat of Jersey, hosting exceptional shopping, restaurants, galleries and nightlife.

Andrew Baird

Having worked in some of the best kitchens in the UK during his training and taking on the position of Head Chef at Longueville Manor at an early age, Andrew turned his back on books and the media and set out to be innovative and individual. He immersed himself in local ingredients, of which Jersey has some of the finest in Europe, together with regional methods of cookery. His involvement with the local farming and fishing communities ensures that he has a true understanding of where all of his ingredients have originated and this in turn translates to the finest quality contemporary dishes on the plate.

Longueville Manor

{ *It was on the island of Jersey that exiled French author Victor Hugo wrote some of his most beautiful poems and you will understand why when you visit this magical island edged by wild beaches.*

And a poetic atmosphere envelops you the moment you pass through the gates of this 13th century manor house. Majestic fountains and little wooden bridges in the grounds, silky soft fabrics and old-style baths in the suites — here there is no lack of those delightful little details that really count. You will appreciate your own exile between a game of lawn tennis and a stroll through the forest among hundred-year old sycamores and oaks.

POACHED TAIL OF JERSEY LOBSTER WITH LUMO-CURED HAM CHOWDER, GARDEN VEGETABLES & MICRO SALAD

BY ANDREW BAIRD

This dish is a tasty assembly of our prized local lobster, our home grown garden vegetables with a burst of flavour from the Lumo ham and plum tomatoes.

Serves 4

Preparation time: 1 hour (excluding stock and tomato confit)

Cooking time: 10 minutes

This dish is made with six components
1. Lobster
2. Lumo ham cannelloni
3. Plum tomato infusion
4. Preparation and cooking of vegetables
5. Preparation and cooking of the couscous
6. Preparation of the chicken stock

INGREDIENTS

4 x 300g	Bobby lobsters (Bobby = lobster without claws)
160g	Lumo cured ham
1 x 20g	Perigord truffle
8	vine ripened plum tomatoes
	olive oil

chicken stock:

1	carrot
1	onion
1	celery stick
1	leek
4	bay leaves
12	peppercorns
50g	parsley
2 litres	water
600g	chicken bones

garden vegetables:

4	baby fennel
8	baby carrots
8	mange tout
8	fine French beans
4	garden asparagus
4	lemon grass
4	caper berries

cous cous:

1	red pepper
1	courgette
100g	couscous
100ml	chicken stock (see recipe)

to finish:

20g	blue maw seeds
20g	pine nuts
10g	red aramath
10g	baby sorrel
10g	chervil
10g	shizo cress
	walnut oil
	balsamic
	salt and pepper

METHOD

lobster:

If available, buy baby lobster without claws. These are often far cheaper than "select".

Straighten the lobster tail and tie a knife or similar metal object to the tail to keep it straight during cooking.

Heat a large pan of salted water to boiling point. Place the trussed lobster into the water for 7 minutes.

Remove from the heat and drain off the water. Refresh until cool in cold water and drain well. Remove the head and peel the tail. Carefully remove the intestine and rinse. Slice into five slices and put aside.

chicken stock:

Peel carrots and onion. Wash the leek and celery and keep whole. Place in a heavy pan with all the other ingredients, bring quickly to the boil and skim. Simmer on a gentle heat for 3 hours skimming all the time. Once cooked, pass through a chinoise quickly.

garden vegetables:

Peel the carrots. Peel the asparagus. Top and tail mange tout and French beans. Trim the fennel. Cook lightly in an emulsion of seasoned chicken stock and olive oil for a few minutes until tender. Drain and leave to cool.

cooking the cous cous:

Peel and dice the red pepper. Heat in a little olive oil until tender. Add the chicken stock, salt, pepper and diced courgette. Bring to simmer. Remove from heat and place in a bowl and cover until cool. Once cool stir through with a fork.

lumo ham cannelloni:

Lay two layers of cling film on a flat surface. Making an oblong, place the Lumo Ham on the film. Place the dressed cous cous down the centre. Slowly draw the far side of the cling film towards you, wrapping the cous cous to form a cylinder. Unwrap and leave aside.

plum tomato confit:

Bring to the boil a large pan of boiling water. Remove vine and stalks from the tomatoes. Place tomatoes in water for 10 seconds. Immediately place in cold water – the skin should be easy to remove. Drain and cut into quarters. Place on a tray and rub with olive oil.

Load tray into a preheated oven at 150°C for 4 hours to achieve an intense tomato flavour. Cut into oblongs and leave aside.

to assemble:

Place the tomato confit and cannelloni parallel to each other on an oblong plate. As shown run

a line of blue maw seeds down the long edge of each plate. Place the sliced lobster tail on top of the tomato confit and dress with sliced perigord truffle, baby fennel, shizo cress and chervil. Place the remainder of the baby vegetables and salad on top of the Lumo ham cannelloni. Use your flair to dress the plate with balsamic, herbs and oil.

ROAST FILLET OF ANGUS BEEF WITH OXTAIL RAVIOLI, GRILLED FOIE GRAS & WOODLAND MUSHROOMS

BY ANDREW BAIRD

This is a dish created with the finest ingredients available. Angus beef is some of the best beef in the world and with the foie gras and ceps, the combination is just divine.

Serves 4

Preparation time: 5 hours (including cooking of oxtail and chicken stock)

Cooking time: 20 minutes

Special equipment:
Pasta machine.

Planning ahead:
Not all butchers will stock the finest beef and oxtail, so order ahead.

INGREDIENTS

400g	Angus Beef fillet
1kg	oxtail on the bone cut into 10cm sections
60g	foie gras
200g	ceps
20g	morels
2	bok choy
100g	haricot beans
*6 litres	chicken stock (recipe x3)
*250g	pasta dough (recipe x1)
*250ml	red wine/oxtail sauce (recipe x1)
*250ml	cep purée (recipe x1)
*100ml	cep cream (recipe x1)
100g	carrot
100g	leek
100g	celery
20g	onion
4	bay leaf
12	peppercorns
1	bottle red wine
50g	tomato purée
1	egg yolk
olive oil	
200g	smoked bacon
30ml	cream (single)
5g	chives

chicken stock (x3):

1	carrot
1	onion
1	celery stick
1	leek
4	bay leaves
12	peppercorns
50g	parsley
2 litres	water
600g	chicken bones

pasta dough:

250g	pasta flour
2	whole free range organic eggs
3	egg yolks from organic free range eggs
1g	saffron stems
10ml	water
5g	salt

cep purée:

250g	ceps
30g	shallot
1	garlic clove
200ml	chicken stock
50ml	double cream
50ml	Madeira wine
15g	unsalted butter
salt and pepper to taste	

cep cream:

40ml	cep purée
60ml	chicken stock

METHOD

chicken stock:

Peel carrots and onion. Wash with the leek and celery, keep whole. Place in a heavy pan with all the other ingredients, bring quickly to the boil and skim. Simmer on a gentle heat for 3 hours skimming all the time. Once cooked, pass through a chinoise quickly.

cooking oxtail and making sauce:

The sauce for this dish comes from a reduction made from the liquor that the oxtail is cooked in. Trim the oxtail of any excess fat. Ideally the oxtail should be cut into 10cm sections. Your butcher will be happy to do this.

Peel carrot and onion. Wash leek and celery and roughly chop.

Roast oxtail in a preheated oven at 200°C for 15 minutes. Remove from the roasting tray and place in a deep saucepan. Drain any excess fat from the roasting tray and add the roughly cut vegetables. Turn the oven down to 180°C and cook for 10 minutes. Add 50 g of tomato purée and stir in. Add mixture to the saucepan with the oxtail.

Deglaze the roasting tray with the red wine. This simply means removing all the meaty bits. Bring the wine to simmering point and then pour this into the oxtail mix. Bring everything to the boil and reduce volume by half. Cover the oxtail with chicken stock (see recipe) and simmer for approximately 4 hours, making sure you don't reduce. Top up if necessary with water.

Once cooked, remove oxtail from the liquor and cool before removing the meat from the bones. Take care to discard any gristle and fat. Pass the liquid through a chinoise and reduce to approximately 1 litre. This should give you a nice balance of oxtail and red wine flavours.

Once the oxtail has cooled — flake it with the back of a fork and roll into small balls. You will need approximately 1 teaspoon of sauce per oxtail ravioli. Cover and place in fridge until you have made the ravioli.

pasta dough:

Sieve the pasta flour and place in a bowl or food processor.

Beat the whole egg and egg yolks and pass through a chinoise.

Infuse the saffron stems in 100ml of hot water. Leave to cool. Add 3 tablespoons of the saffron infusion to the pasta flour together with the eggs and salt. Process in food processor or knead by hand until the mix comes together. Don't worry if at this stage it is still slightly dry. Place in a plastic bag — a freezer bag is ideal and rest for 2 hours.

Remove from the bag and knead again. It should come together to form a smooth pasta dough.

cep purée:

Peel and slice the shallots. Crush the garlic. Place butter in a heavy-bottomed pan and melt over a medium heat. Add shallots and garlic. Wash and roughly cut the ceps. After 4-5 minutes the shallots and garlic should be sweated down without any colour. Add ceps and continue cooking. You will see the ceps soften. At this point add the Madeira wine. The alcohol will evaporate and reduce only slightly. Add the chicken stock. Bring back to the boil and reduce until the mixture becomes sloppy. At this stage add the cream. Bring back to the boil and liquidise. Pass through a muslin or chinoise. Season to taste and it is ready to use.

cep cream:

Simply mix the ingredients together and blend with a hand blender. Heat and hand blend just before serving.

ravioli:

Bring the pasta dough to room temperature. This will take a good hour.

Using a pasta machine, roll out the dough on its finest setting. Dust the work surface with flour to stop it sticking. Using a set of round cutters, select one approximately 70mm and cut forming eight circles.

Place the ball of oxtail in the centre and using a little egg yolk around the edge place the second circle on top. Take care to expel all air.

Cook and serve by adding a few drops of olive oil and a good pinch of salt to a pan of simmering water. Cook for approximately 3 minutes. Drain and serve immediately.

haricot beans:

If using dried haricot beans soak overnight. Cover with chicken stock (see recipe), add a bay leaf and the smoked bacon. Simmer for approximately 1 hour until tender. At this stage remove bacon and bay leaf and reduce the chicken stock until it has almost disappeared. Add cream and simmer until the sauce coats the beans. Serve with a few snipped chives.

the assembly:

Cut the beef fillet into four equal 100g pieces. Season with salt and pepper and using a heavy duty frying pan seal and colour the beef all over. Place in the oven for 4 minutes at 180°C. Leave to rest.

Cut the bok choy in half and blanch in salted water for 2 minutes. Drain and coat in warm butter and season.

Using a large round main course plate, warm the cep purée and using a dessert spoon place an elongated tear drop around the plate as shown in the picture.

Season the foie gras and pan fry until golden on both sides. Using the foie gras oil in the pan, gently sauté the morels and ceps and place on plate as shown. Add the bok choy – opening up the leaves to form a half moon shape. Heat and add a dessert spoon of the creamed haricot beans together with the pâté of foie gras and woodland mushrooms. Heat the red wine/oxtail sauce, cep cream and ravioli. Cut the beef fillet into two and place on top of the bok choy and finish with the ravioli, red wine sauce and cep cream.

HAZELNUT SABLE WITH "JIVARA" CHOCOLATE, SESAME ICE CREAM & A BALSAMIC REDUCTION
BY ANDREW BAIRD

"Jivara" chocolate is one of the finest available. Delicately combined with a hazelnut sablé and sesame ice cream, with the contrasting flavour of reduced balsamic, an outstanding dessert.

Serves 4

Preparation time:	3 hours
Cooking time:	40 minutes

Special equipment:
Ice-cream machine.

Planning ahead:
Depending on your ice cream maker, you may need to make it 24 hours ahead.

INGREDIENTS

hazelnut sablè:

400g	peeled roast hazelnuts
570g	unsalted Jersey butter
225g	sugar
700g	flour
7g	salt
2	vanilla pods
200g	egg yolks

jivara chocolate cream:

250g	milk
250g	whipped cream
100g	egg yolks
50g	sugar
250g	chocolate "Valrhona Jivara"

sesame ice cream:

1 litre	milk
200g	cream
50g	milk powder
6g	salt
2g	agar agar
150g	egg yolk
120g	sugar
40g	trimoline

balsamic reduction:

20ml	balsamic vinegar

METHOD

hazelnut sablè:

Chop hazelnuts and mix with butter, sugar and salt. Place in a mixer and beat until the mix becomes pale. Fold in flour and egg yolks and sugar mix together with the seeds from the vanilla pods. Place between two sheets of silicone paper and roll out to approximately 3mm. Place in a refrigerator and chill for 20 minutes.

Cut into oblong shapes and bake in the oven at 180°C for approximately 8-10 minutes. Leave to cool.

jivara chocolate cream:

Whisk egg yolks and sugar in a mixing bowl until they become pale.

Heat milk and cream to 85°C then put onto egg yolks with sugar mix and slowly mix until luke warm.

Warm the chocolate until it just melts and add to the mixture. Leave to cool.

Once cool place in the refrigerator in a piping bag ready to use.

sesame ice cream:

Mix egg yolks, milk powder, agar agar and sugar until pale. Heat milk and cream to 85°C. Pour over sugar and egg mixture. Return to a heavy-based saucepan and heat until it coats the back of a spatula. Add pectin, trimoline and salt then pass through a conical strainer. Add sesame seed and leave to cool. Then ideally freeze and Pacojet or churn in a traditional ice-cream machine.

balsamic reduction:

Simply reduce the balsamic vinegar over heat until a syrupy consistency is obtained.

Berkshire

{ ### Royal Residence in the Royal County

This historic county is often referred to as the Royal County of Berkshire due to the presence of the royal residence of Windsor Castle, its usage dating back to the 19th century. Windsor provides quick links to London as well as its own amusements such as LEGOLAND Windsor – sparking the imagination of both young and old. Continuing southwards into the Royal County of Berkshire is Newbury, a traditional market town now gaining a new lease of life and famed for its horse racing. This prestigious sport has long been associated with the town and the Berkshire Downs include some of the country's most successful stables. Home to a multitude of Michelin-starred restaurants Berkshire offers the finest dining together with the opportunity to explore local farm shops, orchards, bakeries and even a wine estate.

Alain Roux started in the pastry industry as an apprentice in 1984. He spent two years honing his pastry skills at Pâtisserie Millet in Paris, following the Roux family tradition. His first steps towards entering the family business were taken by working over the next six years at five different Relais & Châteaux restaurants in France. In 1992 he made the best move of his career, to The Waterside Inn at Bray to be under the guidance of the best teacher, his father, Michel.

Promoted to Sous Chef in 1995, Alain then became Joint Chef Patron at The Waterside Inn in 2001 and now runs the kitchen full time, bringing his own style to the menus and retaining the coveted 3 Michelin stars.

The Waterside Inn

{ *While Michel Roux, the father, now takes the time to "inhale the sweet aroma of grapes and write books", Alain – the son – has brilliantly taken over the helm of The Waterside Inn.*

Resolutely creative French cuisine like roasted scallops on sliced baby artichokes, infused with honey, orange and lemon and sprinkled with crab meat; or the salmon en papillote with pine needles and a star aniseed sauce. On the terrace, in the shade of a willow tree, or in the inn's cosy rooms, let yourself be soothed by the calm of the River Thames... And if you feel a desire to explore the surrounding area, you can visit Windsor Castle or stroll around Savill Garden, one of the finest in England.

RELAIS & CHATEAUX

Serves 4

Preparation time: 20 minutes
Cooking time: 35 minutes

Special equipment:
N/A

Planning ahead:
N/A

INGREDIENTS

soup base:

40g	butter
4	shallots, sliced
100g	celeriac, diced
400g	chestnuts, cooked and peeled
100ml	Champagne
1.5 litres	chicken or vegetable stock
100ml	milk
	salt and pepper

garnish:

1	large chicken breast, poached then rolled in 1 tbsp chopped tarragon and sliced
4 tbsp	diced golden bread croutons
4	whole small chestnuts, cooked, peeled and warmed up in a steamer

VELOUTE DE CHATAIGNES AU CHAMPAGNE, ET SUPREME DE VOLAILLE A L'ESTRAGON

CHESTNUT & CHAMPAGNE SOUP, GARNISHED WITH TARRAGON-FLAVOURED CHICKEN BREAST
BY ALAIN ROUX

METHOD

soup base:

Melt the butter in a large saucepan, stir in the shallots and celeriac, then cook gently for 5 minutes. Add the chestnuts and cook for a further 10 minutes. Pour in the Champagne and the stock, then bring to the boil. Simmer gently for about 20 minutes. Add the milk and blend in a food processor until smooth, then pass through a fine sieve into a clean pan. Adjust the consistency with a little additional stock or, even better, with more Champagne. Season to taste with salt and pepper.

to serve:

In a warm soup plate, place some slices of chicken and pour in the hot soup. Sprinkle over a few golden croutons and a whole small chestnut. Serve.

CEVICHE DE NOIX DE SAINT-JACQUES, GUACAMOLE EPICE ET FEUILLES DE MACHE

CEVICHE OF SCALLOPS MARINATED IN VIRGIN OLIVE OIL & YUZU JUICE, GARNISHED WITH A SPICY GUACAMOLE & LAMB'S LETTUCE

BY ALAIN ROUX

Serves 4
Preparation time: 30 minutes
Cooking time: 10 minutes

Special equipment:
N/A

Planning ahead:
N/A

INGREDIENTS

scallops:

8	scallops
4 tbsp	yuzu juice
2	pinches Maldon salt flakes
2	pinches Espelette pepper

guacamole:

1	avocado peeled, stoned and diced
1	small tomato, coarsely chopped
2	spring onions, sliced

juice of ½ lime
a little green chilli pepper, cut in small brunoise
a little red chilli pepper, cut in small brunoise
salt and pepper

yuzu vinaigrette:

4 tbsp	olive oil
4 tbsp	yuzu juice
1 tbsp	pomelo pulp
1 tbsp	diced segment of tangerine
1	pinch black peppercorns, crushed
1	pinch pink peppercorns, crushed
salt	

garnish:

12	tortillas

a few basil shoots
a few coriander shoots

1 tbsp	green flying fish roe
1 tbsp	basil oil
8	bunches of lamb's lettuce leaves

METHOD

scallops:

Thinly slice the scallops and place them on a tray. Coat with the yuzu juice, then season with the salt and pepper. Marinate for 5 minutes, turn the scallops over and marinate for a further 5 minutes.

guacamole:

In a bowl, crush the avocado with a fork. Add the remaining ingredients. Mix gently and season.

yuzu vinaigrette:

In a bowl, using a whisk, mix the oil and yuzu juice. Add the remaining ingredients and mix with a spoon. Season.

to serve:

Place the guacamole in the centre of the plate with the tortillas. Arrange the scallop slices in front and dress nicely with the vinaigrette and all the garnishes around.

FILET DE TURBOT CUIT EN FEUILLE DE VIGNE, AGREMENTE DE RAISINS BLANCS, EMULSION AU VERJUS

FILLET OF TURBOT BAKED IN A VINE LEAF, SERVED WITH WHITE GRAPES & A 'VERJUS' EMULSION

BY ALAIN ROUX

Serves 4
Preparation time: 45 minutes
Cooking time: 15 minutes

Special equipment:
N/A

Planning ahead:
N/A

INGREDIENTS

turbot:

4 x 120g	fillets of turbot
salt and pepper	
4	vine leaves, blanched
16	white grapes, peeled and sliced
1 tbsp	olive oil
a little coarse salt	
1 tbsp	argan oil

'verjus' emulsion:

¼	celery stick, diced
1	shallot, sliced
20g	butter
75ml	verjus
75ml	fish stock
2 tbsp	double cream
salt and pepper	

garnish:

4 tbsp	celeriac purée
a few celeriac chips	
4	slices of cucumber, diamond shape and blanched
4	large celeriac dice, cooked 'à l'Anglaise'
4	white grapes, peeled
a few shoots of red amaranth	

METHOD

turbot:

Season the turbot and place it on a vine leaf. Arrange the slices of white grapes over and drizzle the olive oil on top. Wrap the fish totally in the leaf and place it on a roasting tray whose bottom is covered with coarse salt. Cook in an oven at 180°C for about 10 minutes. When cooked, gently open the vine leaf and drizzle over the argan oil.

'verjus' emulsion:

In a saucepan, sweat the celery and shallot with 10g of butter. Deglaze with the verjus and reduce by half. Add the stock and reduce again by half. Pour the cream and whisk in the remaining butter. Season and emulsify the sauce using a hand blender.

to serve:

Place the fish on a warm plate. Add the purée topped with a few celeriac chips. Arrange, on the side, a 'diamond' cucumber with a celeriac dice and a white grape. Finish with a few shoots of red amaranth and a drizzle of sauce on the fish.

MIGNON DE CHEVREUIL ROTI EN FEUILLANTINE AUX SAVEURS DE CHAMPIGNONS SAUVAGES, BOUQUETS DE BROCOLIS, SAUCE A L'HERMITAGE AU VINAIGRE DE CASSIS

ROASTED LOIN OF VENISON IN A PASTRY CRUST WITH WILD MUSHROOMS, GARNISHED WITH FLORETS OF BROCCOLI, HERMITAGE WINE SAUCE WITH BLACKCURRANT VINEGAR

BY ALAIN ROUX

Serves 4
Preparation time: 1 hour
Cooking time: 40 minutes

Special equipment:
N/A

Planning ahead:
N/A

INGREDIENTS

venison:

500g to 600g	loin of fallow deer
1 tbsp	clarified butter
salt and pepper	
8	large spinach leaves, blanched, refreshed and drained

chicken mousse:

150g	chicken breast
salt	
cayenne pepper	
1	egg white
400ml to 500ml	double cream

wild mushroom farce:

600g	duxelles of girolle and black trumpet mushrooms, cooked
400g	chicken mousse
2 tbsp	chopped parsley

wrapping:

400g	puff pastry
4	herb crepes, cut in a square shape
a little egg wash	

sauce:

30g	clarified butter
300g	venison bones (and/or trimmings)
½	carrot, diced
½	celery stick, diced
½	leek, diced
375ml	red Hermitage wine
100ml	blackcurrant vinegar
750ml	venison or veal stock
10g	butter
salt and pepper	

garnish:

100g	wilted spinach leaves
100g	blackcurrants, poached in a light syrup
12	florets of broccoli, cooked 'à l'Anglaise'
30 to 40 small girolle mushrooms, pan fried.	

METHOD
venison:

Season the loin with salt and seal in a hot frying pan on all sides with clarified butter. Cook for 4-5 minutes in a hot oven at 180°C or longer if you prefer the meat medium. Season with pepper and allow to cool on a wire rack. Wrap and cover the cold loin of venison with the spinach leaves. Keep in the fridge.

chicken mousse:

Cut the chicken in small cubes and pass through a food processor for 2 minutes, then rub through a fine sieve. Place the chicken flesh in a bowl over ice, add the salt, cayenne and egg white, beat well and slowly add the cream, beating constantly.

wild mushroom farce:

In a bowl, mix all the ingredients together and keep in the fridge.

wrapping:

Roll the puff pastry to a rectangle large enough to enclose the venison and 2mm thick. Place onto a piece of baking paper then cut the crepes large enough to enclose the venison plus a little extra and lay on top of the pastry.

Spread an even layer of the farce on top of the crepe, about 1cm thick, then place the venison on top. Fold the crepes coated in the farce over the top of the venison. Trim the open ends, egg wash and fold in like an envelope. Turn the venison over and egg wash the presentation side. Place into the fridge and allow to rest for at least 15 minutes.

Egg wash a second time and score the pastry in a criss cross pattern with a sharp knife. Cook in a preheated oven at 180°C on a lined baking sheet for approximately 15-20 minutes depending on your liking. Remove from the

oven and place onto a wire rack to rest for 5 minutes before serving.

sauce:

In a large heavy-based but shallow pan add the clarified butter and heat. Fry the venison bones over a high heat until golden brown, then remove any excess fat. Add the diced vegetables to the bones and continue to fry. When the vegetables have taken on a little colour, deglaze

with the Hermitage wine, add the vinegar and reduce by two-thirds.

Add the stock and bring to the boil. When boiling, skim off any excess fat from the surface and reduce the heat to a simmer. Simmer for approximately 30 minutes, skimming the surface often. After the sauce has had sufficient time to cook, pass through a fine sieve and muslin into a clean saucepan and bring back to the boil.

Reduce to your desired consistency and taste. Season with salt and pepper. Finish with the butter at the last second.

to serve:

On a warm plate, spread the wilted spinach leaves and place two slices of cooked loin of venison on top. Arrange all other garnishes around and drizzle over the sauce.

ENTREMETS AU CHOCOLAT NOIR ET AIRELLES, SORBET A LA LIQUEUR D'ORANGE

DARK CHOCOLATE & CRANBERRY DESSERT SERVED WITH AN ORANGE LIQUEUR SORBET
BY ALAIN ROUX

Serves approximately 20
Preparation time: 1 hour 20 minutes
Cooking time: 15 minutes

Special equipment:
Baking tray 40 x 30cm. Frame 40 x 30cm.
Sorbet/ice-cream machine.

Planning ahead:
For the cranberry jelly the frozen cranberries,
150g caster sugar, water and juice of 2 oranges
must be macerated for 12 hours in the fridge.

INGREDIENTS

chocolate biscuit (serves approximately 30):

35g	cocoa paste extra 100%
30g	butter
35g	flour
15g	cocoa powder
3	egg whites
45g	caster sugar
150g	almond paste
40g	caster sugar
4	egg yolks
2	whole eggs

cranberry jelly (serves approximately 30):

500g	frozen cranberries
150g	caster sugar
125ml	water
juice of 2 oranges	
750ml	water
10g	pectin NH
25g	caster sugar

whipped ganache (serves approximately 20):

125ml	whipping cream
15g	glucose
15g	trimoline
100g	Guanaja chocolate, chopped
200ml	whipping cream

orange liqueur sorbet (serves approximately 20):

600ml	orange juice
175ml	sorbet syrup
juice of 1 lemon	
65ml	Grand Marnier

chocolate 'leaves' (serves approximately 20):

40	'leaves' Guanaja chocolate, cut in 9 x 3cm rectangles

garnish (serves approximately 20):

120	cranberries, poached in a light syrup
60	small candied orange zest

METHOD

chocolate biscuit:

Melt together the cocoa paste and butter at 45°C. Sieve together the flour and cocoa powder. Make a French meringue with the egg whites and 45g caster sugar to a ribbon consistency. Mix together the almond paste with the 40g caster sugar and warm up to 50°C in a microwave oven. Using an electric mixer, beat the warm almond paste/sugar with a flat paddle and add the egg yolks and whole eggs little by little, until well mixed, to a ribbon consistency. Then, using a spatula, mix and add the cocoa paste/butter, followed by the flour/cocoa powder and immediately fold in the meringue. Spread the mixture with a palette knife onto a 40 x 30cm baking tray, lined with silicone paper. Bake in a hot oven at 180°C, for 7-8 minutes. When cooked, but still moist, slide the biscuit onto a wire rack and leave to cool. Cut into 9 x 3cm rectangular shapes.

cranberry jelly:

Mix the pectin and 25g caster sugar together. Pour the macerated cranberries in a saucepan. Bring to the boil and simmer for 5 minutes. Pass through a conical strainer into another saucepan and add the 125ml water. Warm up to 50°C, then add the 'pectin/sugar'. Bring to the boil and simmer for 5 minutes or until thick enough to coat a spoon. Pour into a 40 x 30cm frame and freeze. When the jelly is frozen, cut into 9 x 1.5cm rectangular shapes.

whipped ganache:

In a saucepan, bring to the boil the 125ml whipping cream, the glucose and trimoline. Pour onto the chocolate and whisk until homogeneous. Add the 200ml whipping cream little by little and keep whisking for a further minute. Keep in the fridge until very cold. When needed, whisk the ganache until light and a ribbon consistency. Put the ganache into a piping bag with a plain 0.5cm nozzle.

orange liqueur sorbet:

Mix all the ingredients together and churn in a sorbet/ice-cream machine following the manufacturer's instructions.

to assemble:

On a rectangle biscuit place a rectangle of jelly in the middle and pipe along it some ganache. Place on top a 'leaf' of chocolate. Repeat again, by placing a rectangle of jelly, some ganache and finish with another 'leaf' of chocolate. That's the entremets done!

to serve:

Place the entremets on a plate with the sorbet next to it. Garnish with a few poached cranberries, a little of the juice and several candied orange zest.

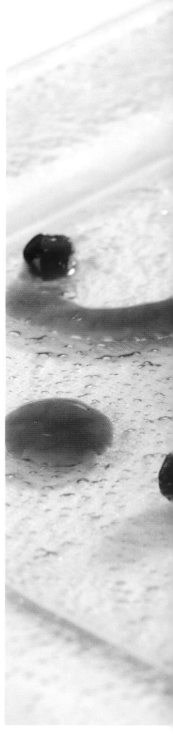

Heston Blumenthal
Grand Chef Relais & Châteaux

Heston Blumenthal has been described as a culinary alchemist for his innovative style of cuisine. His research pushes the boundaries of British gastronomy and enables a greater understanding of the way we register taste and flavour and the effects that nostalgia has on the palate. – a flair, which is prominent in the dishes at his restaurant, The Fat Duck. Heston opened The Fat Duck in Bray in August 1995, which has since gained three Michelin stars and worldwide acclaim for his multi-sensory approach to gastronomy. Heston is entirely self-taught. His formative years were spent travelling to various restaurants, vineyards, cheese makers and butchers throughout France carrying out extensive, thorough and determined research – a characteristic which soon became the trademark of his success.

'Cooking principles: excellence, openness and integrity'

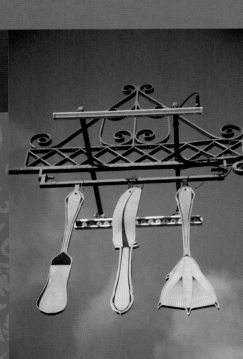

The Fat Duck

{
Snail porridge, mock turtle soup, nitro-scrambled egg and bacon ice cream, "Sound of the Sea"… As you will have guessed by now, Heston Blumenthal's cooking is unique.

His Fat Duck restaurant is a building dating back 450 years with minimalist décor, in the English countryside just a few miles outside London. From a very young age, this "culinary alchemist" has had a modern approach to his cooking – the study of the physical phenomena that affect the taste and flavour of a dish – and he likes nothing better than to endlessly develop new possibilities. This includes his current research into historic British gastronomy in a bid to recreate dishes inspired by the past. One of his multi-sensory creations is a seafood dish with a twist. The seafood is presented amid a selection of seaweeds awash on a beach of delicious sand comprising tapioca, toasted breadcrumbs, miso oil and crispy anchovies with waves of sea foam lapping the shore and then the whole dish is served with an iPod in a shell so you can immerse yourself completely in the world of the ingredients on your plate! For those who like fun when they go out for a meal, this is definitely the place to come …

SNAIL PORRIDGE, JABUGO HAM
BY HESTON BLUMENTHAL

Serves 2

INGREDIENTS

duck ham:

1	bay leaf
15g	black peppercorns
15g	coriander seeds
50g	sel gris (grey salt)
5g	sprigs of thyme
5	Gressingham duck breasts, fat scored

parsley butter:

550g	unsalted butter
85g	garlic, minced
10g	lemon juice
50g	Dijon mustard
40g	ground almonds
15g	table salt
240g	curly leaf parsley
	clarified butter
40g	ceps, cut into 1cm dice
60g	shallots, cut into brunoise (2mm squares)
80g	reserved duck ham, cut into brunoise (2mm squares)

chicken bouillon:

3kg	chicken (2 good-sized chickens)
250g	carrots, peeled and finely sliced
250g	onions, finely sliced
100g	celery, finely sliced
75g	leeks, white and pale green parts only, finely sliced
10g	garlic, crushed
3	cloves
10g	black peppercorns
50g	sprigs of thyme
20g	parsley leaves and stems
3g	bay leaves

braised snails:

100g	*Helix pomatia* snails (shelled weight)
2	cloves
120g	onion, cut in half
40g	carrot, cut in half
90g	leeks, cut in half
2	sticks of celery
30g	garlic bulb, cut in half
2	bay leaves
50g	sprigs of rosemary
50g	sprigs of thyme
120g	water
250g	dry white wine
50g	parsley leaves and stems

walnut vinaigrette:

75g	walnut vinegar
145g	grapeseed oil
5g	Dijon mustard

snail porridge:

10g	fennel, shaved paper-thin
	reserved walnut vinaigrette
	table salt
	black pepper
	fleur de sel
30g	unsalted butter
12	reserved braised snails
30g	reserved chicken bouillon
10g	porridge oats, sieved to remove the powdery bits
30g	reserved parsley butter, at room temperature
20g	Jabugo ham, cut into chiffonade (long, thin strips)
	pinch of micro parsley and micro coriander to garnish.

METHOD

duck ham:

Snip the bay leaf into eight pieces. Grind the peppercorns and coriander, combine with the sel gris, thyme and bay leaf. Spread a layer of this mixture over the bottom of a roasting tray and place the duck breasts on top. Cover completely with the remaining salt mixture, then refrigerate for 24 hours.

Brush the salt cure from the breasts, wrap them in muslin and tie securely with string. Hang in a cellar or other cool place for at least 20 days. Remove the duck from the muslin and refrigerate until needed.

parsley butter:

Melt 50g of the unsalted butter in a pan, add the garlic and sauté until pale gold and fragrant. Add the lemon juice to the pan, then transfer the mixture to a Pacojet beaker along with the mustard, ground almonds, salt and the remaining 500g unsalted butter.

Chop the parsley, sprinkle on top of the butter mixture and run the beaker through the Pacojet machine. Remove the beaker and freeze the mixture until completely solid. Run the frozen mixture through the Pacojet, then freeze solid again. Repeat this process until all trace of the parsley has disappeared. After the final use of the Pacojet, at which point the mixture will have an ice cream consistency, set aside the butter at room temperature until needed.

Heat some clarified butter in a pan, add the ceps and sauté until caramelised.

Strain and set aside.

Wipe the pan clean, then heat some more clarified butter in it. Add the shallots and cook over a very low heat for 30-40 minutes, until very soft and translucent.

Fold the caramelised ceps, the cooked shallots and the duck brunoise into the reserved parsley butter. Refrigerate or freeze until needed.

chicken bouillon:

Place the chickens in a large pan and cover with cold water. Bring to the boil, then carefully remove them and discard the water. Rinse the chickens under cold running water to remove any scum.

Put the chickens in a pressure cooker and add just enough cold water to cover them. Bring to a simmer, skimming off any scum on the surface. Add the vegetables, cloves and freshly crushed peppercorns to the pan. Put the lid on, bring to full pressure and cook for 30 minutes.

Remove the pan from the heat, allow to depressurise, then remove the lid. Add the thyme, parsley and bay leaves and leave to infuse for 30 minutes. Strain the bouillon through a fine sieve lined with several layers of damp muslin. Refrigerate or freeze until needed.

braised snails:

Rinse the snails in several changes of water to remove any grit. Preheat the oven to 120°C.

Press a clove into each half of the onion, then place in an ovenproof casserole with all the other ingredients, apart from the snails and parsley, and bring to a simmer on the hob.

Add the snails, cover with a cartouche (circle of paper to stop a skin forming) and place in the oven for 3-4 hours. Remove the casserole from the oven, add the parsley and set aside to cool.

Drain the snails from the liquid and trim away their intestines and white sac.

Refrigerate until needed.

walnut vinaigrette:

Combine all the ingredients, mix thoroughly and set aside until needed.

snail porridge:

Dress the fennel with the vinaigrette, season with table salt, freshly ground pepper and fleur de sel and set aside.

Heat 20g of the butter until foaming, then sauté the snails and season with table salt and freshly ground pepper. Add the remaining butter to the snails, then remove from the heat and keep warm.

Heat the chicken bouillon in a small saucepan. When hot, stir in the oats. Once they have absorbed the liquid, add the parsley butter and season to taste with table salt and freshly ground pepper. Adjust the consistency of the porridge with chicken bouillon if necessary until it resembles wet rice pudding. (It is important not to overcook the oats or else they will become starchy and lose their texture.)

to serve:

Divide the porridge between two warm plates and cover with the Jabugo ham. Place the warm snails on top, add the dressed fennel and micro salads to serve.

SADDLE OF VENISON, CELERIAC & SAUCE POIVRADE, CIVET OF VENISON WITH PEARL BARLEY, VENISON & FRANKINCENSE TEA

BY HESTON BLUMENTHAL

Serves 4

INGREDIENTS

venison consommé:

2kg	venison bones
900g	Syrah wine
100g	olive oil
180g	carrots, peeled and finely sliced
120g	shallots, finely sliced
80g	celery, finely sliced
90g	leeks, finely sliced
140g	tomatoes, cored and chopped
35g	garlic, sliced
2	bay leaves
3g	sprig of thyme
	parsley leaves
	black peppercorns
2g	juniper berries
2.4kg	water
	tarragon leaves
	table salt

frankincense hydrosol:

50g	golden frankincense tears
100g	water

frankincense dilution:

100g	vodka
0.4g	reserved frankincense essential oil

confit of vegetables:

100g	extra virgin olive oil
140g	carrots, peeled and finely sliced
130g	onions, finely sliced
80g	leek, white and pale green parts only, finely sliced
30g	celery, finely sliced
5g	garlic, thinly sliced

tomato fondue:

500g	ripe vine tomatoes
	table salt
2	sprigs of parsley
2	sprigs of thyme
4	black peppercorns
½	star anise
1	clove
25g	extra virgin olive oil
80g	onions, chopped
10g	garlic, minced
8g	sherry vinegar
2g	tomato ketchup
	few drops of Worcestershire sauce
	few drops of tabasco sauce
	zest of ¼ lemon
	small pinch of saffron

sauce poivrade:

2.5kg	venison bones
900g	red wine (preferably Syrah)
50g	reserved confit of vegetables
50g	reserved tomato fondue
preheat the oven to 180°C/Gas 4.	

gastrique:

15g	honey
2g	red wine vinegar
	reserved venison consommé
0.2g	bay leaf
0.4g	sprig of thyme
1g	juniper berries
0.5g	pink peppercorns
0.3g	black peppercorns

blood cream:

500g	venison bones (with some meat still attached)
500g	whipping cream

celeriac purée:

1kg	celeriac, peeled
200g	unsalted butter
400g	whole milk
	table salt
	black pepper

celeriac fondants:

2kg	celeriac, peeled
375g	unsalted butter
10g	table salt

civet base:

500g	chicken bouillon
10g	groundnut oil
300g	pearl barley
40g	shallots, chopped
1g	garlic, minced
150g	Madeira

red wine jelly discs:

100g	Shiraz wine
50g	Maury wine
0.8g	gellan F
0.08g	gellan LT100

venison medallions:

1	saddle of red deer, 10-18 months old (approximately 6.5kg)
	extra virgin olive oil
10g	sprigs of thyme

red wine foam:

This should not be prepared more than 12 hours before use.

200g	Shiraz wine
100g	Maury wine
8g	soy lecithin

grelot onions: (per portion)

1	grelot onion

butter emulsion:

250g	unsalted butter
150g	water
5g	table salt

to serve:

(per portion)
reserved venison medallions
fine sea salt
fleur de sel
black pepper
reserved celeriac purée
clarified butter
reserved celeriac fondants
10g   chicken bouillon
2   reserved grelot onion halves
reserved butter emulsion

reserved sauce poivrade
2g   freshly sliced white truffle
reserved blood cream
20g   white chicken stock
reserved civet base
5g   cryogenically frozen foie gras, cut into 1cm dice
5g   venison marrow, removed from the bone, soaked in lightly salted water to remove traces of blood and cut into 10mm cubes
15g   foie gras parfait, cubed

1g   sherry vinegar
reserved red wine jelly discs
reserved red wine foam
reserved venison consommé
8 drops   reserved frankincense dilution

METHOD

venison consommé:

Preheat the oven to 180°C. Place the venison bones in a pan and roast for 30 minutes or so, until lightly coloured. Pour the wine into a large pan, bring to the boil, then flame off the alcohol. Set aside until needed. Heat a large pressure cooker and add the olive oil. Add the vegetables and sweat until they are just starting to colour. Add the roasted bones, the flamed wine, bay leaves, thyme, 10g parsley, the juniper berries and 2g black peppercorns and cover with the water. Put on the lid, bring to full pressure and cook for 2 hours. Leave to cool before opening, then skim the fat from the surface. Pass the stock through a fine sieve lined with damp muslin into a large, rectangular container. Cover and freeze until solid. Line a perforated tray with a double layer of muslin large enough to hold the frozen stock in a single flat layer. Turn the stock on to the muslin-lined tray and place this over another tray to catch the stock as it defrosts.

Transfer to the fridge and allow to thaw slowly over 36-48 hours. Discard the gelled mass left in the top tray. Pour the filtered consommé into a large pan and reduce by half. Remove from the heat and allow to cool. Weigh the consommé, and for every 500g, add 7g tarragon, 5g parsley, 0.5g peppercorns and salt to taste. Cover and leave to infuse in the fridge for 12 hours. Strain the finished consommé through a fine sieve and divide into 65g portions. Refrigerate until needed.

frankincense hydrosol:

Set the bath of a rotary evaporator to 50°C. Combine the frankincense and water in the evaporating flask, attach and submerge in the bath. Using a pump, run iced water through the condensing coils. Begin rotating the flask and pull the vacuum to below 50mbars. Run the rotary evaporator for 3 hours. Collect the liquid in the receiving flask, remove the essential oil from the surface with a spoon or pipette and reserve.

frankincense dilution:

Combine the vodka and essential oil and mix thoroughly with a hand-held blender. Refrigerate in an air-tight container until needed.

confit of vegetables:

Heat the olive oil in a saucepan over a medium heat, add the carrots and onions and cook until pale golden in colour. Add the leek, celery and garlic and cook until a rich caramel colour has developed. Set aside until needed.

tomato fondue:

Bring a pan of water to the boil. Make a small incision in the tomatoes and blanch in the water for 10-15 seconds. Plunge into iced water to cool. Drain, remove the skin and cut the tomatoes in half. Scoop out and discard the cores. Place the flesh and seeds in a sieve set over a bowl. Sprinkle with ½ teaspoon salt, toss to combine and leave for 1 hour. Reserve the juice in the bowl, then chop the flesh into small dice and set aside. Make a bouquet garni by placing the parsley, thyme, peppercorns, star anise and clove in a muslin bag and tying securely. Set aside. Heat the olive oil in a pan, add the onions and sweat for 10 minutes. Add the garlic and bouquet garni and sweat for 5 minutes. Add the tomatoes and their juice, the vinegar, ketchup, Worcestershire sauce, Tabasco and lemon zest. Cook over a low heat for 2-3 hours, stirring regularly. After about 1-1½ hours of cooking, add the saffron. The fondue should have a nice dark colour and a jammy consistency. Keep refrigerated until needed.

sauce poivrade:

Place the venison bones in a pan and roast for 1 hour, or until lightly coloured. Place in a storage container. Pour the wine into a large pan, bring to the boil, then flame off the alcohol. Pour over the bones, adding enough water so that they are just covered. Add the confit of vegetables and tomato fondue, then cover and refrigerate for 48 hours. Transfer the bone mixture to a pressure cooker and top up with water to cover if necessary. Put on the lid, bring to full pressure and cook for 2 hours, skimming regularly. Take off the heat and leave to cool completely before removing the lid. Strain the liquid through a fine sieve into another pan. Bring to the boil and reduce to 10 per cent of the original amount. Pass through a fine sieve and set aside until needed.

gastrique:

Place the honey in a pan and warm over a medium-high heat until it begins to caramelise. Add the vinegar, reserved consommé, bay leaf, thyme, juniper berries and pink peppercorns. Return the pan to the heat and simmer for 5 minutes. Add the black peppercorns, freshly cracked, and infuse for a few minutes, until the aroma is sufficiently strong. Strain the sauce through a fine sieve lined with a double layer of damp muslin and refrigerate until needed.

blood cream:

Place the bones and cream in a saucepan and bring to 50°C. Cover and hold at this temperature for 30 minutes. Strain through a chinoise and refrigerate the cream until needed.

celeriac purée:

Using a mandoline, slice the celeriac as thinly as possible. Melt the butter in a large saucepan over a medium heat and add the celeriac. Cook until completely soft, stirring to avoid it catching. When soft, add the milk and simmer for 5 minutes. Transfer to a blender and blitz to a purée. Pass the purée through a fine sieve using the back of a ladle and pour into a PacoJet beaker. Freeze completely, then pass through a PacoJet machine. Repeat this process three times, freezing between each processing. Transfer the purée to a pan and heat gently while stirring. Season to taste with salt and freshly ground pepper, then set aside to cool. Cover and refrigerate until needed.

celeriac fondants:

Preheat a water bath to 83°C.

Cut the celeriac into slices 15mm thick, then cut each slice into rectangles measuring 3 x 4cm. Place in a sous-vide bag in a single layer with the butter and the salt and seal under full pressure. Place the bag in the water bath and cook for 4½ hours (until cooked through but not mushy). Remove and cool at room temperature for 15 minutes. Transfer to room-temperature water for 15 minutes, then place in iced water until thoroughly chilled. Keep refrigerated until needed.

civet base:

Line a tray with baking parchment and refrigerate until cold. Heat the chicken bouillon to just below simmering and keep hot. Place the oil in a pan over a medium heat and, when hot, roast the pearl barley until golden and nutty. Add the shallots and sweat until softened. Add the garlic and cook for 2 minutes. Pour in the Madeira, bring to the boil, then flame off the alcohol and reduce to a syrup.

Pour 200g of the hot chicken bouillon on to the barley and cook over a medium heat until the barley is just soft. Add more bouillon if required to achieve this.

Remove from the heat and spread the barley on to the chilled tray. When cool, divide into 22g portions and refrigerate until needed.

red wine jelly discs:

Cover a large, flat board with cling film, stretching it to ensure that there are no creases or air bubbles. Pour the wines into a pan, bring to the boil, then flame off the alcohol. Using a hand-held blender, add both gellans. Return to the heat and bring to the boil, stirring. As soon as the gellan has dissolved, pour on to the prepared board, tilting to spread the gel in a thin, even layer. Leave to set. Using a cutter 6cm in diameter, cut circles out of the jelly. Stack them between squares of baking parchment, place in a covered container and refrigerate until needed.

venison medallions:

Remove the individual loins from the saddle, keeping the rib bones attached. Then trim away the small fillets and reserve for another use, and French the individual bones. Place the loins in a sous-vide bag with the olive oil and thyme and seal under full pressure. Refrigerate for 48 hours. Remove the marinated loins from the sous-vide bag and wipe off any excess oil. Place several layers of cling film on a work surface and wrap it firmly around the loins, twisting the ends to tighten the package into a cylindrical shape. Refrigerate for at least 4 hours. Transfer the venison to a board, remove the cling film and cut the meat into 150g portions. Wrap each medallion in cling film, place in individual sous-vide bags and seal under full pressure. Refrigerate until needed.

red wine foam:

Pour the wines into a pan, bring to the boil, then flame off the alcohol. Remove from the heat and add the lecithin, stirring to dissolve. Cover until needed.

grelot onions:

Trim away any stalk on the onion and remove all but 0.5cm of the green top. Peel away the first two layers of the onion to expose the tender core. Remove as much root as possible, but keep the onion intact. Seal in a sous-vide bag at 15mbar, then cook in a microwave on full power for about 1 minute – long enough for the onion to be cooked through but still firm. Plunge the bag into iced water to prevent the grelot from overcooking. Once cool, remove from the bag and slice in half. Refrigerate until needed.

butter emulsion:

Combine the ingredients in a small pan and place over a medium heat. Emulsify with a hand-held blender and keep warm.

to serve:

Preheat a water bath to 60°C and another to 50°C. Place the venison medallions in the hotter water bath and cook until the internal temperature of the meat reaches 54°C. Transfer to the cooler water bath for 10 minutes.

Gently reheat the celeriac purée, adjust the seasoning, then cover and keep warm.

Place a small sauté pan on a high heat and add the clarified butter. Remove a fondant from the sous-vide bag and colour one side in the butter. Remove from the heat and pour off the butter. Add the chicken bouillon to the pan, gently shaking to coat the fondant. Keep warm.

Preheat a small sauté pan until very hot. Sear the cut side of a grelot half until golden and slightly charred. Keep warm. Cut the root end off the other half of grelot and separate the layers. Place in a small saucepan with enough butter emulsion to warm through. When hot, drain on kitchen paper and season. Keep warm.

Heat 30g of the sauce poivrade in a small saucepan and swirl in 1 teaspoon of the blood cream, heating gently to lightly thicken the sauce.

Place the white chicken stock in a small pan, bring to a simmer and add 22g of the civet base. Stir and cook until the bouillon has been absorbed. Add 15g of both the sauce poivrade and the celeriac purée to bind the civet base. Stir and allow to reduce slightly. Add the diced foie gras and venison marrow, then remove from the heat. Add the foie gras parfait and sherry vinegar and adjust the seasoning.

Remove a venison medallion from the bag and drain on kitchen paper, leaving the cling film wrapping on the meat. Leave to rest in a warm place.

Place the civet mixture in a small, warm bowl and position a jelly disc on top of it. Using a hand-held blender, froth the red wine foam and spoon over the jelly.

Cut the venison medallion across the grain into five slices, each 1cm thick. Remove the cling film and season the meat with fine sea salt, fleur de sel and sifted black pepper.

Place 60g of the celeriac purée on a warm plate. Place the grelots in butter emulsion on top of the celeriac purée. Trim the edges of the celeriac fondant, cut into three equal triangles and arrange on the plate. Place the slices of venison over the grelot. Place the seared grelot on the plate next to the venison. Spoon over 15g of the sauce poivrade, garnish with the white truffle, and serve.

Meanwhile, make the venison and frankincense tea. Heat 65g of the venison consommé to 65°C, add the frankincense drops and serve after the venison and civet as a kind of palate cleanser.

THE BFG! (ALSO KNOWN AS THE BLACK FOREST GATEAU!)
BY HESTON BLUMENTHAL

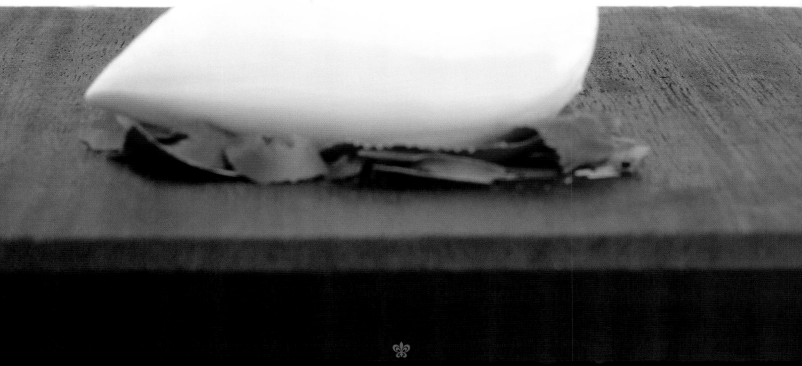

Serves 4

INGREDIENTS

kirsch ice cream:

500g	full-fat milk
120g	egg yolks
200g	unrefined caster sugar
80g	kirsch
350g	sour cream

roast almond paste:

200g	whole blanched almonds
5g	egg white
5g	table salt

almond base:

40g	Amedei Toscano chocolate (32% cocoa solids), chopped
40g	amarena cherries
100g	reserved roast almond paste
15g	reserved chopped almonds
50g	feuilletine (caramelised puff pastry)

apricot pâté de fruit:

200g	unrefined caster sugar
3g	yellow pectin
250g	apricot purée
25g	glucose syrup
3g	malic acid
5g	amaretto liquor

kirsch ganache:

50g	unsalted butter
500g	Valrhona Guanaja chocolate (70% cocoa solids)
450g	UHT cream
70g	invert sugar syrup
110g	kirsch
3g	table salt

chocolate sponge:

225g	whole eggs
125g	unrefined caster sugar
50g	plain flour
30g	cornflour
30g	cocoa powder

soaking syrup:

100g	griottine cherries, in syrup
15g	kirsch

wood-effect base:

100g	unsalted butter
60g	plain flour
5g	baking powder
30g	sifted icing sugar
3g	table salt
60g	whole egg
30g	honey
15g	whole milk

wood grain:

100g	cocoa powder
20g	cornflour
180g	water
	reserved wood-effect base

dried vanilla cherry stems:

2	vanilla pods

chocolate shavings:

100g	Amedei Chuao chocolate (70% cocoa solids)

white chocolate mousse:

7.5g	leaf gelatine (170 bloom)
300g	white chocolate
500g	whipping cream
60g	kirsch
40g	egg yolks
10g	unrefined caster sugar
125g	full-fat milk
	reserved chocolate sponge moulds

dark chocolate mousse:

This should be made while the white chocolate mousse is setting.

5g	leaf gelatine (170 bloom)
150g	Amedei Chuao chocolate (70% cocoa solids)
200g	whipping cream
50g	egg yolks
50g	unrefined caster sugar
2g	table salt
150g	whole milk
	reserved chocolate sponge moulds

the flocage:

This makes enough to cover three gateaux, but the surplus can be stored for later use.

500g	chocolate (70% cocoa solids)
200g	cocoa butter
	reserved gateau

METHOD

kirsch ice cream:

Pour the milk into a pan, bring to a simmer and remove from the heat. Place the egg yolks and sugar in the bowl of a food mixer and beat for 5 minutes. Pour in the warm milk, mixing gently to combine. Return the mixture to the pan and place over the heat, stirring, until it reaches 70°C. Hold at this temperature for 10 minutes to pasteurise. Cool over an ice bath. Cover and mature in the fridge for 8-24 hours. Stir in the kirsch and sour cream, then churn in an ice-cream machine to -5°C. Place a sheet of cling film on the surface of the ice cream, then cover and store in the freezer until needed.

roast almond paste:

Preheat the oven to 180°C and line an oven tray with silicone paper. Combine all the ingredients in a bowl and spread over the prepared tray in a single layer. Bake for 10-15 minutes, or until golden brown. Remove and leave to cool. Roughly chop 15g of the almonds and set aside. Place the rest in a food processor and blitz until puréed. Set aside.

almond base:

Melt the chocolate in a bain-marie or microwave. Chop the cherries to roughly the same size as the almonds and stir into the chocolate along with the almond paste and chopped almonds. Fold in the feuilletine until the mixture comes together – it's important not to overmix. Line a baking tray with parchment and spread the mixture on it to a thickness of about 5mm. Score into strips measuring 12 x 7cm, then cover and refrigerate.

pâté de fruit:

Combine the sugar and pectin in a bowl. Place the apricot purée in a saucepan, bring to the boil and whisk in the pectin mixture. Whisk in the glucose syrup and continue to cook on a medium to high heat until it reaches 107°C. Set aside.

Dissolve the malic acid in the amaretto, then whisk into the apricot mixture, working quickly, as the syrup will now start to set. Pour into a bowl and leave to cool. When the gel has set, blitz with a hand-held blender until smooth and store in a piping bag until needed.

kirsch ganache:

Cut the butter into small pieces and set aside, covered, to reach room temperature. Finely chop the chocolate and melt gently in a bain-marie or microwave until it reaches about 50°C, but not more than 55°C. Set aside. Place the cream, invert sugar syrup, kirsch and salt in a saucepan and bring to the boil. Remove from the heat and very carefully add to the melted chocolate in three stages with the aid of a hand-held blender. (The aim is to emulsify, not to incorporate any air.) Line a 36 x 26 x 5cm tray with baking parchment. Blend the butter into the chocolate mixture, then pour into the prepared tray, cover and leave to set at room temperature for 48 hours. Cut the ganache into rectangles measuring 11 x 6cm, then cover and refrigerate.

chocolate sponge:

Preheat the oven to 180°C. Place the eggs and sugar in a bowl and whisk until thick and glossy. Add the remaining ingredients and fold together. Line a 29 x 19 x 3.5cm baking tray with parchment. Pour the cocoa mixture into the tray and bake for 15 minutes, or until firm to the touch. Cool on a wire rack, then cut into rectangles measuring 11 x 6 x 1.5cm. Using a round cutter 1cm in diameter, cut out two parallel rows of four holes in each rectangle and set aside.

soaking syrup:

Drain the cherries and set aside. Weigh out 40g of the syrup, add to the kirsch and mix thoroughly. Reserve until needed.

wood-effect base:

Preheat the oven to 180°C. Melt the butter in a small saucepan over a medium heat, stirring frequently, until it begins to brown and develops a nutty aroma. Strain the beurre noisette through a fine sieve and set aside.

Sift together the flour, baking powder, icing sugar and salt. Stir in 50g of the beurre noisette, then mix in the egg, honey and milk, incorporating them separately. Refrigerate until needed.

wood grain:

Preheat the oven to 180°C. Place the cocoa, cornflour and water in a bowl and whisk to a smooth paste. Using a home decorating tool designed for creating a wood-grain effect, dip the edge of it into the paste and using a rocking motion spread it over a silicone baking mat. Place in the freezer until set (about 1 hour). Allow the wood-effect base to come to room temperature, then spread it over the wood grain as thinly as possible. Place in the oven and bake for 8-10 minutes, or until golden brown. Transfer to a rack, leave to cool and store in an air-tight container until needed.

dried vanilla cherry stems:

Top and tail the vanilla pods, split in half lengthways and scrape out the seeds (save for another use). Cut each pod in half widthways, and cut these into three lengthways strips. Tie a knot at the end of each strip to give the effect of a cherry stem. Set aside in a warm, dry place until needed.

chocolate shavings:

Run a small sharp knife along the block of chocolate to make shavings. Store in the freezer until needed.

white chocolate mousse:

Soak the gelatine in cold water and set aside. Chop the white chocolate and gently melt in a bain-marie or microwave. Set aside. Lightly whip the cream and kirsch to soft peaks and set aside. Whisk the yolks and sugar together for 5 minutes and set aside. Heat the milk in a saucepan to 60°C. Slowly pour it into the egg mixture while whisking constantly then return to the pan. Heat gently, stirring constantly, until it reaches 70°C, and hold at this temperature for 10 minutes. Squeeze the gelatine dry, then add to the saucepan and stir to dissolve. Pour the mixture into the melted chocolate and stir together. Fold in the cream, then pour immediately over the sponge in the moulds to a depth of 1cm. Refrigerate for about 1 hour to set.

dark chocolate mousse:

Soak the gelatine in cold water and set aside. Chop the chocolate and gently melt in a bain-marie or microwave. Set aside. Lightly whip the cream to soft peaks and set aside. Whisk the egg yolks, sugar and salt together until pale in colour (about 5 minutes). Heat the milk in a saucepan to 70°C, then slowly pour it into the egg yolks while whisking constantly and return the mixture to the pan. Heat gently, stirring constantly, until it reaches 70°C, and hold at this temperature for 10 minutes. Squeeze the gelatine dry, then add to the saucepan and stir to dissolve. Pour the mixture into the melted chocolate and stir together. Fold in the cream, then pour immediately over the white chocolate mousse to the top of the moulds. Level the surface with a palette knife, then freeze for 3-4 hours, until completely set.

assembly:

To build the gateau, part 1
(4-5 portions)
reserved almond base
reserved apricot pâté de fruit
reserved kirsch ganache
reserved chocolate sponge
8 reserved griottine cherries
reserved soaking syrup

Place a 12 x 7 x 6cm metal mould on a baking tray lined with parchment. Place an almond base strip in the bottom of each mould. Pipe a line of the pâté de fruit 1cm wide along the centre of it. Top that with a rectangle of ganache, followed by a rectangle of chocolate sponge. Place a cherry in each hole. Drizzle a little of the soaking syrup over the sponge and reserve.

To build the gateau, part 2
(4-5 portions)
reserved frozen gateau

Using a Parisian scoop 20mm wide, scoop out two parallel rows of four shallow indentations in the chocolate mousse layer of the gateau. Using a blow torch, warm the outside of the mould and invert the contents on to a tray. Turn it over so that the holes are on top. Using an offset palette knife, smooth the sides of the gateau.

the flocage:

Chop the chocolate and cocoa butter and melt gently in a bain-marie or microwave. Pour into a paint spray gun and, working quickly, spray the gateau evenly on all sides. Refrigerate until the centre has defrosted (about 2-3 hours).

To build the gateau, part 3
(4-5 portions)
kirsch
reserved wood-effect base
reserved gateau
reserved chocolate shavings
reserved soaking syrup
8 amarena cherries, drained
reserved vanilla cherry stems
reserved kirsch ice cream

Pour the kirsch into an atomiser and secure the spraying nozzle. Place the wood-effect base on a serving tray and sit the gateau on top. Surround with the chocolate shavings, then push a skewer into each indentation to a depth of 2-3cm. Using a pipette, fill the skewer holes with the soaking syrup, making sure that it does not spill out. Place a cherry in each indentation, stalk end up. Stick a vanilla stem into each cherry and serve with the kirsch ice cream. Spray the kirsch atomiser into the air above the place settings.

Daniel Galmiche

Born in Lure in the Comte region of Eastern France, Daniel was enthralled with cooking from an early age. His grandparents ran a small self-sufficient organic farm and he used to hunt for game with his father. After leaving school, Daniel worked alongside the Michelin-starred chef Yves Lalloz on a three-year apprenticeship at the Hotel Beausite, Luxeuil les Bains. He worked at L'Ortolan, Le Gavroche, Le Meridien Penina, Portugal and Duxton Hotel in Singapore among other places before joining The Vineyard at Stockcross in 2009. Daniel has held a Michelin star for 20 years. By those in the know, he is described as the "king of contemporary French cooking".

"*Eating out is one of the greatest pleasures of life and I have made it my mission to communicate this.*"

The Vineyard
at stockcross

{

The Vineyard at Stockcross, a restaurant with rooms or a luxury country house retreat? We'll let you decide but one thing is certain – this haven for fine food and excellent wine is like no other.

It is a luxury hotel, so why not start your very own gastronomic affair right here with us? Privately owned by Sir Peter Michael, The Vineyard at Stockcross is located just outside Newbury, Berkshire and one hour from central London. The 49 rooms and suites range from the original and traditional style hunting lodge bedrooms through to the contemporary and spacious atrium suites. The Vineyard's connection with fine wine is all too evident with a cellar that contains 23,000 unique wines and one of the most impressive wine lists the culinary world has to offer. Add to this one of the most highly rated boutique spas in the UK that is on hand to pamper and relax you and you'll be looking for a reason to extend your stay. The unrivalled privacy at The Vineyard allows for unique events from stunning wedding celebrations or executive board meetings to team-building events, conferences and even car launches.

⚜

SCALLOP CARPACCIO & SCALLOP TARTARE

CARPACCIO DE SAINT-JACQUES ET SON TARTARE
BY DANIEL GALMICHE

This recipe, is very refreshing, light, and interesting. One thing though, in The Vineyard, we are very much working toward sustainability, I know, some people will not think or care about it, but put it that way, if you do, you will have scallop for a long time to come. So worth it …

At The Vineyard we only buy hand-dived scallops, not dredged, if you do this too you will be enjoying scallops for a long time to come! The advantage of this is that you will enjoy a beautiful, firm, delicious flesh and it is for that reason we use this recipe in the restaurant. I personally love scallops with lime and lemongrass, but you need to find this out yourself. Remember, ingredients are the key, then the rest will come.

Serves 4
Preparation time: 45 minutes
Cooking time: N/A

Special equipment:
Mandoline (optional).

Planning ahead:
The jelly can be made in advance. Start to roll the scallops the day before.

INGREDIENTS

scallops:

8	large scallops
4	small scallops
1 tbsp	crème fraîche
zest of 1 lime	
juice of 1 lime	
sea salt	
pepper	
½	bunch chives, chopped
1	Granny Smith apple, peeled and chopped into small dice (brunoise)
1 tsp	olive oil

apple jelly:

1	stalk lemongrass
500ml	clear apple juice
25g	vegetable gelatine powder

croutons:

1	thin large slice of white bread (tin loaf)
olive oil	

to serve:

olive oil	
zest of 1 lime	
salt and pepper	
1 tsp	Aquitaine caviar
4	sprigs of chervil

METHOD

scallops:

Wrap the large scallops in four parcels of cling film (two scallops per person) and roll tight. Put into the freezer.

While this is setting make the tartare – cut the four small scallops into small cubes and keep in an ice-cold container. When needed add the crème fraîche, lime zest, a few drops of lime juice, season to taste and add the chives, apple brunoise (10g) and the olive oil. Keep aside.

apple jelly:

Infuse the lemongrass in the apple juice for 40 minutes, then remove the lemongrass. Pour the apple juice into a small pan and bring to a simmer, add the gelatine powder, whisk in quickly then pour onto a small shallow plate or tray until set. Cut into cubes once set and keep them covered in the fridge.

croutons:

Brush the bread with olive oil, cut into rectangles and place on a tray. Put in the oven at 140°C for 8-10 minutes.

to serve:

Using a meat slicer or other sharp utensil (like a mandoline) cut some thin slices of the frozen scallop and arrange in a square shape on a cold plate. Brush with olive oil and add some grated lime zest, seasoning and then the caviar. Place the scallop tartare in the centre with the apple jelly and croutons on top. Garnish with the chervil.

Serves 4
Preparation time: 1 hour 40 minutes
Cooking time: 45 minutes

Special equipment:
Vacuum pack, water bath, Thermomix, 4 small rings.

Planning ahead:
The veal shin needs to be cooked the day before.

INGREDIENTS

veal shin:

1	small veal shin (10/12 portions)
1	small carrot, chopped
1	onion, chopped
3	cloves garlic
2	sprigs of thyme

white wine, as required
chicken stock, as required

1	handful tomatoes, diced
4 tbsp	veal jus

salt and pepper
olive oil, as required
thin slices of carrot to make bands

veal rack - boneless:

1	small rack of veal (400g)
200g	pancetta, sliced but not too finely

olive oil, as required

10g	thyme

sweetbreads:

150g	sweetbreads

veal jus from the veal shin

40g	carrots
30g	truffle matignon (mini brunoise - dice)

artichokes:

2	baby artichokes
½	bunch chives, chopped
1	slice pancetta
10ml	chicken stock
4	baby carrots

dry pancetta:

4	thin slices of pancetta

breadcrumbs:

½	small bunch of parsley, washed and stems removed
50g	breadcrumbs

truffle & Swiss chard tian:

1	large Swiss chard braised with pancetta, carrots, onions, thyme and garlic
40g	truffle, sliced

mashed potatoes:

6	large Agra potatoes
300g	sea salt
80g	butter
40g	whipping cream

TRIO OF VEAL, SMOKED MASH, JUS WITH TRUFFLES

DECLINAISON DE VEAU, FUMEE, JUS AU TRUFFLES
BY DANIEL GALMICHE

This is one of my favourite recipes on our menu as I really love veal. There is only one problem with veal and that it that it is expensive so sometimes difficult to source a good cut! You will see in this recipe that we use three different parts of the veal, so when it is on the plate it gives you three different flavours, which equals a lovely, balanced dish.

At The Vineyard we use French veal, from a small farm in Brittany, as we know the farmer looks after his cattle; this is extremely important to us too. This recipe is a long task, but well worth it, and if you are like me, you will love it. We usually use at least 70 per cent of British produce here at The Vineyard where possible but I am yet to find a farmer who can supply me with the standard of veal that I looking for, but I will carry on searching! Anyway, I am sure you will have fun making this one but most of all enjoy eating it. The result will delight you. Bon appétit!

METHOD

veal shin:

Seal the veal shin and put the garnish (carrot, onion, garlic and thyme) in a pan and sweat it down. Deglaze with the wine then add chicken stock and cook in the oven at 120°C for about 4 hours - this needs to be done the day before. When the veal shin is cooked and falling apart, remove from the liquid and shred while still warm. Add the tomatoes and the veal jus, season the mix then roll in cling film in cylinder shapes. Keep in the cool part of your fridge. Slice just before you cook the veal rack and seal both ends of the cylinders of shin in a warm pan with a few drops of olive oil, then add chicken stock to braise and make sure it is hot enough. When ready to serve, cut out the cling film and wrap in a carrot band.

veal rack – boneless:

Roll the veal in pancetta then place in a vacuum bag with the olive oil, thyme and lime zest. Cook in a water bath at 54°C for 35 minutes then quickly colour in a pan just before serving.

sweetbreads:

Blanch quickly then refresh in iced water, remove the outer skin then roast until golden brown and finish in veal jus with the carrots and truffle matignon.

artichokes:

Sauté the artichokes with the chives in a medium-sized pan, add the pancetta, deglaze briefly with the stock, add the four baby carrots and braise until tender.

dry pancetta:

Dry in the oven at 140°C for 20 minutes.

breadcrumbs:

Mix the parsley and breadcrumbs together in a Thermomix.

truffle & Swiss chard tian:

Lay the Swiss chard in a small ring and top with the truffle.

mashed potatoes:

Cook the potatoes with their skins on in the salt in the oven at 200°C, pass through a sieve then add the butter and cream.

to serve:

Assemble the dish as shown in the picture.

Serves 4
Preparation time: 1 hour
Cooking time: 30-45 minutes

Special equipment:
Vacuum pack, steam oven, Thermomix, corer,
Pacojet, siphon.

Planning ahead:
The apple cylinder needs to be started the day
before. The apple crisps need to dry overnight.

INGREDIENTS

light apple compote:

500g	Braeburn apples
1	litre apple juice
1	lemon
1	cinnamon stick

apple cylinder:

4	Granny Smith apples
caster sugar, as required	
200g	30% sugar syrup

apple crisp:

1	Granny Smith apple
100g	water
5g	ascorbic acid (vitamin C)

triangles of puff pastry:

200g	puff pastry
80g	icing sugar
2	egg yolks

vanilla ice cream:

500g	semi-skimmed milk
200g	whipping cream
1	vanilla pod
8	egg yolks
100g	caster sugar

apple jelly:

375g	apple juice
25g	caster sugar
9g	vegetable gelatine
green colouring, as required	

tatine espuma:

reserved juice from the compote	
100g	double cream

caramelised apples:

2	Braeburn apples
caster sugar, as required	

'DECONSTRUCTED' APPLE TARTE TATIN
BY DANIEL GALMICHE

A fresh approach on a classical French dessert. This is a lovely, light and refreshing dish which we wanted to make interesting to look at as well as to eat without forgetting the traditional take from the 'tatin sisters'. All the different elements are there, but in a modern way. Everyone love apples (well most of us) and this dessert is to prove no different and is very popular at The Vineyard as the feedback we receive is great. I am sure you will love it too.

METHOD

light apple compote:

Peel the apples and cut into small cubes. Put the apple juice, apple, lemon and cinnamon stick into a vacuum bag. Cook at 100°C and steam for 25 minutes. Remove the bag from the oven and pour out the juice and keep it to one side for the 'espuma'. Blitz the remaining mixture in a Thermomix until the apple is smooth and then leave to cool in the fridge.

apple cylinder:

Using a corer make four cylinders from the apples and caramelise with sugar quickly. Leave to cool down in the freezer as this will enable the apples to keep the cylindrical shapes. With a small cutter, also cut small discs of apple and put them in the syrup overnight. The next day you will be able to stick them on the cylinder.

apple crisp:

Slice the apple and brush with the water and vitamin C, then leave them to dry overnight.

triangles of puff pastry:

Roll the puff pastry thinly (¾cm), then first cut out triangles 5cm each side (use a cutter if you have one) then with a round cutter make a hole in the centre the size of the apple cylinder. Place the triangles on a silpat and sprinkle over icing sugar. Brush 12 of the triangles with egg yolk and put some more icing sugar on top and another silpat and place on a heavy tray. Cook for 20-25 minutes at 190°C or until light brown in colour.

vanilla ice cream:

Boil the milk, cream and the vanilla pod and infuse for 7 minutes. In a bowl whisk the egg yolks and the sugar together until the mix becomes almost white. Then add the milk/cream mix into the yolks. Put back on to cook until it reaches 82°C, whisking constantly. Cool down on top of a bowl filled with ice then put in a Pacojet tub.

apple jelly:

Boil the apple juice and sugar together, then add the gelatine and green colouring. When it is cooked (gelatine dissolved) put on a flat square plate in a fridge and when set use a round cutter to cut the jelly.

tatine espuma:

Mix together the juice and the cream then put in a siphon and add three gas chargers.

caramelised apples:

Caramelise the apples in sugar until a light brown caramel.

to serve:

Take four glasses and fill each with compote for the first level followed by caramelised apple for the second level. The third level is the espuma then finally the apple syrup from the apple cylinder recipe. For the puff pastry triangles make a pedestal with the apple discs and stack three puff pastry triangles on them with an apple cylinder in the middle hole. Put the vanilla ice cream on the left of the glass. Garnish with the apple jelly and apple crisp.

Devon

Untamed moorland, ancient towns and Riviera

{ 'Glorious Devon' was a promotional slogan created by the Great Western Railway in the 1920s and it remains equally true today. This region of immense contrast from bustling cities to old market towns and tiny villages, of wild moorland to traditional seaside and fishing harbours, of great houses and gardens, is one of total fascination. Its cities reflect a long and eventful history. The walled capital city of Exeter has Roman origins while Plymouth has long been the maritime heart of the nation, forever linked with Sir Francis Drake and the defeat of the Spanish Armada and the departure of the Pilgrim Fathers for a new life in America. The bleak and wild country of the moor could not be a greater contrast to the resorts around Torbay in an area that quickly became known as the 'English Riviera' because of its mild climate, semi-tropical gardens and fine Victorian hotels. Fine local foods are a growing feature of the region, although nothing has supplanted a Devonshire cream tea for a seductive indulgence.

Michael Caines is one of Britain's most acclaimed chefs. AA Chef's Chef of the Year in 2007 and awarded an MBE in 2006 for services to the hospitality industry. In 2000, Michael founded Michael Caines Restaurants and took over food and beverage operations at The Royal Clarence, Exeter, Britain's first hotel. A chance encounter with Andrew Brownsword led to the creation of the ABode Hotel group, of which Michael is an Operational Partner and Director, in overall charge of all food and beverage operations throughout the fast-growing group. Michael is also Executive Chef at Gidleigh Park, the acclaimed and prestigious country house hotel on the edge of Dartmoor at Chagford, Devon, where he has earned his reputation – as well as two Michelin stars, and also at its Michelin-starred sister hotel, The Bath Priory Hotel, Restaurant and Spa in Bath. Both properties serve distinctive modern European cuisine utilising the finest local and regional produce and ingredients.

Gidleigh Park

{ *The beautiful Tudor style country house hotel, together with the magnificent 107 acres of mature grounds and woodlands, is set in an idyllic location within the heart of Dartmoor National Park.*

Savour the culinary delights created by two Michelin star, Executive Head Chef Michael Caines MBE, who uses only the finest local ingredients. Alongside its outstanding cuisine, Gidleigh Park has long enjoyed the reputation of having one of the finest wine lists in the UK, with some 1000 bottles from around the world. From the house you can enjoy walks through the grounds and onto Dartmoor itself. In the local area you can enjoy horseback riding, bird of prey flying, clay pigeon shooting and guided tours on foot or by car.

RIVER DART WILD SALMON, OSCIETRA CAVIAR, SALMON JELLY, CUCUMBER, HONEY & SOY VINAIGRETTE, WASABI & GREEK YOGHURT VINAIGRETTE

BY MICHAEL CAINES

This recipe is inspired by two cooking cultures, Chinese and Norwegian. The dill and salmon come straight from gravlax and five-spice powder, honey and soy are pure Chinese. The salmon jelly just melts in the mouth and adds another texture to everything. I like to finish off with micro leaves and herbs from our kitchen garden at Gidleigh: dill, purple basil and borage flowers are particularly good.

Serves 4
Preparation time: 1 hour
Cooking time: 1 hour

Special equipment:
Mandoline.

Planning ahead:
The salmon is best marinated overnight.

INGREDIENTS

salmon:

15g	sugar
15g	sea salt
1	lemon – zested, peeled and segmented (the segments reserved for garnishing)
1	pinch freshly ground pepper
600g	wild salmon fillet, skin on

cucumber:

1	cucumber – peeled, deseeded and cut into 7cm lengths
salt	
1 tbsp	chopped dill
1	splash of groundnut vinaigrette

honey and soy vinaigrette:

50ml	clear honey
1	pinch Chinese five-spice powder
1 tsp	Dijon mustard
10ml	balsamic vinegar
100ml	white wine vinegar
10ml	soy sauce
200ml	extra virgin olive oil
salt and pepper	

wasabi and Greek yoghurt vinaigrette:

25ml	double cream
1½ tsp	wasabi
50ml	Greek yoghurt
salt and pepper	

salmon jelly (stock):

1	salmon carcass
50g	onion, chopped
35g	leeks, chopped
1	clove garlic, crushed
250g	tomatoes, chopped
75g	fennel, finely chopped
2	parsley stalks
½	star anise
1	small sprig of thyme
¼	stick of celery
1 tbsp	white peppercorns, crushed
50ml	Noilly Pratt
100ml	white wine
700ml	water

stock clarification (for salmon jelly):

125g	salmon trimmings
2	egg whites
salt and pepper	
30g	ice
3	leaves gelatine

garnish:

4	lemon segments, cut into 5 equal pieces
handful of micro salad leaves and herbs (eg purple basil)	
18	borage flowers
Keta caviar (salmon roe)	
Oscietra caviar	

METHOD

salmon:

Prepare a marinade by mixing together the sugar, salt, lemon zest and pepper. Place the salmon on a tray and cover with the marinade, then leave it for at least 8 hours. After this wash and skin the fillet, trimming off any brown meat. Cut the fillet in half lengthways, then cut in half twice more, wrap the fish in cling film and place it in the fridge for several hours to firm up, ideally overnight.

cucumber:

Slice the cucumber on a mandoline into 2 x 3mm strips. Trim evenly then place the slices in a colander over a dish and scatter salt over them. The slices should be left for 10 minutes to draw out the water, then rinsed thoroughly with water and dried off with a clean cloth. Place the strips on a tray and freeze the cucumber briefly, then take out and defrost. Cover with a pinch of chopped dill and some groundnut vinaigrette and marinate until ready to serve.

honey and soy vinaigrette:

Put the honey, Chinese five-spice powder and mustard together in a bowl and mix well until blended. Then whisk in, separately, the balsamic vinegar, white wine vinegar and soy sauce. Once the ingredients have been blended together, then use a hand blender and gradually add the olive oil slowly until it is completely mixed. Season with salt and pepper to taste.

wasabi and Greek yoghurt vinaigrette:

Whisk the cream and wasabi together until stiff. Pass the mixture through a fine sieve into a bowl then fold in the Greek yoghurt and season with salt and pepper.

salmon jelly (stock):

Put all the ingredients together in a large saucepan over a medium heat and bring to the boil. Reduce to a simmer and cook for a further 30 minutes, then strain the stock through a colander and then a fine sieve. Pour it back into the saucepan and simmer over a medium heat until it has reduced its volume by one-third.

stock clarification (for salmon jelly):

Next clarify the stock. Blitz the salmon trimmings with the egg whites and salt in a liquidiser. Once mixed together blend in the ice and put to one side. Bring the stock back to the boil, then whisk in the clarification mixture and again bring the stock back to the boil, stirring constantly with a wooden spoon. Reduce to a simmer and leave to cook for 10 minutes, then remove the stock from the heat and pass it through a fine sieve into a clean saucepan. Put this over a medium heat and bring the strained stock back to the boil. Correct the seasoning and add the leaves of gelatine. Line a tray with cling film and pour in the stock to a thickness of 1cm. Put in the fridge to set. Once set, take out and cut into small cubes.

to serve:

Remove the salmon from the fridge. Heat up a saucepan of water to 40°C over a low heat, drop in the salmon (still in its cling film) and poach for 10 minutes. Meanwhile, place some of the cucumber slices on your plates and sprinkle these with keta caviar. Dot some blobs of the honey and soy vinaigrette around the plate, add the lemon segments and fill in the gaps with blobs of wasabi and Greek yoghurt vinaigrette. Add some salmon jelly cubes and then the salmon – three pieces per person – and finish with the micro salad leaves and herbs, borage flowers, keta and oscietra caviars.

SCALLOPS WITH CELERIAC PUREE & SOY & TRUFFLE VINAIGRETTE
BY MICHAEL CAINES

This is a wonderful dish which incorporates the rich soy and truffle vinaigrette with the smooth, creamy flavour of the celeriac. This contrasts beautifully with the meaty scallops which are delicate in flavour against the intense flavour of the soy and truffle. This has become one of my signature dishes over the years.

Serves 4
Preparation time: 2 hours
Cooking time: 45 minutes

Special equipment:
Robot coupe
Blender
Non-stick pan

Planning ahead:
Make the celeriac purée, the soy truffle vinaigrette and the French vinaigrette in advance.

INGREDIENTS

12	scallops
	celeriac purée
	soy and truffle vinaigrette
	mixed salad
	chopped chives
	olive oil
	salt and pepper
	French dressing

celeriac purée:

200g	celeriac, chopped
15g	celery, chopped
15g	onions, chopped
150ml	water
150ml	milk
25g	unsalted butter
pinch of salt and pepper to season	

soy and truffle vinaigrette:

25g	shallots, sliced
50g	button mushrooms
10g	soy sauce
25g	veal glace
30g	olive oil
20g	truffle juice
5ml	truffle oil
2	sprigs of thyme, fresh (80g/bunch)
100g	olive oil

french vinaigrette:

300ml	vegetable oil
100ml	white wine vinegar
salt and pepper	
sprig of thyme	
1 clove garlic	

METHOD

celeriac purée:

In a saucepan sweat the onion, celery and salt with the butter, add the milk and water then the celeriac and pepper. Bring to the boil and reduce to a simmer. Cook out for 30 minutes and then allow to cool. Pass off through a colander and then place into a robot coupe and blend until fine. Remove from the robot coupe and then pace into a blender and blend to a very fine purée.

soy and truffle vinaigrette:

Sweat the shallots in the 30ml of olive oil and a pinch of salt and lightly colour.

Add the mushrooms and thyme and sweat for a further 2 minutes. Add the soy sauce and reduce to nothing, now add the truffle juice and reduce by half.

Add the veal glace and bring to the boil, place into a blender and blend to a fine purée.

Warm 100g of olive oil and add to the pulp, then add the truffle oil.

Correct the seasoning and then pass through a fine sieve. Place into a plastic bottle and use at room temperature.

french vinaigrette:

Mix all the ingredients together in a bottle and shake before using.

to serve:

Pan fry the scallops in a non-stick pan in olive oil.

Dress some celeriac onto the plate, and then some soy vinaigrette.

Now place three scallops onto the plate and top with the salad dressed in the French vinaigrette.

Serves 4
Preparation time: 2 hours
Cooking time: 15 minutes

Special equipment:
A thick-bottomed pan.

Planning ahead:
Braise off the chicory, soak the raisins and also
caramelise the walnuts three days in advance.

INGREDIENTS

4   80g pieces of duck foie gras
braised chicory
raisins soaked in Jasmine tea
dried orange powder
caramelised walnuts
orange segments

braised chicory:

25g   butter
50g   onions, chopped small
200ml   orange juice
50ml   chicken stock
8   baby chicory (or 2 large)
1   garlic clove, peeled and chopped
1   small bay leaf
1   sprig of thyme
salt and pepper
orange dust

raisins soaked in jasmine tea:

5g   tea
200ml   boiling hot water
100g   raisins

caramelised walnuts:

150g   walnuts
200ml   stock syrup

PAN-FRIED DUCK FOIE GRAS WITH BRAISED CHICORY WITH ORANGE & RAISINS
BY MICHAEL CAINES

This is a gorgeous dish. The rich, fatty flavours of the foie gras are cut and contrasted by the citrus orange and sweet, plump raisin fruit. The braised chicory gives a wonderful contrast of texture and slight bitterness on the palate. This is a recent addition to my menus that has proved to be a very popular dish.

METHOD

braised chicory:
Sweat the onions and garlic in the butter with a pinch of salt no colour. Add the orange juice, chicken stock, thyme and bay leaf. Add the baby chicory and bring to the boil, season with salt and pepper. Cover with a parchment paper and braise in the oven until soft. Leave to cool.

Remove the garnish and pass off the liquid, store the braised chicory in the stock.

Take some of the stock and bring to the boil, add a pinch of orange dust and season with salt and pepper, now add a drop of orange juice. Reserve for later.

raisins soaked in jasmine tea:
Infuse the tea with the boiling hot water and leave to stand until the water is warm. Place the raisins into a jar or plastic container and then pass the tea through a fine sieve onto the raisins.

Leave to soak for 3 days before using to allow the raisins to plump up.

caramelised walnuts:
Place the walnuts into the stock syrup and cook until 110°C, remove using a draining spoon and place into a fryer at 190°C until golden brown.

Remove and place onto parchment paper and lightly salt. Once cool, take a few and chop with a knife for the topping of the foie gras.

to serve:
In a hot pan, pan-fry the foie gras colouring both sides, remove from the pan and top with the chopped walnuts, a dusting of orange powder and some sea salt. Leave to rest in a warm place.

Now reheat the chicory in its stock, and warm the raisins in their juices. Cut chicory in half, dress in the middle of the plate, sprinkle the raisins around then place the foie gras on top. Add a few caramelised walnuts, orange segments and then sauce with the butter sauce.

Enjoy!

ROAST PHEASANT WITH LENTILS, & PUMPKIN & CUMIN PUREE
BY MICHAEL CAINES

Love this dish for the autumn and winter, pheasant is surprisingly mild in flavour and not as strong as some might think. The sweetness of the pumpkin with the cumin spices adds another dimension to the mild game flavour that you get from the pheasant. The soft and smoky lentils hold up well against the other flavours, yet bring to the dish an earthy flavour and a soft texture.

Serves 4
Preparation time: 3 hours
Cooking time: 30 minutes

Special equipment:
Blender.

Planning ahead:
Prepare the lentils and also the pumpkin and cumin purée in advance. Ask your butcher to prep your pheasant for oven ready.

INGREDIENTS

2	pheasants oven ready or dressed
	pumpkin and cumin purée (recipe as below)
thyme	
garlic	
salt/pepper	
lentils (recipe as below)	
non-scented oil	
unsalted butter	
sugar	
toasted pumpkin seeds	
200g	button onions

pumpkin and cumin purée:

250g	pumpkin (Crown Prince)
2g	cumin seeds
20g	butter
1 tsp	pumpkin oil
50ml	chicken stock

lentils:

250g	green lentils
1 litre	water
8	cloves garlic, peeled
150g	shallots, peeled
400g	smoked bacon trimmings
1	onion, cut in half and spiked with cloves
150g	carrot cut into 4, lengthways
100g	thinly sliced lardons, blanched
1	small bouquet garni (thyme, bayleaf, parsley stalks and celery bound with leek and tied together with string)
1 (heaped) tsp chicken bouillon	
chopped parsley	
butter	
salt/pepper	

METHOD

lentils:

Place the lentils into a saucepan and cover with water (not the litre), bring to the boil and pass through a colander then refresh with cold water. Place the lentils back in the saucepan and add the litre of water, garlic, shallots, onion, carrots, bouquet garni, bouillon and bacon trimmings. Bring to the boil and reduce to a slow simmer, cook out for approximately 45 minutes. Once the lentils are cooked allow to cool and then remove the garnish (onion, bacon, bouquet garni etc.). Strain the lentils from their juices and place into a pan, heat and add a knob of butter. Now add the blanched lardons and season, finally add some chopped parsley. Keep back for later use.

pumpkin and cumin purée:

Toast the cumin seeds in a dry pan until light brown. Place the butter into a pan and cook the cumin seeds for a few seconds before adding the peeled and chopped pieces of pumpkin. Add a pinch of salt and cook for 10 minutes. Add chicken stock and bring to the boil. Place a lid on top and cook for 20 minutes.

Place into a blender and blend to a fine purée, now add the pumpkin oil and season with salt and pepper.

pheasant:

Stuff the birds with the thyme, two garlic cloves, salt and pepper; season the outside of the bird and then heat a roasting tray and add a drop of non-scented oil and unsalted butter. Place the birds into the tray on their sides and put into a preheated oven at 200°C for 5 minutes, turn onto the other side for a further 5 minutes then finally onto the back with the breast facing up for 5 minutes. Remove from the oven and leave to rest for 10 minutes.

to serve:

Place the button onions in a shallow saucepan and cover with water. Add a pinch of sugar, salt, pepper and a knob of butter. Bring to the boil and reduce the water, colour the onions and place onto a tray. Reheat the pheasant in the oven and then warm the lentils, be careful not to dry them out, then add the button onions and keep warm.

Take the pheasant out of the oven and remove the legs and breast. Dress some pumpkin purée onto the plate, now place the lentils in the middle of the plate and put the portioned pheasant on top.

Serves 4
Preparation time: 1 hour
Cooking time: 30 minutes.

Special equipment:
Hand blender, various moulds.

Planning ahead:
N/A

INGREDIENTS

caramel and cardamom parfait:

200g	caster sugar
40g	glucose
50g	water
15g	butter, melted
30g	warm water
2g	green cardamom seed
100g	double cream
150g	caster sugar
60g	water
240g	egg yolks
300g	double cream

milk chocolate mousse:

360g	milk chocolate
200g	milk
5g	gelatine leaves, soaked
400g	double cream

nougatine:

500g	caster sugar
500g	fondant
500g	glucose
150g	water

CARAMEL & CARDAMOM PARFAIT, NOUGATINE MILK CHOCOLATE MOUSSE

BY MICHAEL CAINES

METHOD

caramel and cardamom parfait:

Make a dark caramel with the 200g caster sugar, glucose and 50g water. Deglaze the dark caramel with the melted butter and warm water.

In the meantime infuse the green cardamom in the 100g double cream.

Make a pate a bombe with the egg yolks and 150g caster sugar by cooking the sugar and 60g water at 121°C and pouring it over the whisking egg yolks. Whisk until cold.

Lightly whip the 300g double cream.

Pass the infused cream into a sieve then fold into the pate a bombe. Lightly add the cream. Place in a mould and put in the freezer to set.

milk chocolate mousse:

Melt the chocolate on a bain marie. Bring the milk to the boil then add the soaked gelatine. Add little by little this mix to the melted chocolate, creating an elastic centre. This texture should be kept throughout the mixing. Smooth using a hand blender. When the mixture is between 35°C and 45°C add the cream. Place into rectangular moulds.

nougatine:

Bring all the ingredients to a caramel then pour onto a tray. When cold break into pieces and blitz the nougatine until it forms a fine powder. Sprinkle the powder onto a baking tray then flash in a hot (200°C) oven for a couple of minutes. Cut into rectangular shapes the same size as the mousse while the nougatine is still warm. Leave to cool down.

to serve:

Sandwich the mousse between two nougatine rectangles. Serve with the parfait.

Dorset

Hardy's Wessex and the dramatic ruin

Dorset would appear to be one of England's least known regions but with its unspoiled villages, historic towns, idyllic scenery, literary associations and coastline it must surely be one of the most rewarding. This is the country of the author Thomas Hardy and its towns feature under disguised names including 'Casterbridge' for Dorchester and 'Budmouth' for Weymouth. Hardy would still recognise the lonely hill country and heathland of his day, for it remains little changed. Dorchester is the county town, serving the immediate area with good shopping and the Dorset County Museum holds the original Hardy manuscript of *The Mayor of Casterbridge*. Another of the iconic sights of Dorset is the dramatic ruin of Corfe Castle, perched high above the village and the restored railway below. As well as its stunning coast and countryside, Dorset is fast becoming equally as famous for its produce with its chocolate on sale at Harrods, its cheese sold in the food halls at Harvey Nichols and its meat used by the most famous of chefs. Of course, no visit to Dorset would be complete without trying the age-old classic, Dorset Apple Cake.

Steven Titman

Steven Titman has developed a cuisine of international fame since joining Summer Lodge Country House & Hotel as Head Chef in 2004. He prefers to use a wide variety of locally sourced, fresh produce to create dishes which allow the flavours to speak for themselves. Steven began his career at Longueville Manor in 1994 as Chef de Partie before moving abroad to Germany in 1998 to work at the Restaurant a la Table in Dortmund. He returned to working at a Relais & Châteaux property in the form of The White Barn Inn in Maine, USA in the autumn of 2000 where he continued to work as Chef de Partie and later progressed to become the junior Sous Chef.

'Dorset is a gourmet's paradise, fuelled by an abundance of superb local ingredients and wonderful home-cooked food'

RELAIS & CHATEAUX

Summer Lodge
Country House & Spa

{ *Deep in the heart of the rolling Wessex countryside, little changed from the days it was immortalised in the novels of Thomas Hardy, and only a short drive from the dramatic rocks and fossils of the world renowned Jurassic Coast, Summer Lodge affords a magical escape from the prosaic realities of the 21st century.*

Set in four acres of idyllic gardens, with a croquet lawn, indoor pool, health spa, and a small collection of richly furnished guest rooms and suites, it's a small world into itself — and one you won't want to leave. Add in a restaurant of international repute, a cellar master who was runner-up in the Best Sommelier of the World awards 2007, plus service that manages to be wonderfully discreet yet impressively thoughtful, and it's easy to see why guests come from so far and wide.

Serves 4
Preparation time: 25 minutes
Cooking time: N/A

Planning ahead:
The grapefruit segments need to marinate in the olive oil overnight.

Special equipment:
N/A

INGREDIENTS

2   pink grapefruits, segmented and drained
extra virgin olive oil
2   bunches coriander (save a little for chopping and 8 leaves for drying)
1   lobster (preferably from Portland) approx 700g in weight, boiled for 6 minutes and removed from its shell
120g   white crab meat (preferably from Portland - pick through this and check there is no shell)
1   pinch chopped chives
20   green beans, cooked and sliced
1   lime, zest and juice
2 tbsp mayonnaise
4 tbsp crème fraîche
salt and pepper
sherry vinegar
2 tbsp pomegranate seeds
2   oranges, segmented and drained

GATEAU OF PORTLAND CRAB & LOBSTER WITH GRAPEFRUIT SALAD, CREME FRAICHE & CITRUS DRESSING
BY STEVEN TITMAN

A lovely light, refreshing dish ideal for the warm summer evenings.

METHOD

Place the grapefruit segments in a bowl and cover with olive oil, then place in the fridge overnight.

In a pan of boiling salted water blanch the coriander for 2 minutes then refresh in iced water. Squeeze it dry and mix in a blender to make a purée.

Cut four good slices from the lobster tail and two nice pieces from each claw. Chop the remaining lobster and mix with the crab meat. Add the reserved coriander (chopped), chives, beans and the lime zest. Bind with the mayonnaise and some of the crème fraîche. Season to taste with salt, pepper and lime juice.

Stretch some cling film tightly over an empty plate and lightly grease with olive oil. Place the eight reserved coriander leaves on the plate and microwave for approximately 1½ minutes, until crispy.

Strain the marinated grapefruit through a sieve. Mix the oil with a splash of sherry vinegar (3 parts oil to 1 part vinegar) and mix in the pomegranate seeds.

to serve:
Place a ring on a serving plate and pack the crab and lobster mixture into the ring, leaving ½ cm at the top. Next add the grapefruit and press down with the back of a spoon. Carefully remove the ring. Place the orange segments on the plate, arrange the lobster slices on top and finally dress with the pomegranate dressing. Garnish with the dried coriander leaves.

SOY-INFUSED LOIN OF EXMOOR VENISON WITH MARINATED RED CABBAGE, CELERIAC & SZECHUAN PEPPER JUS

BY STEVEN TITMAN

The aromas from the soy and Szechuan pepper complement the richness of the meat and the creaminess of the celeriac.

Serves 4
Preparation time: 30 minutes
Cooking time: 40 minutes

Planning ahead:
The loin needs to marinate for 6 hours (3 hours if vacuum packing).

Special equipment:
Vacuum packing equipment (optional).

INGREDIENTS

700g	venison (preferably from Exmoor) loin, trimmed
16 tbsp	light soy sauce
1 tbsp	Szechuan peppercorns
2	shallots, chopped
2	cloves garlic
1	sprig of thyme
8 tbsp	olive oil
100ml	red wine
500ml	veal or chicken stock
250g	unsalted butter
1	celeriac, peeled and diced
250ml	full-fat milk
250ml	double cream
2	large sweet potatoes, cut into cylinders or rectangles
1	small red cabbage
6 tbsp	sherry vinegar
2 tbsp	golden raisins
salt and pepper	
3 tbsp	light soy sauce
1 tbsp	sesame oil
½ tsp	sesame seeds
2	heads of baby bok choy, separated into leaves

METHOD

Place the venison loin in a bowl and add the 16 tablespoons of light soy sauce and half the Szechuan peppercorns. Leave to marinate for 6 hours (if you can vacuum pack this then shorten the marinating time to 3 hours).

Cook one shallot, the garlic and thyme in a little oil. Add the red wine and reduce until almost evaporated. Add the stock and continue to reduce until it reaches the required sauce consistency. Strain the sauce and infuse for 10 minutes with the remaining Szechuan peppercorns. Strain again.

Cook the remaining shallot in a little butter then add the celeriac. Add the milk and cream and bring to a simmer. Continue to simmer until the celeriac is soft, then strain and blend to make a purée.

Slice the butter approximately 2cm thick and place in a shallow pan. Add the sweet potatoes and place on a moderate heat. Cook, turning regularly, until the potatoes are golden brown and cooked through.

Finely slice the red cabbage and place in a bowl. Heat the vinegar and add the raisins, cover with cling film and leave the raisins to 'swell' until cool. Mix the raisins, vinegar and red cabbage together and add a little olive oil, salt and pepper to taste.

Remove the venison from the marinade and wrap tightly in cling film, making sure to tie both ends so that the packet is waterproof. Heat a pan of water to approximately 55°C and place the venison into it. Cook for 30 minutes, keeping the temperature of the water as close to 55°C as possible.

Place the 3 tablespoons of soy sauce, sesame oil and seeds in a pan with the bok choy and cook gently until the leaves are wilted.

to serve:
In a hot pan quickly sear the venison until coloured on all sides. Place the purée, red cabbage and sweet potato on the plate, carve the venison and place on top of the red cabbage. Finish with the wilted bok choy and the sauce.

Serves 4
Preparation time: 15 minutes (not including
                    the ice cream)
Cooking time: 4-5 minutes

Planning ahead:
The ice cream can be made a day or two
in advance.

Special equipment:
Ice-cream machine
4 ramekins

INGREDIENTS

butterscotch ice cream:

250ml	double cream
75g	light brown sugar
25g	butter
250ml	full-fat milk
6	egg yolks

toffee sauce:

165g	light brown sugar
112g	butter
250ml	double cream

soufflé:

2	egg whites
20g	sugar
60g	banana purée (approximately 2 bananas pushed through a fine sieve)

HOT BANANA SOUFFLE WITH TOFFEE SAUCE & BUTTERSCOTCH ICE CREAM
BY STEVEN TITMAN

Two great flavours that are classically served together prepared here in a new and interesting way.

METHOD

butterscotch ice cream:

Bring half of the cream to the boil. In a dry pan heat 70g of the sugar to a caramel, then add the boiling cream and whisk in the butter. Bring the milk and remaining cream to the boil, then add the caramel to it. In a bowl mix the remaining sugar and the egg yolks together, then slowly add the boiling milk and cream mixture. Return the mixture to the pan and cook gently until thickened (keep stirring to stop the eggs from 'scrambling' on the base of the pan). Leave to cool and then churn in an ice-cream machine according to the manufacturer's instructions.

toffee sauce:

Place the sugar and butter in a pan and heat until the sugar is dissolved. Leave to cool slightly then whisk in the cream and strain.

soufflé:

Preheat the oven to 180°C. Butter and sugar four ramekin dishes.

Whisk the egg whites until they form soft peaks, then add the sugar and gently fold into the purée. Pour the soufflé mixture into the ramekins and bake in the oven for 4-5 minutes.

to serve:

Place the soufflé on a plate with a scoop of ice cream. Serve the toffee sauce on the side or break open the soufflé and pour a little inside!

RELAIS & CHATEAUX

Hampshire

{ *Historic hunting forest and maritime heritage*

Hampshire could once boast Winchester as the seat of its Saxon and Norman kings and it still has reminders of times long past in the New Forest. Once a Royal hunting forest and still one of the largest areas in the south, it was the scene of the accidental killing of the Norman King William II in 1100. Today the forest is populated by the ubiquitous New Forest Ponies, five species of deer, wild donkeys and an abundance of wildlife. Unlike its days as a Royal hunting forest with access forbidden, the vast majority of the forest is now freely accessible. Nearby Southampton continues to be an important port, with both cargo ships and passenger liners, including the new QM II, berthing here. Hampshire has an abundance of fine foods, all grown, produced and reared in the county; top quality meat and cheeses, fresh trout, tempting chocolate and fresh watercress to name a few.

Luke Matthews

Luke has been at Chewton Glen since 1993; he spent ten years as Senior Sous Chef and then in November 2003 was appointed Executive Chef. Luke is a local man, having attended school, and subsequently college, in Bournemouth. After finishing his apprenticeship, aged 20, Luke had a brief sojourn at Chewton Glen with Chef Pierre Chevillard which was an inspiring catalyst in his early career path. He then worked in the Channel Islands before moving to one of the first gastro-pubs in Oxfordshire then heading to the South of France as Sous Chef at Hotel Les Bories, Gordes. Following on from another 18 months at Bishopstrow House in Warminster he finally came home to Chewton Glen, again in the capacity of Senior Sous Chef before taking over as Executive Chef.

'I am driven by satisfying my guests. Many of them enjoy simple food made with top quality ingredients and cooked with the same care as the more complex dishes'

Chewton Glen

> The cheerful and welcoming sage green shutters and sweeping lawns are the first thing to greet visitors to Chewton Glen.

This sets the tone for what is certain to be a pleasant and relaxing stay in an elegant and modern setting where you instantly feel at home. Captain Marryat wrote his most famous novel *The Children of the New Forest* here. It was the charm of Chewton Glen that inspired these stories and breathed life into their characters. This wonderful story continues today throughout the hotel rooms and lounges in this unique forest and coastal dual location. Chewton Glen also boasts exceptional leisure and recreational facilities – the fame of its spa has long spread beyond the borders of the United Kingdom – as well as offering children's activities during the school holidays.

DRESSED DORSET CRAB, APPLE & CELERIAC REMOULADE, RYE CRISP
BY LUKE MATTHEWS

A simply stunning starter using the finest local crab.

Serves 4
Preparation time: 1½ hours
Cooking time: 5 minutes

Special equipment:
Liquidiser, 50mm ring.

Planning ahead:
N/A

INGREDIENTS

dressed crab:

200g	white crabmeat
25g	mayonnaise
juice and zest of 1 lemon	
salt and pepper, to taste	

dressed brown meat:

100g	brown crabmeat
20g	mayonnaise
salt and pepper, to taste	

brown meat sauce:

100g	brown crabmeat
150g	mayonnaise
juice of ¼ lemon	
1	pinch cayenne pepper

dressing:

1 tbsp	caster sugar
2 tbsp	rice wine vinegar
2	cloves garlic, finely chopped
½	red chilli, finely chopped
6 tbsp	fish sauce
6 tbsp	water
6 tbsp	lime juice

radish carpaccio:

½	mooli
1	black radish

apple and celeriac remoulade:

100g	apples
100g	red radish
100g	celeriac
1 tbsp	mayonnaise
1 tbsp	whole grain mustard
salt and pepper, to taste	

rye bread crisp:

1	slice rye bread per person
olive oil, as required	

METHOD

dressed crab:

Mix the first three ingredients together well and season with salt and pepper.

dressed brown meat:

Fork the crabmeat then mix in the mayonnaise and season.

brown meat sauce:

Purée the brown meat in a liquidiser then mix in the rest of the ingredients.

dressing and radish carpaccio:

Mix all the dressing ingredients together and leave to infuse for 1 hour. Thinly slice six rings of both mooli and black radish per plate, then marinate these in the dressing for 10 minutes.

apple and celeriac remoulade:

Julienne the apples, radish and celeriac. Mix together with the mayonnaise and mustard, then season.

rye bread crisp:

Preheat the oven to 175°C. Thinly slice the bread, lay on a tray with greaseproof paper and sprinkle with olive oil. Place another tray on top and then put in an oven at 175°C for about 5 minutes until crisp, but check regularly.

to serve:

Using a 50mm ring layer the white meat on the bottom and then top with brown meat. Arrange the radish and mooli on a plate then top with the crab ring and a quenelle of the apple and celeriac remoulade. Finish the plate by piping the brown meat sauce around. Serve with the rye crisp.

TRONCON OF HALIBUT WITH CAPERS & PRESERVED AMALFI LEMONS
BY LUKE MATTHEWS

Cooking fish on the bone is always preferable and this dish is a fantastic way to enjoy halibut.

Serves 4
Preparation time: 45 minutes
Cooking time: 25 minutes

Special equipment:
N/A

Planning ahead:
The lemons should be prepared 1 week in advance. They will keep for a month in the fridge.

INGREDIENTS

preserved lemons:

5	Amalfi lemons
juice of 3 lemons	
¼	cup salt

parsley root purée:

500g	parsley roots
75g	butter
water, to cover	
2 tbsp	double cream
salt and pepper, to taste	

halibut:

1 tbsp	olive oil
1	large knob butter
salt and pepper, to taste	
4	halibut steaks

to serve:

6 tsp	Lilliput capers
6 tsp	chopped parsley
1	preserved lemon (see above)

METHOD

preserved lemons:

Cut the lemons lengthways into quarter segments, leaving them attached still at the bottom. Rub in the salt and lemon juice then put into a preserving jar. Marinate for 1 week before use. They will keep for a month in the fridge.

parsley root purée:

Peel and finely chop the parsley roots, add the butter along with the water and simmer until soft. Remove from the heat and strain, then liquidise till very smooth, adding the cream and some of the cooking juice if required to gain a spreading consistency. Season with salt and pepper and keep warm.

halibut:

Preheat the oven to 175°C. Melt together in a frying pan the oil and butter, season the fish and sauté till golden on each side, then place the pan in the oven for a couple of minutes.

to serve:

Remove the fish from the pan and allow it to rest for 2-3 minutes, then add the capers, parsley and lemon to the pan and heat gently. Spread some of the warm purée onto a plate, lay the fish onto the purée and spoon over the lemon and capers, drizzling a little of the butter around.

TAHITIAN VANILLA & ORANGE PANNA COTTA, SEASONAL BERRIES

BY LUKE MATTHEWS

A surprisingly refreshing and delicate dessert to complete any dinner party.

Serves 4
Preparation time: 1 hour, plus chilling
Cooking time: 5 minutes

Special equipment:
Fine sieve, 50mm rings.

Planning ahead:
N/A

INGREDIENTS

350ml   double cream
50ml   full-fat milk
1   Tahitian vanilla pod
zest of ½ orange
1   leaf gelatine
55g   caster sugar

to serve:

300g assorted seasonal berries

METHOD

Bring the cream and milk up to the boil with the vanilla, add the orange zest and cover with cling film. Infuse for 30 minutes. Soak the gelatine in iced water. Add the sugar to the cream mixture and bring up to the boil again. Take off the heat and dissolve the soaked gelatine into it. Pass through a fine sieve to remove the zest. Allow to cool over a bowl of ice until it is starting to set, then mix well so that the vanilla is floating and well dispersed. Set in 50mm rings lined with cling film and place in the fridge to set.

to serve:

Once set, gently turn out onto serving plates and garnish with berries.

British-born Luke Holder spent 10 years of his childhood growing up in Dubai. That, together with a year-long backpacking stint through South-East Asia, really inflamed his already big passion for food and cooking. On his return to the UK in 1998 Luke began working for Chris Galvin at the very exclusive Orrery restaurant in London. He went on to work at Sugar Reef, The Sloane Club, and the Oxo Tower on the South Bank, all in London. Luke then opened a fine-dining restaurant in Thailand followed by a brief spell working in Dubai alongside one of the most exciting chefs of his generation, Stephane Buchholzer, and concluded with a year cooking in the kitchen of three Michelin-starred Enoteca Pinchiorri, Florence. It was his experience cooking in Italy that changed his philosophy on food forever and firmly placed his focus on cooking locally and seasonally at the highest level. He brought this philosophy back to the UK in 2008 when he took on his first UK Head Chef role at The Lakeside Park Hotel, Isle of Wight. In January 2010 Luke became Head Chef at Lime Wood Hotel.

Lime Wood

Hotel & Restaurant

{ *Situated in the secluded heart of the New Forest National Park, only 90 minutes from London, the Lime Wood look is the emblematic English country house of your dreams but with a dynamic and contemporary approach.*

On the site of a former 13th century hunting lodge, the classic Regency building has been carefully refurbished and a new wing added. The décor gives pride of place to local materials, combining antiques with individual design pieces. Sculptures in the garden, game and mushrooms from the forest on the menu all add up to the charm of an aristocratic residence combined with modern laid-back luxury.

Serves 8
Preparation time: 1 hour
Cooking time: N/A

Special equipment:
Vacuum bags, water bath, chinoise.

Planning ahead:
N/A

INGREDIENTS

langoustine citrus cure:

250g	granulated sugar
250g	salt
zest of 1 lemon zest	
zest of 1 lime	
zest of 1 grapefruit	
zest of 1 orange	
20g	coriander seeds
18	live langoustines

pickled cucumber:

200g	granulated sugar
300g	Chardonnay vinegar
1	cucumber

pink grapefruit and foie gras dressing:

1	large pink grapefruit
60g	foie gras

garnish:

coriander cress

CARPACCIO OF KRIEL CAUGHT LANGOUSTINES WITH PINK GRAPEFRUIT, CUCUMBER & FOIE GRAS DRESSING

BY LUKE HOLDER

A superb summer dish that is both rich and elegant. It is a great way to eat langoustines and with the grapefruit and cucumber it is refreshing on a hot day. It takes a little time and thought in its preparation but is very simple to serve once ready.

METHOD

langoustine citrus cure:

Blend the sugar and salt with the citrus fruit zests and coriander seeds. Place the langoustines in the freezer for 40 minutes to kill them. Peel the langoustine meat from the shells and de-vein the tails. Place the tails under the citrus cure for 9 minutes, then wash off and pat dry. Roll out some cling film on a flat surface. Arrange nine langoustines head to tail, three deep and three long on the cling film. Then place the next layer of six langoustines on top, two deep, three long. Finally add the remaining three langoustines on top, one deep, three long. Roll the cling film tightly around the langoustines then place in the freezer to set.

When it comes to serving, slice on a machine to 2mm thick.

pickled cucumber:

Heat the sugar and vinegar together until the sugar has dissolved, then allow to cool. Peel the cucumber and dice into 5mm squares. Vacuum pack the cucumber with the sweet pickle. Reserve until needed.

pink grapefruit and foie gras dressing:

Peel then cut the grapefruit segments down and pick out the individual grapefruit sacks, reserving them in grapefruit juice. Vacuum pack the foie gras and place in a water bath at 53°C for 20 minutes until all the fat has rendered out of the foie gras. Pass the fat off through a fine chinoise. Mix the foie gras fat with the individual grapefruit sacks and reserve until needed.

to serve:

Place the sliced langoustines on a plate. Dress them with the pickled cucumber, grapefruit and foie gras dressing and add a little coriander cress to finish.

Serves 4
Preparation time: 1½ hours
Cooking time: 30 minutes

Special equipment:
Thermomix, vacuum bags, water bath.

Planning ahead:
N/A

INGREDIENTS

beetroot purée:

500g	beetroot
500ml	beetroot juice
50ml	Cabernet Sauvignon vinegar

baby beetroot:

12	baby beetroot
1	sprig of thyme
25ml	olive oil
1	pinch rock salt

beetroot jus:

500ml	beetroot juice
500ml	port
3	star anise
1 litre	game stock
200ml	base jus

venison coffee crust:

50g	roasted coffee beans
2	venison loins
2	sprigs of thyme
25ml	olive oil

garnish:

butter, melted
fresh micro basil

LOIN OF NEW HOUSE GAME ESTATE VENISON, BEETROOT, COFFEE & BASIL
BY LUKE HOLDER

Here in the forest we are blessed with an abundance of great game. Nothing speaks of the forest more than venison. The classic combination with venison is bitter chocolate, here we substitute the chocolate with coffee and add Thai basil for its anise qualities. The anise flavours add to the gamey depth of the dish.

METHOD

beetroot purée:

Wash, peel and dice the beetroot and place in a pan. Cover with the beetroot juice and vinegar and cook on a slow heat for 1½ hours until the beetroot is tender. Blend in a Thermomix for 6 minutes until smooth. Pass through a fine sieve then hang in muslin to remove any excess liquid.

baby beetroot:

Wash and peel the baby beetroot. Vacuum pack the beetroot with the thyme, olive oil and rock salt, steam for 22 minutes, then refresh in ice water.

beetroot jus:

Place the beetroot juice, port and star anise together in a pan and reduce by two-thirds. Once reduced, add the game stock and base jus and reduce until glossy and thick.

coffee crust:

Roast the coffee beans in the oven at 180°C for 2 minutes then add to a mortar and pestle and crush to a fine powder.

venison loins:

Vacuum pack the venison loins with the thyme and olive oil and cook in a water bath at 53°C for 12 minutes. Remove from the bag and seal in a hot pan, then allow to rest for 2 minutes. Roll the venison loins in the coffee powder crust, carve and serve.

to serve:

Arrange the venison on each plate, add the beetroot brushed with a little melted butter, some purée and jus, and serve with the fresh micro basil.

Serves 4
Preparation time: 1 hour
Cooking time: 12-15 minutes

Special equipment:
Ice-cream machine or Pacojet, 4 soufflé dishes.

Planning ahead:
The sorbet can be made in advance.

INGREDIENTS

crème fraîche sorbet:

250ml	crème fraîche
188ml	cold syrup (made up of 105g sugar, 13g glucose and 96ml water brought to the boil and chilled)
15ml	lemon juice

date purée:

100g	Medjool dates
100ml	sugar syrup
1	pinch cinnamon
1	pinch all spice
butter, as required	
100g	green pistachios, crumbled

soufflé base crème patisserie:

2 tbsp	plain flour
2 tsp	caster sugar
½ tsp	cornflour
1	medium egg yolk
1	medium whole egg
4 tbsp	milk
6	Medjool dates
1 tbsp	double cream

meringue:

6	medium egg whites
85g	caster sugar

PISTACHIO & MEDJOOL DATE SOUFFLE WITH CREME FRAICHE SORBET
BY LUKE HOLDER

Perfect for those cold autumn winter nights when there is not much fruit around. The Medjool date is an amazingly sweet date which offers a richness akin to caramel but is of mother nature's own doing. Offset with the pistachio and cut with the cool fresh acidity of the crème fraîche sorbet this dish just works.

METHOD

crème fraîche sorbet:
Combine all the ingredients together and either churn in a traditional ice-cream machine or freeze and finish with a Pacojet.

date purée:
Simmer the dates with the sugar syrup and spices until the dates are soft, then blend. Take four 200ml soufflé dishes and brush them completely with softened butter. Chill the dishes for 5 minutes, then, as an insurance policy so the soufflé doesn't stick to the dish, apply a second coat as before. Roll with the crumbled pistachios. Pipe in the date purée just enough to cover the bottom.

soufflé base crème patisserie:
Mix together the flour, sugar and cornflour. Put the egg yolk and whole egg into a bowl, stir, then beat in half of the flour mixture to give a smooth paste. Tip in the rest of the flour mixture and mix well.

Pour the milk, dates and cream into a pan and bring just to the boil, cook for 5 minutes until the dates are soft. Remove from the heat and blend.

Return the date milk to the pan with the crème patisserie. Cook, stirring over a medium-low heat for 5 minutes to a smooth, thick paste. Remove from the heat. Leave until cold, beating occasionally with a wire whisk.

meringue:
Preheat the oven to 190°C. Whisk the egg whites to soft peaks with an electric whisk. Sprinkle in the sugar as you are mixing. Keep whisking to give stiff, firm peaks to give volume to the soufflés.

Stir 2 tbsp of egg whites into the crème patisserie. Carefully fold in a third of the rest, cutting through the mixture. Fold in another third (take care not to lose the volume); fold in the rest.

Spoon the mixture into the dishes to fill them by three-quarters, then gently press a spoon in to make sure it fills all the gaps. Fill the dishes to the top with the mixture, then bang each dish on to the surface so the mixture fills the sides.

Take a palette knife and pull it across the top of each dish so the mixture is completely flat. Take a little time to wipe any splashes off the outside of each dish, or they will burn on while cooking.

So that the mixture won't stick to the top of the mould, and to give a straight finish, go around the top edge of the mixture with your finger. Bake the soufflés for 12-15 minutes.

The soufflés should have risen by about two-thirds of their original height and jiggle when moved, but be set on top.

to serve:
Serve the soufflé immediately with a quenelle of sorbet.

Sussex

Where downland meets the sea

{

The passage of time has dealt kindly with Sussex for, in spite of being so close to the capital, it has retained its character, whether in its countryside and villages, its towns or resorts. Brighton, often known as 'London by the Sea', owes its individuality and reputation to the Prince Regent who built the Royal Pavilion that has long defined the resort, contrasting with the genteel and elegant Eastbourne. Great castles, houses and gardens are as much a feature of the county as picturesque villages that remain seemingly little altered. Local produce, excellence in environmental practice and special diet alternatives feature strongly in Sussex. Another food highlight is the classic fish and chips, made from fresh fish caught locally along the Sussex coast. A legendary aspect to the food and drink culture of Sussex is the Sussex Breakfast featuring free-range eggs and locally reared and produced sausages, bacon, preserves and yoghurts.

In 2006 James joined Amberley Castle as Head Chef, and felt that Amberley's breathtaking location, nestled at the foot of the South Downs, was the perfect location for him to strive to achieve his first Michelin star, having worked in Michelin-starred restaurants for his entire career. James has a modern European take on food, utilising local produce within a 30 mile radius of the Castle, and works with a young, enthusiastic team that brings new ideas and possibilities with endless combinations of flavours and styles to his kitchen.

Amberley Castle

{ *After nine hundred years standing proud in the unspoilt county of West Sussex, known as "the garden of England", this castle with its storybook battlement towers has weathered the attacks of enemies and of time itself.*

Today the battles of the past have made way for an enchanted peace, but certain historic traditions remain. Every night, just before midnight, the impressive portcullis is lowered ever so slightly as if to protect your slumber that little bit more. Indeed you will be sleeping in a princely suite with a four-poster bed and mullioned windows overlooking gardens full of blossom trees. The food is also fit for a king and is served in a dining room with vaulted ceilings and decorated with tapestries and suits of armour. Take a journey back in time in this uniquely romantic setting.

SALAD OF BEETROOT, FENNEL, GOAT'S CURD, BLACK OLIVE REDUCTION, POWDER & PICKLED BEETROOT SORBET

BY JAMES DUGAN

Seasonal local produce kept simple with the introductions of creamy textures and sharp vinegar flavours keeping it well balanced.

Serves 4
Preparation time: 1½ hours
Cooking time: 30 minutes

Special equipment:
Ice-cream machine.

Planning ahead:
N/A

INGREDIENTS

baby beetroots:

16	mixed variety baby beetroots
4 tbsp	olive oil
2	sprigs of thyme
1	bay leaf

beetroot sorbet:

3	large beetroots
200ml	red wine vinegar
100ml	water
150g	caster sugar
50g	glucose
50g	trimoline
salt and pepper	

fennel:

4	baby fennel, topped, tailed and peeled
2 tbsp	olive oil
1	pinch salt
1	pinch pepper

black olive oil:

100g	black olives
100ml	extra virgin olive oil
salt and pepper	

black olive paste:

2	shallots, diced
50ml	olive oil
1	clove garlic, puréed
½ tsp	thyme leaves
1	bay leaf
150g	back pitted olives

black olive powder:

100g	black olives, dried

garnish:

200g	goat's curd
10g	fennel leaves
10g	mustard leaves

METHOD

baby beetroots:

Peel the beetroots, keeping the sprouting top intact. Warm the oil, add the beetroots and sauté gently. Add the thyme and bay leaf, then place in the oven at 180°C for approximately 15 minutes until soft (check with a knife tip). Once cooked keep warm.

beetroot sorbet:

Peel the beetroots and place them in a pan. Cover with the vinegar, water, sugar and glucose, bring to the boil and simmer until the beetroots are cooked. Remove from the heat, add the trimoline and blitz in a blender until smooth. Pass through a sieve, then correct the seasoning. Once cool churn in a ice-cream machine according to the manufacturer's instructions.

fennel:

Blanch the fennel in boiling salted water until cooked, refresh in ice water, toss in the oil and season to taste.

black olive oil:

Place the olives and oil together in a blender, blend until smooth then pass through a sieve. Season and place in a squeezy bottle.

black olive paste:

Sweat the shallots in the oil and after a few minutes add the garlic, thyme, bay leaf and then the olives. Blend to a smooth paste and pass through a sieve.

black olive powder:

Dry the olives out on a sheet of silicone paper in the microwave on a medium heat until crisp, then blitz to a powder in a blender.

to serve:

Warm the beetroots and fennel under the grill. To plate up the salad, firstly make quenelles of the goat's curd and black olive paste, lay over the beetroots and fennel, dust with the black olive powder and drizzle over the black olive oil dressing. Finish with a quenelle of beetroot sorbet and garnish with the mustard and fennel leaves.

ROAST LOIN OF RABBIT, POLENTA, BLACK PUDDING, SPINACH & ROOT VEGETABLE SAUCE

BY JAMES DUGAN

A fantastic use of black pudding and rabbit, one of my favourite dishes and great for the autumn/ winter months.

Serves 4
Preparation time: 3 hours
Cooking time: 1 hour

Special equipment:
N/A

Planning ahead:
The rabbit loins need to be prepared and refrigerated a few hours in advance. The polenta discs, herb purée and confit garlic should all be made in advance.

INGREDIENTS

rabbit loins:

4	rabbit loins
8	slices Parma ham
150g	black pudding
100g	crepinette

polenta:

300ml	chicken stock
4 tbsp	olive oil
2	shallots, finely diced
1	clove garlic, puréed
1 tsp	thyme leaves
100g	polenta
1 tsp	grated Parmesan
1 tsp	mascarpone
salt and pepper	

herb purée:

2	bunches basil
2	bunches tarragon
3 tbsp	olive oil
½ tsp	Dijon mustard
salt and pepper	

root vegetables:

100g	carrots
100g	swede
100g	celeriac
olive oil	

confit garlic:

8	cloves garlic
100ml	butter
salt and pepper	

rabbit sauce:

3 tbsp	olive oil
2	rabbit carcasses, chopped small
4	shallots, chopped
2	garlic cloves, crushed
1 tsp	English mustard
2	bay leaves
6	sprigs of tarragon
80ml	white wine
250ml	veal stock
1 litre	chicken stock

to serve:

olive oil, as required	
60g	spinach
butter, as required	
16g	girolle mushrooms
300ml	rabbit sauce (see above)

METHOD

rabbit loins:

Trim the loins free of sinew. Lay two Parma ham slices out overlapping, lay the loin across then lay the black pudding moulded to the same shape and size as the loin on top and roll up in the ham into a tight sausage shape. Lay down the crepinette and wrap the loins in it and refrigerate for a few hours.

polenta:

Bring the chicken stock to the boil. In a separate pan heat the oil then add the shallots, garlic and thyme. After a few minutes add the polenta then the hot stock, stirring frequently. Cook for about 10 minutes until done, remove from the heat and fold through the Parmesan and mascarpone, season to finish. Lay on a tray lined with silicone and use a rolling pin to get a thickness of 1cm, and allow to cool. Use a 50mm cutter to cut out discs, then refrigerate.

herb purée:

Heat a pan of boiling water and add a generous amount of salt, add the herbs and boil for 2 minutes, then remove and refresh in ice water. Pat the herbs dry and place in a blender with the oil, mustard and seasoning. Blitz in a blender and pass through a sieve, then place in a squeezy bottle.

root vegetables:

Dice the carrots, swede and celeriac into 5mm cubes, pan fry gently in the oil with no colour, then drain on a towel.

confit garlic:

Peel the garlic, melt the butter and lightly season it, then add the garlic and cook gently but don't let the butter boil. When the garlic is soft (approximately 30 minutes) remove and allow to cool.

rabbit sauce:

Heat the oil in a large pan add the chopped rabbit bones and cook until a rich brown colour

is achieved. Add the shallots and garlic and after 5 minutes add the mustard, bay leaves and thyme. After 5 more minutes deglaze with the wine, reduce by half then finish with both stocks. Bring the sauce to a slow simmer, skim regularly and after 3 hours pass off through a sieve and reduce to the desired consistency.

to serve:
Preheat the oven to 180°C.

Roast the loin in a pan until evenly coloured, then place in the oven for 5 minutes. Remove and let it rest for 5 minutes. Meanwhile pan fry eight polenta discs until golden and crisp in oil, wilt the spinach in butter and cook the girolles

separately in butter too, then drain. Warm the sauce with the vegetables. Place two polenta discs on one side of the plate with a quenelle of spinach and a girolle mushroom and confit garlic on top. Cut the rabbit loin into three and place on the opposite side of the plate, pour the sauce up the middle and drizzle with the purée.

THE BANOFFEE PIE
BY JAMES DUGAN

Being invented in West Sussex, Banoffee Pie –
one of the all-time great desserts – was a tricky
contender to replicate in a different light, but
the chestnuts and salt angle really worked.

Serves 4
Preparation time: 12 hours
Cooking time: 1½ hours

Special equipment:
Ice-cream machine.

Planning ahead:
The ice cream can be made in advance.

INGREDIENTS

biscuit base:

60g	dark chocolate
60g	butter
44g	eggs
50g	caster sugar
½	vanilla pod
30g	plain flour
½	banana
30g	chestnuts

banoffee mix:

250ml	full-fat milk
40g	chestnuts
2	bananas
60g	egg yolks
60g	caster sugar
1½	gelatine leaves
190g	double cream

cocoa jelly:

234g	water
167g	sugar
14g	cocoa powder
14g	eau de vie
3	gelatine leaves

salt caramel:

95g	caster sugar
95g	glucose
95g	full-fat milk
75g	butter
2.5g	salt
112g	whipping cream

banana ice cream:

2	over-ripe bananas
1 tsp	lemon juice
60g	caster sugar
125g	whipping cream
125g	full-fat milk
1	small pinch salt

glazed bananas:

4	bananas
50g	caster sugar

METHOD

biscuit base:

Melt the chocolate and butter together. Beat together the eggs, sugar and vanilla,
fold in the flour followed by the chocolate and butter, and finally the banana and
chestnuts. Place in a lined mould 30 x 7 x 3cm.

banoffee mix:

Warm the milk, chestnuts and bananas together, blitz in a blender and pass through a
fine sieve. Mix the egg yolks and sugar together then pour over the hot milk. Mix and
cook out to 83°C, remove from the heat, pass through a sieve and cool over ice. Soak
the gelatine then dissolve it in the milk mix. Cool over ice, once fully chilled whisk the

cream to a soft peak consistency and fold the milk mix into it. Lastly pour the mix over the biscuit base and chill until set.

cocoa jelly:
Warm all the ingredients together apart from the gelatine. Soak the gelatine, add to the cocoa mix, pass through a sieve and chill in a refrigerator. Once the jelly resembles an oil consistency pour over the set banoffee mousse and allow to fully set.

salt caramel:
Heat all the ingredients except for the cream in a pan to 120°C . Once it reaches that temperature add the cream, remove from the heat and chill in a refrigerator.

banana ice cream:
Blend all the ingredients together, pass through a sieve and churn in an ice-cream machine according to the manufacturer's instructions.

glazed bananas:
Slice the bananas into cylinders, toss in the sugar and glaze with a blow torch until caramelised.

to serve:
Cut a slice of pie onto the plate, spoon over a little salt caramel mix, place the glazed banana next to the pie and finish with a spoon of ice cream.

Rupert Gleadow

Our oak-panelled, intimate restaurant is at the heart of the Manor. Chef Rupert Gleadow's culinary skills are highly rated by food guides such as Zagat 2010 (28/30), *The Good Food Guide* and *the AA* which has awarded Gravetye the coveted three rosettes.

Rupert honed his skills in a variety of countries, including France, Australia and his native Scotland before coming to Gravetye four years ago as head chef. His cuisine is described as 'modern British' although you will find influences from far afield. Rupert prides himself on the use of locally sourced organic produce where possible, with much being available from Gravetye's own garden and local farms.

We are incredibly fortunate to have a one-acre walled kitchen garden, which during the summer months provides 95 per cent of all the fruit and vegetables we use in the kitchen.

Gravetye Manor

{ *Gravetye Manor is a truly enchanting place. Close to the pleasures of London, yet far from its hustle and bustle.*

This beautiful Elizabethan manor sits proudly among the winding pathways and abundant flower beds of William Robinson's own garden, the grandfather of the English natural garden. From the hushed quiet of the wood-panelled restaurant to the crackle of log fires, guests cannot fail to be charmed by this most quintessential English country house. Summer or winter, the sweeping countryside views, first-class cuisine and attentive yet unobtrusive service will ensure an unforgettable experience.

SEARED FILLET OF ENGLISH RED MULLET, KING PRAWN & SQUID INK RAVIOLI, SOFT SHELL CRAB TEMPURA, CHORIZO OIL

BY RUPERT GLEADOW

Serves 4
Preparation time: 1½ hours
Cooking time: 30 minutes

Special equipment:
N/A

Planning ahead:
N/A

INGREDIENTS

pasta:

250g	'00' pasta flour
8	egg yolks
1	dash milk
1	dash olive oil
3	sachets squid ink
1	pinch salt

filling:

¼	red chilli, de-seeded
1	clove garlic
1	banana shallot
8	king prawns, cooked
1 tsp	mascarpone
1	dash lime juice

vegetable garnish:

8	baby beetroot
8	small onions
8	baby nave (turnips)
8	leaves pak choi
2	large carrots

carrot and vanilla purée:

8	baby carrots
300ml	orange juice
1	vanilla pod

mullet:

4	fillets red mullet
butter, for frying	

crab tempura:

tempura flour	
iced water, as necessary	
1	soft shell crab
seasoned flour	

chorizo oil:

100g	chorizo
100ml	vegetable oil

METHOD

pasta:

In a mixing machine with a dough hook attachment, put all the pasta ingredients and mix for at least 10 minutes on medium speed. Remove from the mixer and knead by hand for a further 2-3 minutes. Wrap in cling film and place in the fridge to rest.

filling:

Finely dice the chilli, garlic, shallot and prawns before adding to the mascarpone. Season to taste and add the lime juice.

ravioli:

Using a pasta machine, roll the pasta out as thin as you can. Place eight mounds of the filling on the pasta sheet. Using a pastry brush, run some water round the edge of the

mounds before folding the pasta over and carefully pressing the pasta round the prawn mix, ensuring there is no air between the pasta sheets. Using a pastry cutter, cut the ravioli out of the sheet. Place on a floured tray and put in the fridge.

crab tempura:

Put the tempura flour in a mixing bowl and add the iced water until the batter has the consistency of double cream. Cut the soft shell crab into four pieces and lightly dust with seasoned flour.

carrot and vanilla purée:

Dice the carrot and boil in the orange juice until very soft. Remove the seeds from the vanilla pod and purée the carrot and vanilla seeds, adding orange juice as necessary.

chorizo oil:

Dice the chorizo and warm in the vegetable oil. Allow to infuse and then pass through a sieve.

to serve:

Cook the baby vegetables in a pan of boiling salted water. Remove while they still have some bite to them and set aside.

First halve and then pan fry the red mullet fillets in a little butter. Blanch the ravioli in the boiling water for two minutes. Deep fry the battered crab pieces until golden.

Assemble on the plate, brushing the vegetables with a little melted butter.

GARDEN BLACKBERRY SOUFFLE, ELDERFLOWER SORBET & POACHED BLACKBERRIES

BY RUPERT GLEADOW

Serves 4
Preparation time: 1 hour
Cooking time: 30 minutes

Special equipment:
Ice-cream machine, 4 soufflé moulds.

Planning ahead:
N/A

INGREDIENTS

sorbet:

300ml	water
200ml	elderflower cordial
300g	sugar
1	lemon, juice only

pastry cream:

1	egg
2	egg yolks
80g	cornflour
15g	flour
570ml	milk
70g	sugar

soufflé base:

350g	pastry cream
100g	reduced blackberry purée (see recipe below)
4	egg yolks

soufflé:

caster sugar for dusting	
4	egg whites

reduced blackberry purée:

570ml	water
500g	sugar
1kg	blackberries, reserve 16 for serving

METHOD

sorbet:

Boil all the ingredients until the sugar has dissolved. Cool before putting into an ice-cream machine until firm. Place in the freezer until required.

pastry cream:

Mix the egg, yolks, cornflour and flour in a mixing bowl. Boil the milk and sugar and add to the bowl. Return to the saucepan and cook slowly on the stove until thick, stirring all the time.

reduced blackberry purée:

Boil all the ingredients together and reduce to half. Strain through a sieve and cool.

soufflé base:

Take 350g of the cooled pastry cream and add 100g of the blackberry purée and the egg yolks. Reserve in the fridge.

soufflé:

Butter four soufflé moulds and dust with caster sugar. Take four heaped tablespoons of the base and put into a mixing bowl. Whip four egg

whites to a soft peak and carefully fold into the base. Spoon into the moulds and level off with the back of a knife. Put into the oven at 180°C for 9 minutes.

to serve:

While the soufflés cook, warm 16 fresh blackberries in a pan with a spoonful of sugar. Arrange on a plate alongside the soufflé and a ball of the sorbet.

Oxfordshire

Dreaming spires and the Royal County

The dreaming spires of the ancient University City of Oxford, the oldest in England, continue to draw academics, undergraduates and visitors alike from all over the world. Still at the heart of the city, the University occupies its square mile, just as it has done since its inception in around 1200. The Thames, known as the Isis here, is a key part of the sporting and social life of the University and its colleges. South of the city is the old market town of Abingdon, again situated on the Thames, the river being popular for pleasure boating. Driving through the county of Oxfordshire you will discover farms, vineyards, allotments, orchards, dairies, smallholdings and plenty of farm shops where you can buy products from locally produced wines and organic vegetables to home-made sausages, pies, cakes, chutneys and jams.

Raymond Blanc
Grand Chef Relais & Châteaux

Raymond Blanc is acknowledged as one of the finest chefs in the world; his exquisite cooking has received tributes from every national and international guide to culinary excellence. At the age of 28, Raymond Blanc opened his first restaurant, "Les Quat' Saisons" in Summertown, Oxford. After just one year, the restaurant was named Egon Ronay Restaurant of the Year and a host of other accolades including Michelin stars followed. It was in 1984, however, that he fulfilled a personal vision, creating a hotel and restaurant in harmony when he opened Le Manoir aux Quat' Saisons in Great Milton, Oxford. Le Manoir is the only country house hotel in the UK which has achieved two Michelin stars for a total of 25 years.

'Perfection in food, comfort, service and welcome'

Le Manoir
Aux Quat' Saisons

{ *"The good doesn't interest us, only the sublime does" says Raymond Blanc. With his formidable team Raymond Blanc has created a modern classic. Le Manoir's experience aims to overwhelm all of your senses.*

The innovative food is right at the heart of it; drawing its character from seasonal ingredients, often gathered from the magnificent organic vegetable garden. The hotel matches the excellence of the cuisine; each room is unique, elegant and hugely comfortable... a place to celebrate life and oneself; French art de vivre at its best. Also home to the "The Raymond Blanc Cookery School."

Serves 4
Preparation time: 15 minutes
Cooking time: 2 minutes

Special equipment:
N/A

Planning ahead:
The vinaigrette can be made several
days in advance.

INGREDIENTS

2	bunches baby leeks, trimmed and washed
15g	Dijon mustard
15g	white wine vinegar
30g	water
1g	sea salt
½ g	pepper, white, freshly ground
45ml	groundnut oil (or any unscented oil)
20g	sliced black truffle (*1)

LEEK & TRUFFLES WITH MUSTARD VINAIGRETTE
BY RAYMOND BLANC

This is a perfect light starter with the minimum of ingredients.

METHOD

Slice only the green part of the leeks at an angle ½ cm thick and blanch in boiling water for 1-2 minutes and refresh in ice water.

In a large bowl mix the mustard, vinegar and water. Season with the salt, pepper and slowly add the oil, whisking all the time. Taste and correct the seasoning.

Drain the leeks thoroughly and put in a separate bowl, mix in 4 tablespoons of the mustard dressing. Taste and add more if you need to. (*2)

Arrange the leeks in the middle of four starter plates in a neat circle. Top with the slices of truffle and spoon around a little of the remaining dressing.

Chef's notes (*):

*1   Fresh truffles will always be better if you are lucky enough to get hold of some. But you can buy quality preserved truffles in good delis and supermarkets.

*2   You need just enough to coat and lightly season the leeks.

Variation:
You could replace the truffle with sautéed langoustines, prawns, scallops, cooked and sliced Jerusalem artichokes.

Serves 4
Preparation time: 20 minutes and
                1 hour marinade
Cooking time: N/A

Special equipment:
Japanese mandoline.

Planning ahead:
The tuna can be marinated a week in advance
and frozen until needed.

INGREDIENTS

8	hand-dived scallops medium, thinly sliced
100g	tuna, marinated (see below), cut into 1mm thin strips
4	pinches salt
4	pinches cayenne pepper
15ml	Seville orange juice
20ml	extra virgin olive oil
4g	banana shallots, finely diced, washed and drained
2g	chives, chopped
8g	caviar Oscietra
100g	fennel salad (see below)
2g	shiso cress, 6 leaves each
4g	micro herb

tuna marinade:

100g	tuna loin trimmed
4.5g	grey salt
3g	Seville orange zest, grated
2g	lemon zest, grated
2g	basil stalks, chopped
2g	black peppercorns, crushed

fennel salad:

100g	fennel, finely sliced
4	pinches sea salt
5ml	Seville orange juice
15ml	extra virgin olive oil
2g	lime zest, blanched 3 times in boiling water and chopped fine
8g	ginger, sliced fine and blanched 3 times in boiling water
½ g	cayenne pepper
5g	fennel seeds, soaked overnight and toasted in a dry pan
20g	rocket leaves

CEVICHE OF TUNA & SEA SCALLOP WITH SHAVED FENNEL SALAD
BY RAYMOND BLANC

My cuisine is very much modern French but at all times seasonal, using tastes and textures from elsewhere to enrich my French traditions. This light summer dish is a perfect example – the tuna is from the Mediterranean.

METHOD

tuna marinade:

On a large piece of clingfilm (big enough to wrap around the tuna twice) place the piece of tuna, mix together the rest of the ingredients and evenly sprinkle on both sides of the fish. Tightly wrap in the clingfilm and leave to marinate in the fridge for 1 hour.

Wash off the marinade, pat dry and store in the freezer tightly clingfilmed.

fennel salad:

In a large bowl mix all the ingredients together except for the rocket. Taste, correct the seasoning and put to one side until needed. This should only be done up to 10 minutes before you are ready to serve, and mix in the rocket at the last minute to prevent it from wilting.

ceviche:

On a large square plate, arrange the sliced scallops into three lines running from the top to the bottom. In between the scallop rows place the sliced tuna.

Season the scallops only with the salt and pepper.

On top of each row of scallops place a thin line of shallot, chives and three small amounts of caviar evenly spaced.

Finish with a small amount of fennel salad in the middle and garnish with the Shiso and micro herbs.

BRAISED FILLET OF TURBOT, OYSTER, CUCUMBER & WASABI JUS
BY RAYMOND BLANC

This has been a classic dish at Le Manoir for many years. But as with all Manoir dishes it is about details which are not always easy to duplicate in your own home. I have 40 chefs in my kitchen. Maybe the best way to enjoy it is at Le Manoir.

Serves 4
Preparation time: 20 minutes
Cooking time: 15 minutes

Special equipment:
Blender
Sieve

Planning ahead:
You can have all the ingredients sliced and your wine weighed out the day before.

INGREDIENTS

fish:

4 x 150g	turbot, filleted and portioned, brushed with butter, lemon, salt and pepper (*1)
20g	butter, unsalted
50g	½ shallot, small peeled and sliced
2g	sea salt (1 pinch)
0.5g	white pepper (1 pinch), freshly ground
120g	button mushrooms, washed and sliced
100ml	dry white wine (Chardonnay)
80ml	water

vegetable garnish and oysters:

20g	butter, unsalted
30ml	water
200g	spinach, washed
85g	cucumber ribbons (*2)
60g	samphire grass
4	whole native Colchester oysters, size 2, opened and kept in their juices in a small saucepan.

sauce:

200ml	strained cooking liquor, see above
60g	cucumber skin
12g	wasabi paste
1g	lecithin – soya based (*3) (optional)
40g	butter
1g	lemon juice

METHOD

sauce and fish:
Preheat the oven to 190°C.

In a sauté pan on a medium heat, sweat the shallots in the butter for 2 minutes. (*4)

Add the sliced mushrooms and sweat for a further minute.

Add the wine and boil for approximately 5 seconds – taste. (*5)

Place the fillets of fish on the mushrooms, bring the liquid to the boil and cover with a lid

Cook in the preheated oven for approximately 5 minutes. Remove from the oven, spoon out the fish on to a large buttered serving dish and keep warm. (*6)

Strain the juices into a large jug blender, pressing on the shallots and mushrooms to extract as much juice as possible. Reserve.

finishing the sauce:
In a large jug blender, blitz together the hot cooking juices, cucumber skin, wasabi paste, lecithin, butter and lemon juice. Strain and reserve.

vegetable garnish and oysters:
Divide the butter and water into two saucepans. Spinach in one and cucumber and samphire in the other. Add a tiny pinch of salt to the spinach. Cover with a lid.

On a high heat bring the pans of vegetables to a quick boil. The spinach will take 1 minute, the cucumber and samphire 30 seconds. Just barely warm the oysters in their own juices. Place the turbot back in the oven for 1 minute. And bring your sauce to the boil.

serving:
Place the spinach in the middle of each plate, with the cucumber and samphire around. Top with the fish and oyster, spooning the sauce over and around.

Chef's notes (*):

*1   Peel the cucumber, reserving the skin, then use a mandoline or a sharp knife to cut ribbons from the cucumber, turning as you go, until you are left with the seeds, which can be discarded.

*2   This can be done a few hours in advance. The melted butter mixed with the lemon juice and salt will season the fish first. Then the fish is refrigerated; the butter will solidify and prevent the salt from curing the fish.

*3   Lecsithin is an emulsifier that you can find in many vegetables, seaweeds, eggs etc. Here we are using a natural extract of soya beans in a powdered form. Once emulsified with liquid it will produce a light airy sauce. It is optional.

*4   By sweetening the shallots you will convert the starches into sugars adding a sweetness to your sauce.

*5   The wine is boiled in order to remove some of the alcohol content and to reduce the acidity. The aim is to leave enough acidity to give depth of flavour; if reduced too much, the sauce is likely to be very flat.

*6   Once the fish has been taken out of the oven, it is rested for 3 minutes. This will allow the residual heat to finish cooking the fish perfectly, and also some of the juices to escape. This will be used to enrich the sauce.

Variation:
The fish could be portioned on the bone and cooked which would provide more flavour to the sauce. The bones of the fish could be chopped up and softened with the sliced mushrooms to provide more depth of flavour.

This dish offers many variations: tomatoes, mustard, basil and leek could also be used. Fillets of brill, plaice, lemon sole, etc. can be used instead.

ROASTED WINTER VEGETABLES
BY RAYMOND BLANC

This is a lovely way to cook and present your seasonal vegetables, using what is available and as local as possible you can maximise the vitamins, minerals, flavour and textures.

Serves 4
Preparation time: 20 minutes
Cooking time: 2 hours

Special equipment:
N/A

Planning ahead:
All elements of this dish can be cooked a day in advance and reheated to order.

INGREDIENTS

roasted beetroot, pumpkin and onions:

2	candy beetroot, washed and quartered
2	golden beetroot, washed and quartered
160g	pumpkin discs, cut 3cm round and high
	baby onions, peeled and trimmed
30g	olive oil
30g	water
	sea salt and freshly ground black pepper

pumpkin purée:

200g	pumpkin, peeled and diced 2cm
10g	unsalted butter
2g	sea salt
1g	black pepper, freshly ground
5ml	hazelnut oil

mushroom fricassée:

5g	shallot, finely chopped
15g	unsalted butter
2g	garlic, finely chopped
100g	seasonal mushrooms (chanterelles, trompettes, girolles)
10g	flat leaf parsley, chopped
1	squeeze lemon juice
	sea salt and freshly ground black pepper

garnish:

15g	butter
30ml	water
100g	spinach
8	parsnip ribbons, deep fried
12	sage leaves, deep fried
100ml	Port reduced by two-thirds
100ml	red wine until it thickens (*1)

METHOD

roasted beetroot, pumpkin and onions:
Preheat your oven to 110°C.

In a small casserole with a lid, sweeten the vegetables on a medium heat in the olive oil with a little seasoning for 5 minutes. Add the water and cook in the preheated oven for 40 minutes to 1 hour until they are soft but still hold their shape. (*2)

pumpkin purée:
In a medium-sized saucepan on a medium heat, gently cook the pumpkin in the butter, with a little seasoning and cover with a tight-fitting lid. Stir regularly to ensure it does not stick to the bottom.

When the pumpkin begins to break down and release its moisture, turn up the heat to evaporate as much of the liquid as possible, stirring all the time.

Purée the pumpkin in a food processor until smooth, taste, correct the seasoning and add a little hazelnut oil to finish.

mushroom fricassée:
This should be cooked at the last moment when you are ready to plate up.

Sweat shallots in the butter on low heat for 1 minute. Add the garlic, turn up the heat and add all the wild mushrooms apart from the black trumpets, cook for 30 seconds, then add the trompettes. Add a pinch of salt and pepper and cook for 1 minute, stir in the parsley and add a squeeze of lemon juice.

to finish the dish and garnish:
Preheat your oven to 180°C.

Reheat your beetroot, pumpkin and onions in the oven for 8-10 minutes.

Warm your purée in a small pan and cook your mushrooms.

In a separate medium saucepan, bring the butter and water to the boil, creating an emulsion; add a pinch of salt and the spinach. Cook until it has just wilted, drain and keep warm.

To dress the plates, spoon the pumpkin purée in the middle of each plate and spread it lengthways, avoiding the edges. Arrange all the other ingredients on top of the purée and spoon the red wine and port reduction around.

Chef's notes (*):
*1   Reduce the wines until they coat the back of your spoon; taste and add a little caster sugar if the concentrated tannins of the wines becomes too overpowering.

*2   This slow method of cooking the vegetables ensures all the starches are converted into sugars giving maximum flavour and will leave them with a soft melting texture without becoming a purée or falling to pieces.

Variation:

This dish can be made all year round by using the best seasonal vegetables. Replace the beetroot, pumpkin and onions with carrots, celeriac, Jerusalem artichokes, new season garlic cloves, butternut squash, grelot onions, small red thai shallots. Use seasonal mushrooms, ceps, girolles, chanterelles, trompettes, morels, oyster, pied bleu.

Serves 4
Preparation time: 40 minutes
Cooking time: 25 minutes

Special equipment:
Ice-cream machine, 7cm pastry rings, piping bag, silicone tray, mandoline.

Planning ahead:
You can make the ginger sauce and dried pear slices a day in advance.

INGREDIENTS

almond clafoutis:

100g	ground almonds
100g	icing sugar
6g	cornflour
100g	unsalted butter, softened
1	medium egg
3g	vanilla extract

caramel croustillant:

35g	milk, full cream
75g	unsalted butter
95g	caster sugar
2g	Pectin powder NH
30g	glucose powder
15g	plain flour

caramelised pear:

2	whole pears, Comice, peeled, halved, cored and cut with 7cm pastry ring. (keep the trimmings for the sorbet)
32g	unsalted butter
150g	caster sugar
30ml	white wine, Chardonnay

ginger sauce:

60ml	whipping cream
60ml	milk, full cream
8g	fresh ginger, grated
20g	caster sugar
2	egg yolks, organic
¼ leaf	gelatine, softened in cold water

dried pear slices:

½	Comice pear (small and slightly under ripe)
15ml	stock syrup (100g caster sugar, 100ml water boiled)

pear sorbet:

400g	Comice pear purée (freshly made)
20ml	lemon juice
10ml	alcohol, eau de vie de Poire William
1g	vitamin C powder
50g	caster sugar (according to sweetness)

pear dice:

100g	Comice pear, peeled, cored and diced 5mm
20ml	alcohol, eau de vie de Poire William
3g	fructose
dash	lemon juice

CARAMELISED PEAR CROUSTILLANT & ITS OWN SORBET
BY RAYMOND BLANC

One of the new Le Manoir dishes, simple and one of the greatest experiences using Comice pears.

METHOD

almond clafoutis:
Preheat your oven to 160°C.

In a large bowl mix together the almond powder, icing sugar and cornflour. Gradually mix in the softened butter, then, in a separate bowl beat together the egg and vanilla extract and add this to the mixture. Reserve in the fridge for a minimum of 1 hour to let it set slightly.

Line a tray with greaseproof paper, lightly grease the pastry rings and using a piping bag evenly fill the rings by one-third.

Cook for about 8-10 minutes until lightly golden.

caramel croustillant:
Preheat your oven to 180°C.

In a medium saucepan heat together the milk and butter to a gentle simmer.

In a bowl mix together the sugar, pectin, glucose. Mix this into the hot milk and bring to the boil. Remove from the heat and add the sieved flour.

Pour onto a tray between two sheets of greaseproof paper, roll thin and freeze for 30 minutes in order to remove the top layer of paper.

Bake in the preheated oven for 7-8 minutes.

Allow to cool slightly before you cut out your 7cm discs and reserve.

caramelised pear:
In a non-stick pan, bring the butter and sugar to a light brown caramel. Add the pieces of pear and colour on both sides for 2 minutes each. Pour in the wine and simmer until just soft in the middle, take off the heat and leave to cool before draining off the cooking liquor.

Reserve until needed.

ginger sauce:
In a medium pan, bring the milk and cream to a simmer and infuse with the freshly grated ginger for 30 minutes. In a bowl mix together the egg yolks and sugar. Strain off the milk and whisk into the egg mixture. Pour back into the saucepan and cook on a medium heat for 2 minutes until it coats the back of the spatula, stir in the drained gelatine and cool over an ice bain-marie. Reserve in the fridge until needed.

dried pear slices:
Preheat your oven to 110°C.

Using a mandoline, slice the pear lengthways as thin as possible, place directly onto a Teflon tray. Brush with the stock syrup and cook for about 30 minutes until dry and crisp with no colour.

pear sorbet:
In a blender blend all the ingredients together and churn in an ice-cream machine straight away. Reserve in the freezer until needed.

pear dice:
Mix all the ingredients together just before you are ready to serve.

to serve:
In each medium serving bowl pour a small amount of ginger sauce into the middle, top with the warm clafoutis, the warm caramelised pear half and cover with the caramel croustillant. Garnish with the pear dice, pear sorbet and a dried pear slice.

NORTH WAREHOUSE

Gloucestershire

{ *A county of warmth and character*

Gloucestershire has much to offer, comprising part of the Cotswold Hills, part of the flat fertile valley of the River Severn and the entire Forest of Dean, offering no shortage of sights. Gloucestershire boasts a spectacular range of natural beauty, loved and known by people across the world. The city of Gloucester is home to the historical cathedral and Victorian Docks, and renowned for combining a rich historic past with a modern city. Gloucestershire is typically known for its double Gloucester cheese, which has a mellow flavour and is popular in recipes for the ease with which it melts. At one time it was referred to as Berkeley cheese and has been made in the Vale of Gloucester for over a thousand years. Other speciality dishes include Squab Pie, commonly made with either lamb or mutton, and Gloucester Pancakes, made from suet dough, a wonderfully warm filling food suitable for autumnal weather.

Andrew Birch

Andrew, a Welsh lad born and bred, has been cooking since he left school 10 years ago. After leaving college, he worked at Salford Hall Hotel under the direction of Head Chef Chris McPherson followed by a return to his native city of Swansea and the famous Morgans Hotel. By 2004 it was time to leave home, spread the wings and he landed at the Tanner brothers' famous restaurant in Plymouth where, after three promotions, he rose to become Chef Tournant. March 2008 saw Andrew take up the Island life at St Martins Hotel on the Isles of Sicily working for Head Chef Kenny Atkinson as his Junior Sous Chef but Island life wasn't for him and he soon realised he was a landlubber and returned to the mainland.

In August 2008 Andrew took up the role of Junior Sous Chef for Chef Martin Burge at fellow Relais & Châteaux property Whatley Manor then became Head Chef at the famous Ribby Hall in Lancashire.

Andrew started at Lower Slaughter Manor in April 2011 as Head Chef. His style of cooking is completely seasonal, using local produce whenever possible combined with technical ability in creating memorable dishes.

RELAIS & CHATEAUX

Lower Slaughter Manor

{ *In one room, the décor is a deluge of crystals. In another, a sea of cushions. Opulent, gently lit, with wall hangings and sofas everywhere, Lower Slaughter Manor envelops you in its warmth and romanticism.*

An address that is all about elegant hedonism, with tennis, beauty treatments, fishing, horseback riding or bike rides in one of the most beautiful and untouched parts of England. Hope that it rains and that the earth exhales the perfumes that make this country so bewitching.

RELAIS & CHATEAUX

SEARED FOIE GRAS, SPICED WALNUTS WITH ORANGE & WATERCRESS

BY ANDREW BIRCH

Serves 4
Preparation time: 10 minutes
Cooking time: 30 minutes plus chutney
                      cooking time, which will
                      be variable.

Special equipment:
Hand blender, chinoise, squeezy bottle, deep fryer.

Planning ahead:
N/A

INGREDIENTS

seared foie gras and orange dressing:

1	lobe foie gras
4	heads chicory
1	splash oil
150g	sugar
1	star anise
500ml	orange juice
20ml	pomace oil
1	large gellespas
salt and pepper	

spiced walnuts:

50g	walnuts
100ml	stock syrup
1	pinch five spice

to serve:

watercress sprigs

METHOD

seared foie gras and orange dressing:
Portion the foie gras into 60g pieces and set aside in the fridge.

Finely shred the chicory, place in a heavy-based saucepan with a splash of oil on a high heat and add the sugar. Cook out and caramelise quickly, then add the star anise and half the orange juice. Turn the heat to low and allow it to slowly tick over. Stir frequently until it reaches a chutney consistency. When cool place in a plastic container in the fridge.

To make the dressing take the pomace oil, the rest of the orange juice and the gellespas and blend, pass through a fine chinoise and set aside in a squeezy bottle.

spiced walnuts:
Place the walnuts in a saucepan with the stock syrup on a medium heat and cook out for 20 minutes, stirring occasionally. Drain for 10-15 minutes on a cooling rack. Deep fry on 160°C for 3-4 minutes and allow to go quite dark but not burnt. Cool on a rack and sprinkle with the five spice.

finishing the foie gras:
Season the foie gras and place into a heavy-duty frying pan on a very high heat for 25-30 seconds or until golden-brown. Flip it over and baste with its own juices for 30 seconds. Place on a warm metal tray and set aside in a warm area to warm through.

to serve:
Arrange the watercress on a plate and place the foie gras on top of the chutney. Chop a few walnuts and sprinkle over the dish. Dress with the orange dressing.

ROASTED JOHN DORY, SUMMER VEGETABLES WITH A VERMOUTH FOAM

BY ANDREW BIRCH

Serves 4
Preparation time: 45 minutes
Cooking time: 45 minutes

Special equipment:
Blender, fine chinoise, melon baller, vacuum pack bag, hand blender (Bamix).

Planning ahead:
The diced cucumber jelly needs to vac pack for 6 hours.

INGREDIENTS

roasted John Dory:

1.8-2.3kg John Dory fish from a good fishmonger – filleted but skin on
salt and pepper
oil, as required
juice of 1 lemon

cucumber jelly and pickled cucumber:

8	cucumbers
5g	agar agar
50ml	white balsamic vinegar

saffron potato balls:

2	large maris piper potatoes
2g	saffron
100ml	reduced fish stock
25g	butter
25g	cream
50g	milk
	vermouth, to taste
	salt, to taste
	juice of 1 lemon

summer vegetables:

100ml	fish stock
25g	butter
50g	fresh peas
50g	fresh broad beans, shelled
50g	concasse
12	asparagus spears
50g	samphire
2	baby gem lettuces

METHOD

roasted John Dory:

Place the John Dory on a chopping board, skin-side down and remove the skin with a sharp flexible knife. This will leave you with three muscles, two large and one small. Run a knife down the natural line of each muscle. Repeat with the other side of the John Dory. Plunge it into iced water and wash thoroughly, drain and set aside.

cucumber jelly and pickled cucumber:

Blitz seven cucumbers and pass through a fine chinoise. Measure out 1 litre of this cucumber juice. Place 750g of the juice in a saucepan on a low-medium heat. Place 250g in a saucepan on a high heat and bring to the boil. Add the agar agar to the liquid that has come to the boil and allow to cook out for 3-4 minutes. Add the hot liquid to the warm liquid and mix, then place in a shallow metal tray and place in the fridge to set. Cut into 1cm dice when cool.

Peel the remaining cucumber and cut in half lengthways. Scoop out the seeds. Place in a vacuum pack bag with the vinegar and seal. Leave for 6 hours. Open the bag and drain the cucumber on a cloth. Cut into 1cm dice.

saffron potato balls:

Peel the potatoes and wash under cold water. Scoop out balls with a melon baller. Place in a small saucepan of salted water with the saffron. Bring to the boil and then take off the heat and allow to cool in the liquid. Put the fish stock, butter, cream, milk and vermouth into a saucepan and place on a low-medium heat. Do not boil. Season with salt and add lemon juice to taste.

summer vegetables:

Place the fish stock and butter in a saucepan and add the peas, broad beans, concasse, asparagus, samphire, baby gem lettuce leaves and the cooked saffron potato balls. Put on a low-medium heat.

to serve:

Season the John Dory with salt and pepper and place in a hot frying pan with oil and cook on a high heat for 3-4 minutes. Flip the fish over, take off the heat and squeeze lemon juice over. Drain the vegetables and arrange in a bowl.

Add the diced cucumber jelly and pickled cucumber. Arrange the John Dory on the vegetables, use a hand blender to foam the sauce from the potatoes and spoon it over.

Serves 4
Preparation time: N/A
Cooking time: 1 hour

Special equipment:
Blender, sugar thermometer.

Planning ahead:
N/A

INGREDIENTS

dark chocolate tasting:

110g	70% dark chocolate
162g	double cream
1	egg yolk
10g	butter

white chocolate tasting:

185g	white chocolate
325g	double cream
¾	leaf gelatine
1	egg white

milk chocolate tasting:

100g	milk chocolate
100g	caster sugar
40g	milk
agar agar	

caramel crunch:

150g	liquid glucose
150g	icing sugar
125g	milk chocolate
12g	cocoa powder

hazelnut crumb:

150g	hazelnuts
100g	plain flour
150g	demerara sugar
100g	butter

TASTING OF VALRHONA CHOCOLATE WITH CARAMEL CRUNCH & HAZELNUT CRUMB

BY ANDREW BIRCH

METHOD

dark chocolate tasting:

Melt the dark chocolate over a bain marie. Bring the cream to the boil and pour over the egg yolk. Pour this mixture slowly over the chocolate, add the butter and mix thoroughly. Pour into a mould and place in the fridge to set.

white chocolate tasting:

Melt the white chocolate over a bain marie. Whip 250ml of the cream to a soft peak stage and set aside in the fridge.

Put the gelatine in a bowl of cold water until softened. Boil the remaining cream off the heat and stir into the softened gelatine. Pour this mixture over the melted chocolate and mix thoroughly. Fold the whipped cream gently into the chocolate mixture. Whisk the egg white until just peaking and fold this into the rest of the mixture. Place into a plastic container and into the fridge to set.

milk chocolate tasting:

Melt the milk chocolate over a bain marie. Place the sugar in a saucepan and slowly warm to a caramel. Take off the heat and add the milk slowly while stirring continuously. Pour this mixture over the chocolate. Measure out this liquid to the nearest 100g. Measure 0.8g agar agar to every 100g of liquid. Pour the agar agar into the liquid and place back into a saucepan and bring to the boil, stirring continuously. Pour into a separate container and leave to set in the fridge. When set, blitz to a smooth custard.

caramel crunch:

Place the glucose and icing sugar in a heavy-based saucepan and bring to the boil. Continue heating until it reaches 157°C on a sugar thermometer. Pour this over the chocolate and cocoa powder and quickly pour all the mixture onto a sheet of greaseproof paper. Place a sheet of greaseproof paper over this. Place on a flat baking tray and put in the oven at 160°C for 3-4 minutes. Roll over with the rolling pin until thin. Allow to cool then break into pieces to form tuile.

hazelnut crumb:

Place all the ingredients into a blender and blitz until they are combined. Place on a sheet of greaseproof paper and onto a baking sheet. Cook in a pre-heated oven at 160°C for 10-15 minutes until golden brown. Leave to cool then break into pieces.

to serve:

Unmould the dark chocolate by warming the mould with a warm cloth. Take a scoop of the white chocolate and place next to the dark chocolate. Spoon on the milk chocolate and caramel custard and garnish with the caramel crunch chocolate tuile and hazelnut crumb.

Wiltshire

{

A voyage of mystery

A county of contrasts and diversity, Wiltshire repays the time spent here with interest. Wiltshire is certainly not short of places to go and sights to see, with lively market towns and scenery like no other. The cities of Swindon and Salisbury epitomise Wiltshire and all it has to offer, through experiencing the bustling city culture. Salisbury Plain is famous for being home to one of the most ancient sights in the country, Stonehenge – surrounded by mystery, it never fails to impress. Other famous sights include Salisbury Cathedral, Wiltshire's White Horses, Stourhead and the Kennet and Avon Canal all steeped with history as well as lesser-known gems such as Lacock and STEAM museum of the Great Western Railway. Wiltshire is also full of an array of different local shops, quaint tea rooms, gastro pubs, restaurants and events throughout the year. Wiltshire Ham, lardy cake and Tacklements beer mustard are all delicacies of the county, as well as playing host to regional specialities.

Martin Burge
Grand Chef Relais & Châteaux

Martin Burge was awarded his second Michelin star in January 2009 for the acclaimed cuisine served in 'The Dining Room' at Whatley Manor. Martin's cuisine is classical French with a modern interpretation. His passion for good food is inspired by working with some of the UK's most talented chefs in restaurants including Pied à Terre, L'Ortolan, Le Manoir aux Quat' Saisons and The Landmark. Other accolades include AA four Rosettes and *Which? Good Food Guide* recognising 'The Dining Room' in the Top 20 Restaurants in the UK.

Whatley Manor

{ *Two hours from London, a visit to the Cotswolds will make you feel as if you have stumbled into an enchanted world, of wide open countryside and honey-coloured stone buildings.*

It is known as "the Heart of England", not because of its geographical situation – it is in the south-west – but because of the emotion that it inspires among its visitors. It is here that you will find Whatley Manor; a beautiful private manor house hotel set within 12 acres of English country gardens with a contemporary spa. A place to restore and revive.

SNAILS SET IN GARLIC CASSONADE & TOPPED WITH RED WINE SAUCE INFUSED WITH VEAL KIDNEY, ACCOMPANIED WITH PARSLEY PUREE & GARLIC CROUTONS

BY MARTIN BURGE

Serves 4

Special equipment:
Vac-pac machine and vac-pac bags, muslin cloth, chinoise, 24 small pots.

Planning ahead:
Prepare the cassonade the day before.

INGREDIENTS

snails:

350g	snails, blanched
25g	carrots
15g	celery
15g	onions
10g	leeks
15ml	pernod
12g	garlic
10g	parsley stalks

garlic cassonade:

30g	garlic, peeled
250ml	double cream
100ml	whole milk
2	whole eggs
4	egg yolks
15g	salt
½g	freshly milled white pepper
5ml	lemon juice

red wine sauce infused with veal kidney:

75g	rendered veal suet
250g	shallots, sliced
20g	garlic, peeled
7g	thyme
1	bay leaf
135ml	red wine vinegar
500ml	ruby port
1 litre	red wine
200g	button mushrooms, sliced
3.5 litres	chicken stock
750ml	water
75g	veal glace (reduced veal stock)
200g	veal kidney, diced

parsley purée:

200g	fresh flat leaf parsley leaves
2 litres	water
50g	salt
75g	unsalted butter
¼g	freshly milled white pepper
½g	salt

garlic croutons:

150g	unsalted butter
20g	garlic, peeled
1g	salt
24	bread croutons

METHOD

snails:

Wash the snails in cold water and dry them on a cloth or paper towel. Dice the carrots, celery, onions and leeks into approximately 1cm cubes. Place all of the ingredients into a vac-pac bag and vac-pac on full power.

Place the sealed bag into another vac-pac bag and seal again. Place the bag into a water bath set at 75°C for 7 hours. After 7 hours remove the vac-pac bag and plunge the bag into iced water, allowing to cool completely.

Once chilled open the vac-pac bags, pick out the snails and gently wash and dry them. Store the snails in the fridge until ready to use.

garlic cassonade:

Blanch the garlic three times, this should be done by placing the garlic in a pan of cold water and bringing up to the boil, drain off the hot water and replace with cold — repeat this process three times.

In a saucepan bring up to a gentle simmer the blanched garlic with the cream and milk, and allow to cool to room temperature, infusing the cream with the garlic. Place the infusion with the garlic in a food blender with the eggs and egg yolks and blend until smooth. Add the salt, pepper and lemon juice and allow the mix to rest in the fridge for 24 hours prior to use.

The next day, using a small ladle, skim the foam from the top of the mixture and then the mix is ready to use.

red wine sauce infused with veal kidney:

In a saucepan sweat the shallots with the garlic, thyme and bay leaf in the veal fat until the shallots soften slightly.

Add the vinegar and reduce until all of the vinegar disappears. Add the port and reduce until a syrup is formed. At this stage add the red wine and mushrooms and continue reducing until there is only one-eighth of the original amount of wine.

Add the rest of the ingredients apart from the veal kidney and bring up to the boil, at this stage

using a small ladle to skim off any impurities. Turn the sauce down to a gentle simmer and cook for 2 hours, taking care to regularly remove any impurities from the top by skimming — this will prevent any cloudiness.

Pass the stock through a muslin cloth and reduce until a sauce consistency is achieved. Sauté the veal kidney until golden brown and drain the fat off on paper. Add this to the reduced sauce and gently simmer for 10 minutes, then allow to stand for a further 10 minutes to infuse the kidney flavour.

parsley purée:

Boil the water and salt together, cook the parsley leaves in salted water until soft. Strain the parsley leaves through a colander. Plunge them into iced water to cool them down quickly then remove them and drain on kitchen paper until required.

Set up blender and blend the parsley leaves until smooth. Pass the purée, using a chinoise, and ladle into a saucepan. Add the butter, salt and pepper, and stir over a low heat until the butter has emulsified into the purée.

garlic croutons:

Preheat the oven to 180°C.

Melt the butter with the garlic and salt, and allow to stand for 30 minutes to infuse. Using a pastry brush, apply a thin coat of butter to each side of the crouton.

Bake on a flat tray in the oven, until golden brown. Place the croutons on tissue paper — this draws out the excess butter and prevents the croutons from being greasy.

to serve:

Preheat the oven to 100°C. Place a snail in each pot totalling 24, and cover each one with the garlic cassonade mixture. Place these on a 2.5cm deep tray, and fill the tray with boiling water until the level of water is three-quarters covering the sides of the pots.

Cling film the top of the tray and place in the oven for approximately 45 minutes, until the cassonades are set. Remove from the tray and dry off any excess water on the pots.

On top of each pot pour a teaspoon of sauce to finish.

Serve the warm croutons and parsley purée in suitable dishes.

chef's tip:

Snails can be purchased online. First purge them in salted water then blanch in boiling water for a few minutes. Then remove their shells and cook them in a court bouillon. You can also buy them pre-cooked in their own court bouillon.

We make the croutons from breadsticks sliced on an angle, but they can be made using any shaped bread as long as they are the same thickness.

ROASTED SCALLOP GLAZED WITH SMOKE & SERVED WITH PICKLED COCKLES

BY MARTIN BURGE

I am a huge fan of pickled cockles as they remind me of my childhood days spent at the seaside. It was great fun to create a dish combining them with the hand-dived scallop.

Serves 4

Special equipment:
Liquidiser, vac pac machine, water bath, hand blender, steamer.

Planning ahead:
Prepare on day of serving.

INGREDIENTS

smoke-glazed scallop:

4	large hand-dived scallops
salt and pepper	
20ml	rapeseed oil
10ml	fatty glazed smoke Sosa product

white balsamic pickled cockles:

234ml	water
32ml	white balsamic
34ml	groundnut oil
2g	salt
2g	gellespas Sosa product
1.5kg	cockles
1kg	fish stock

Parma ham crumb:

150g	thinly sliced Parma ham
3.5g	maltosec Sosa product

celeriac purée:

300g	celeriac
60ml	full-fat milk
60ml	whipping cream
1.5g	celeriac salt
3ml	lemon juice

almond purée:

75g	almond paste toasted Sosa range
25ml	water
7.5ml	almond oil
50g	celeriac purée 'base recipe - see above'

braised salsify:

250g	salsify
12.5ml	lemon juice
1.2g	salt
2.5g	sugar
200ml	whipping cream

garnish:

50g	Brussels sprouts

METHOD

white balsamic pickled cockles:
To make the pickling liquor place the water, white balsamic, groundnut oil, salt and gellespas into a container and hand blend the ingredients together until they have completely emulsified. Set the pickling liquor aside until ready to use. Place the cockles into a pan with the fish stock and gently heat the stock up until the cockles just start to open. Strain the cockles through a colander and while they are still hot pick them and place into the pickling liquor. Place the cockle stock back onto the stove and reduce the mixture down to form a glace. Add the glace to the pickled cockles and store in the fridge until ready to use.

Parma ham crumb:
Place the ham into an oven set at 140°C for approximately 15-20 minutes until it becomes crispy. Once cooked place the ham onto kitchen paper and leave under a hot lamp to drain off any excess fat. After approximately 1 hour under the hot lamp blend the Parma ham in a food processor into a fine crumb. Add the maltosec to the powdered parma ham and spread the mix onto kitchen paper and leave for a further 20-30 minutes to allow the maltosec to absorb the oils.

celeriac purée:

Place all of the ingredients into a vac pac bag and cook in simmering water until soft. Place all the ingredients into a liquidiser and blend into a smooth purée. Cool over ice and once cooled store in the fridge until ready to use.

almond purée:

Mix all the ingredients together with a hand blender to form a smooth paste.

braised salsify:

Preheat the water bath to 95°C. Place the salsify, lemon juice, salt and sugar into a vac pac bag and cook in the water bath for 1 hour. Once the salsify is just cooked and soft in texture plunge the bag into iced water to prevent from cooking further. Cut the salsify into the desired pieces and store in the fridge ready to use.

garnish:

Peel the green leaves from the sprouts and set aside until ready to use.

to serve:

Set up a steamer to cook the sprout leaves. In a pan gently heat the cream and salsify together and set aside in a warm place. Gently heat the cockles and the pickling liquor together in a pan and set aside in a warm place. Heat the almond purée carefully in a bain marie, making sure that it's not too hot to prevent any lumps and skin forming. Place the seasoned scallop into a frying pan with the oil and cook on a medium heat until one side is golden brown. Turn the scallops over and then place in an oven set at 190°C until cooked. The cooking time will vary depending on the size of scallop. The scallops will be firm to touch once they are cooked. Brush the scallops liberally with the glazed smoke. When the dish is 1 minute from completion place the sprout leaves into the steamer and cook until they have a slight bite in texture. Season with salt and pepper. Serve as pictured and finish with Parma ham crumb.

Chef's note:

Source the dived scallops in their complete shell as they have a much cleaner taste. A tightly closed shell also indicates that the scallop is alive and therefore very fresh.

ROASTED VENISON FILLET DRESSED WITH CARAMELISED BACON, GAME SAUSAGE & RED WINE SAUCE

BY MARTIN BURGE

Venison is a super red meat to offer on the menu and this recipe makes the most of the seasonal vegetables on offer.

Serves 4

Special equipment:
Hobart mixer, liquidiser, vac pac machine, water bath, food processor, scales, Robot Coupe, fine sieve, micro scales.

Planning ahead:
The venison sausage and smoked bacon need to be made well in advance.

INGREDIENTS

venison sausage:

350ml	red wine
100g	sugar
2g	thyme
1g	bay leaf
1g	orange peel
3g	juniper berries
1kg	venison
500g	pork
420g	pork fat
200g	breadcrumbs
3g	garlic, finely chopped
140ml	water
5g	salt
pepper, to taste	

smoked bacon:

½	side smoked streaky bacon
500ml	olive oil

red wine sauce:

75g	sliced shallots
2g	garlic
2g	thyme
1	bay leaf
20ml	olive oil
50ml	red wine vinegar
150ml	port
300ml	red wine
75g	button mushrooms
1 litre	chicken stock
200ml	water
5g	cumin seeds, toasted

celeriac fondants:

10	celeriac fondants (made with a 40mm cutter)
0.2g	celery salt
salt and pepper	
10g	butter
50g	butter (foaming)

Shiraz mayonnaise:

200ml	Shiraz
12g	sugar
0.1g	salt
1.5g	gellespas Sosa product
24ml	Shiraz

cabbage purée:

800g	shredded cabbage
125g	butter
6g	garlic
1g	vitamin C powder
500ml	double cream
300g	spinach leaves
8g	salt

chocolate gel:

160ml	water
50g	grue (nibbed cocoa)
20g	sugar
13g	cocoa powder
7g	water
0.5g	gellan gum

confit chestnuts:

300g	peeled chestnuts
200g	duck fat
3g	thyme
5g	garlic
1g	bay leaf
5g	salt

METHOD

venison sausage:

In a saucepan reduce the red wine and sugar to a light syrup. Add the thyme, bay leaf, orange peel and juniper to the syrup. Pour the warm marinade over the venison and the pork then place in the fridge for 24 hours. Once the meats are marinated remove the bay leaf and the thyme. Mince the venison and the pork. In a Hobart mixer beat together the minced meats, pork fat, breadcrumbs, garlic, water and salt. This process will take between 10 to 15 seconds. Season the mixture with pepper and allow to rest for 24 hours in the fridge.

smoked bacon:

Place the bacon into a large container of iced water. Soak in the fridge for 24 hours then remove the bacon from the iced water and dry with a towel. Place the bacon and the olive oil into a vac pac bag and cook in a water bath for 42 hours at 68°C. Once cooked chill on ice then remove from the bag and dry with a towel. Trim the edges from the bacon and cut into desired pieces.

red wine sauce:

Sweat the shallots in a pan with the garlic, thyme, bay leaf and olive oil until translucent. Add the vinegar and reduce until there is no liquid remaining. Add the port and reduce again until a syrupy consistency is achieved. Add the red wine and mushrooms, and continue to reduce until 20 per cent of the liquid remains. Add the chicken stock and water then bring to the boil and, using a ladle, skim off the fat and any impurities. Pass the stock through a fine sieve and chill over ice. Using a spoon scrape the fat which has hardened on the surface of the sauce. Return the ingredients to the pan and reduce until a desired consistency is achieved. Pass through a fine sieve and set aside ready for serving. Just before serving add the cumin seeds to the sauce for around 5 minutes then pass through a fine sieve and serve.

celeriac fondants:

Place all of the ingredients into a vac pac bag and seal. Place the sealed ingredients into a water bath set at 95°C for 30 minutes. Once the ingredients have been cooked plunge them into iced water. Just before serving colour the celeriac in a pan with the foaming butter.

Shiraz mayonnaise:

Place the 200ml Shiraz, sugar and salt into a pan and reduce the mixture until 170ml remains. Add the gellespassa and 24ml Shiraz and whisk until the mixture thickens. Strain through a fine sieve and set aside until cool. Store in the fridge until ready to use.

cabbage purée:

In a saucepan sweat the cabbage in the butter with the garlic and the vitamin C powder. When the cabbage is soft add the cream and gently bring to the boil for a few minutes. Put all of these ingredients into a liquidiser and add the spinach then liquidise into a purée. Add the salt then pass the mixture through a fine sieve and set aside in the fridge until ready to use.

chocolate gel:

Place the water and grue into a saucepan and bring to the boil. Set aside and allow the mixture to infuse until it cools down. Pass the mixture through a fine sieve into a saucepan and then add the sugar, cocoa powder and water to the pan. Whisk the ingredients well. Add the gellan gum and bring the mixture up to the boil for 1 minute. Pass the mixture through a fine sieve and set aside in a suitable container in the fridge until set.

confit chestnuts:

Vac pac all the ingredients together. Cook in a water bath set at 80°C for 1½ hours. Remove from the waterbath and chill the chestnuts over ice until ready to use.

to serve:

Place the venison loins into a water bath set at 58°C for approximately 40 minutes. When the venison is cooked remove it from the water bath and leave in the bag. Set aside in a warm place.

Place the sausages into a pan of chicken stock set at 80°C and poach for 5 minutes. Remove the sausages from the stock and place them with the venison in a warm place.

Heat up the chestnuts in their own duck fat and set aside in a warm place.

Place the rapeseed oil and celeriac fondants into a frying pan and gently fry both sides to an even golden brown colour. Leave in the hot pan and set aside in a warm place until ready to serve.

In a frying pan on a medium heat place the rapeseed oil and the bacon and gently caramelise both sides. In the same pan once the bacon has

coloured on one of the sides add the sausages and carefully caramelise them evenly all around.

Remove the venison from the bag and season with salt and pepper. Place the venison loins into a hot frying pan with the rapeseed oil and quickly colour both sides. This should not take more than 1 minute total cooking time. Reheat the cabbage purée in a bain marie the same time as the venison is frying in the pan. At the same time place the sprout leaves into the steamer. Once they are just cooked with a slight bite in texture lightly season with salt and pepper.

Place the reduced Shiraz into a fine squeezy bottle and pipe the wine onto the plate then add the diced chocolate gel. Cut the caramelised venison loin into half and repeat this with the sausage, cutting on a slight angle. Dress the dish as per the picture, placing the cabbage purée first followed by all the other ingredients.

Chef's tip:

To prepare the chestnuts easily prepare a hot fryer. Take a sharp knife and criss cross the shell of the chestnuts then place them in the fryer. Cook no more than four chestnuts at a time and peel while hot.

Serves 4

Special equipment:
Fine sieve, ice-cream machine, 4 martini glasses.

Planning ahead:
The sorbet can be made in advance.

INGREDIENTS

vanilla panna cotta:

2g	gelatine
50ml	full-fat milk
125ml	whipping cream
8g	caster sugar
¾	vanilla pod

coconut granite:

20g	desiccated coconut
100ml	water
96ml	coconut milk
75g	coconut purée
13g	caster sugar
0.5g	salt
9ml	Malibu

Pedro Ximenez jelly:

6g	gelatine
150ml	Pedro Ximenez sherry
15ml	Pedro Ximenez sherry

pineapple sorbet:

500g	pineapple purée
50g	caster sugar
10g	glucose

VANILLA PANNA COTTA TOPPED WITH COCONUT GRANITE & PINEAPPLE SORBET
BY MARTIN BURGE

This pre-dessert is offered to guests while their main desert is being prepared. It gives them an explosive taste of flavour and gets them in the mood for what's to come.

METHOD

vanilla panna cotta:

Soak the gelatine in plenty of cold water ready for use. Place the milk, cream, sugar and split vanilla pod into a pan and bring the mixture up to the boil. Cover the mixture and set aside for 20 minutes, allowing the vanilla to infuse. Squeeze the excess water from the gelatine and then add to the warm mixture until completely dissolved. Pass the mixture through a fine sieve and pour evenly into the martini glasses. Set the panna cotta in a fridge for approximately 2 hours.

coconut granite:

Place the desiccated coconut into a moderately hot oven set at 150°C for approximately 5 minutes until golden brown. Mix the toasted coconut with the water in a pan and simmer for 5 minutes. Pass the toasted coconut through a fine sieve then add the coconut milk, coconut purée, sugar, salt and Malibu. Pour the mixture into a container and freeze. Once the mixture has frozen solid run a fork across the top in a scraping motion, producing flaky pieces of iced coconut.

Pedro Ximenez jelly:

Soak the gelatine in plenty of cold water. Squeeze the excess water from the gelatine and then add to the 150ml Pedro Ximenez until dissolved. Add the remaining Pedro Ximenez to the mixture and allow to completely cool down. Cover the panna cotta completely with a thin layer of the jelly and leave to set in the fridge.

pineapple sorbet:

Place the ingredients into a pan and bring to the boil. Set aside and allow to completely cool down before churning the sorbet in an ice-cream machine. Once the mixture is completely churned and formed store in the freezer ready for use.

to serve:

Remove the panna cotta from the fridge and add the coconut granite. Make a quenelle of the sorbet using a hot teaspoon, place on top and serve immediately.

Chef's note:

When you cut a vanilla pod in half run your knife across the pod to separate the seeds. This process maximises the vanilla flavour from the pod and infuses the ingredients directly.

CHICORY MOUSSE LAYERED WITH BITTER COFFEE & MASCARPONE CREAM

BY MARTIN BURGE

The combination of flavours in this dessert make it sinful, from the layering of the dark chocolate, the booziness of the kahlua and sherry followed by the rich creamy mascarpone mousse.

Serves 4

Special equipment:
Spray gun, blow torch, water bath, vac-pac machine, food mixer, 4 x 50mm diameter hexagonal mould for the mascarpone mousse, 4 x 50mm diameter sphere moulds for the chicory mousse, 60cm x 40cm tray, thermometer, chinoise.

Planning ahead:
The chicory mousse and the joconde sponge may be prepared ahead of time.

INGREDIENTS

chicory mousse:

75g	chicory beans
75ml	full-fat milk
185ml	whipping cream
2	medium egg yolks
20g	sugar
15g	milk chocolate
2.5g	gelatine

coffee syrup:

75ml	espresso coffee
50ml	Kahlua
50g	Pedro Ximenez sherry
20g	caster sugar

joconde sponge:

187g	icing sugar
187g	almonds, ground
5	medium eggs, beaten
35g	unsalted butter, melted
50g	caster sugar
6	medium egg whites
50g	plain flour, sieved
15g	dark chocolate, 70% cocoa, melted

mascarpone mousse:

55g	caster sugar
10ml	water
2	medium egg yolks
85g	mascarpone cheese
2g	gelatine leaf
80ml	whipping cream

chocolate spray:

300g	cocoa butter
300g	dark chocolate, 70% cocoa

to serve:

25g	dark chocolate
24	tempered chocolate leaves (4cm x 3cm)
4	pieces of gold leaf
5g	gold dust

METHOD

chicory mousse:

In a frying pan toast the chicory beans on a medium heat.

Pour the milk and 75ml of whipping cream into a vac-pac bag with the toasted chicory beans. Seal the bag and place in a water bath set at 75°C for 30 minutes.

Remove the bag from the water bath and pass the mixture through a fine sieve or chinoise.

Measure out the infusion to 125ml and discard the remainder.

Whisk together the egg yolks and sugar. Meanwhile bring the infusion to the boil then pour over the egg yolks and sugar. Return to the heat, continuously stirring with a spatula or wooden spoon. The mixture will thicken to make an Anglaise. Pass this chicory Anglaise through a chinoise or fine sieve. Add the chocolate and set aside until required. Take a glass bowl and soften the gelatine in cold water for about 10 minutes.

Squeeze the gelatine to remove any excess water. In a pan add 10ml of whipping cream and the gelatine, heat the mixture up gently until the gelatine has dissolved. Take the gelatine cream off the heat and then pour onto the chicory Anglaise and whisk until well mixed. Whisk the remaining cream to form soft ribbons and then fold into the chicory Anglaise. Mix well. Pour the mixture into half-sphere moulds and freeze.

coffee syrup:

Dissolve the sugar into the coffee. Add the rest of the ingredients. Set aside until required.

joconde sponge:

Preheat the oven to 220°C.

Place the icing sugar, almonds and half of the beaten eggs into a food mixer. Whisk on high speed for 8 minutes. Add the remainder of the eggs and whisk on high speed for another 10 minutes. Add the butter into the mix and set aside.

Line a tray 60cm x 40cm with silicone paper.

Meanwhile make a meringue by whisking the caster sugar and the egg whites until soft peaks are formed. Fold the almond mixture into the meringue. Fold the flour into the mixture. With a palate knife spread the mixture gently and evenly over the tray. Bake in the oven for 10-12 minutes, until firm to the touch.

Leave to cool and then spread a thin layer of melted dark chocolate over the top. Cut the sponge into eight hexagons using the mould as a cutter. Set aside. Discard any remaining sponge.

mascarpone mousse:

Dissolve the sugar and water in a pan and boil to 118°C to make a sugar syrup.

Meanwhile in a mixing bowl add the egg yolks then pour on the sugar syrup and whisk the

mixture to form a sabayon. Set aside. In a separate bowl whisk the mascarpone cheese until soft and smooth. Fold the sabayon into the mascarpone.

In a glass bowl soften the gelatine in cold water for about 10 minutes. Squeeze the gelatine to remove any excess water. In a pan heat up 5ml of cream and add the gelatine until dissolved. Take the melted gelatine off the heat and then pour into the mascarpone sabayon and whisk until combined. In a bowl whisk 75ml of cream to form soft peaks and then fold into the mascarpone sabayon.

Place the joconde sponge on the bottom of the hexagonal mould and soak the sponge with a tablespoon of the coffee syrup. In the mould pipe the mascarpone mousse up to half way. Repeat the layering of the joconde sponge, coffee syrup and the mascarpone mousse. Leave to set in the fridge for 2 hours.

chocolate spray:

Set up a bain marie and melt the cocoa butter and chocolate together until it reaches 50-55°C. Pass the chocolate through a chinoise into a spray gun.

to serve:

Remove the chicory mousse from the freezer. Turn the mousse out of the mould by heating the outside of the mould with a blow torch. Meanwhile melt some dark chocolate over a bain marie. Brush the bottom of each mousse with the melted chocolate. Place the mousse back in the freezer for 10 minutes.

Set up the spray gun. The temperature of the chocolate must be about 50°C so that the gun works efficiently. Remove the frozen mousses from the freezer and spray all over, except the base, making sure they remain frozen while

spraying. Lay the sprayed mousses on a tray lined with silicone paper and place in the fridge to defrost naturally (around 1 hour).

Light the blow torch and heat the outside of the hexagonal mould to assist with removing the mousse from the mould. Place the chicory mousse carefully on top of the mascarpone mousse. Arrange the chocolate leaves around the outside of the mascarpone mousse to form a hexagon. Then place the pieces of gold leaf on top of the dome and sprinkle with a light dusting of gold dust on the edge of the plate.

chef's tip:

Place the spherical moulds for the chicory mousse in the freezer a few hours before filling them. This will ensure that the mousse does not separate during the freezing process.

Hywel Jones

Hywel Jones started his career as Chef de Partie in two three-star Michelin establishments: Chez Nico at 90 and Marco Pierre White. He then developed his skills as Junior Sous Chef at the Michelin-starred Le Soufflé. From there he went on to earn his own Michelin star working at Foliage restaurant at the Mandarin Oriental, Hyde Park where he was Head Chef for five years. He then became Executive Chef at Pharmacy restaurant in Notting Hill before moving to Lucknam Park in 2004. Since Hywel has been Head Chef at Lucknam he has achieved several accolades including Hotel Chef of the Year 2007, Best Restaurant outside London 2006 and one Michelin star.

'An un-spoilt, country house living at its very best'

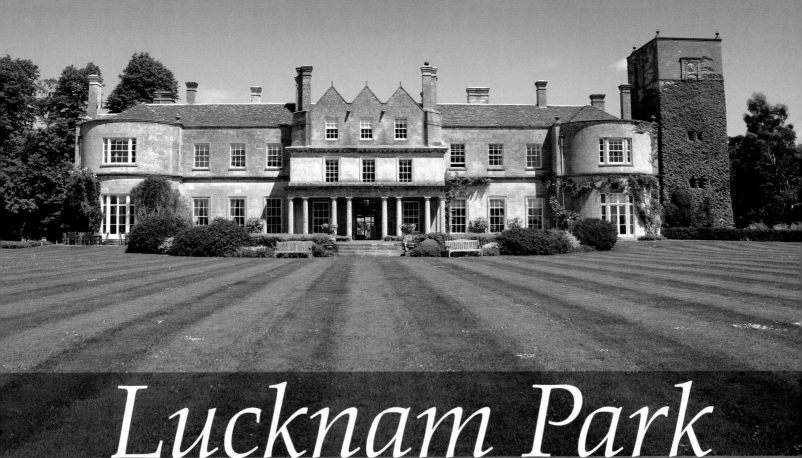

Lucknam Park

{ *Country house living at its very best. The very name conjures up images of trees and tranquillity, of stately nature and magnificent settings.*

A country retreat where five-star luxury invites and indulges with sumptuous bedrooms and outstanding cuisine. The grand ambience of The Park restaurant to the contemporary and stylish all-day dining of The Brasserie. Luxuriate in The Spa now regarded as one of the finest in the UK. Enjoy a beautiful horse ride over the estate, all levels of riders from beginners to advanced are catered for or simply enjoy the 500 acres of gardens and walking trails and perhaps a tour of Bath just 6 miles away. You will leave wanting to return very soon ...

BRAISED TURBOT, BUTTERED ICEBERG & CORNISH CRAB, HANDMADE MACARONI, TRUFFLE BUTTER SAUCE

BY HYWEL JONES

Serves 4
Preparation time: 1 hour
Cooking time: 15 minutes

Special equipment:
Pasta machine.

Planning ahead:
N/A

INGREDIENTS

pasta dough:

265g	pasta flour
1 tsp	olive oil
3	egg yolks
2	whole eggs, beaten

braised turbot:

4 x 140g	fillets line-caught turbot
2	shallots, finely chopped
1	sprig of tarragon
100ml	dry white wine
	drizzle of olive oil
	salt and pepper
125g	unsalted butter
	lemon juice, to taste
1 tbsp	chopped truffle

buttered iceberg and Cornish crab:

80g	fresh white crab meat
1	green iceberg lettuce, outer leaves only
¼	bunch chives, finely chopped
2	tomatoes, peeled and deseeded

to serve:

4	baby artichokes, roasted

METHOD

pasta dough:

Place the flour in a food processor, add in the olive oil, turn on and incorporate the eggs and yolks until a firm dough is formed. Then wrap in cling film and refrigerate for 1 hour.

macaroni:

Using a pasta machine roll the pasta out to setting N1 and cut into 6cm squares. Brush a little egg wash on to one edge and then roll the pasta square around a clean pencil to form a cylinder. Allow to dry for 1 hour and then blanch in boiling salted water. Refresh, drain and store in a fridge until required.

braised turbot:

Preheat the oven to 180°C .

Place the fish in an ovenware dish and cover with the shallots, tarragon, white wine and a drizzle of oil. Season lightly, cover with greaseproof paper and cook in the oven for around 6-8 minutes until the fish is just cooked.

Strain the juices off the fish and reduce by half, whisk in the butter and season with salt, pepper and lemon juice and then finely stir in the truffle.

buttered iceberg and Cornish crab:

Melt a little butter in a pan and add the crab meat, remove from the heat and add the lettuce. Cook gently until it just begins to break down. Add the chives and diced tomato flesh.

to serve:

Spoon the lettuce mix into rings, remove the rings and top with the fish fillets. Heat the macaroni in the truffle butter and arrange on top of the fish. Finish with the artichokes.

LOIN OF MIDDLEWOOD FARM VENISON, BRAISED OXTAIL, BUTTERNUT SQUASH & SLOE GIN
BY HYWEL JONES

Serves 4
Preparation time: 25 minutes
Cooking time: 5 hours (includes slow-cooking the oxtail)

Special equipment:
Fine sieve.

Planning ahead:
The braised oxtail needs to marinate for 24 hours.

INGREDIENTS

venison:

600g	trimmed loin of Brecon venison
oil, as required	

braised oxtail:

1	whole oxtail, cut into pieces
1	carrot
½	onion
1	celery stick
½	leek
1	bouquet garni
1 75cl	bottle red wine
salt and pepper, to taste	
flour, as required	
1 litre	good strength meat stock

sloe gin sauce:

150g	venison trimmings
75g	finely chopped mirepoix vegetables
200ml	sloe gin
500ml	red wine
1 litre	oxtail stock reserved from the braised oxtail
1	bouquet garni
12	juniper berries

butternut squash purée:

100g	butter
1	butternut squash, peeled, deseeded and diced
salt and pepper	
few drops maple syrup and lemon juice	

risotto fritters:

25g	cooked risotto base
2 tbsp	squash purée
sprinkling of grated parmesan	
4	small sage leaves, finely sliced
flour, as required	
breadcrumbs, as required	

to serve:

2	thin slices Carmarthen ham
140g	seasonal mixed greens eg; curly kale, sprout tops
12	small wild mushrooms
butter, as required	

METHOD

braised oxtail:
Cover the meat with the vegetables, herbs and wine and marinate for 24 hours.

Drain and pat the meat dry, then season. Dust with flour and brown in a heavy-bottomed pan. Add the vegetables and continue to cook until golden. Cover with the marinade and reduce by two-thirds. Add the stock. Bring to a simmer and cover. Cook at 130°C for 3-4 hours or until the meat flakes from the bones. Allow to cool in the liquid.

Remove the meat from the bones. Discard any fat and flake the remaining meat. Season lightly and moisten with a little of the cooking liquid. Pass the liquid through a fine sieve and set aside for the sauce.

sloe gin sauce:
Brown the venison trimmings and drain. Colour the vegetables in the same pan and deglaze with 150ml sloe gin and the red wine. Reduce to 250ml. Add the stock and trimmings back to the pan along with the bouquet garni. Simmer gently for 30 minutes, skimming frequently. Pass through a fine sieve. Crush the juniper berries and warm through in the remaining sloe gin. Add to the sauce and leave to infuse for 30 minutes, then pass through a sieve again.

butternut squash purée:
Melt half the butter and cook the diced squash in it until completely soft. Blend to a smooth purée and pass through a fine sieve. Season and whisk in the remaining butter, and adjust with maple syrup and lemon juice to taste.

risotto fritters:
Combine the first four ingredients and form into four even-sized balls. Coat in flour and breadcrumbs.

to serve:
Preheat the oven to 170°C.

Colour the venison loin in a little oil and cook in the oven for around 10-12 minutes or until pink. Roll the flaked oxtail in cling film to form a 2.5cm diameter roll. Wrap in the ham, cut into four pieces and pan fry. Cook the greens and wild mushrooms in a little butter and keep warm.

Deep fry the risotto fritters until golden.

Arrange the greens in the centre of four plates and place a little butternut purée either side.

Arrange the remaining elements around. Reduce the sauce base to the required consistency. Finally carve the venison into four even-sized pieces, place one each on top of the greens and drizzle the sauce over the oxtail.

Serves 4
Preparation time: 45 minutes
Cooking time: Approximately 45 minutes

Special equipment:
200ml tart ring, ice-cream machine, blow torch.

Planning ahead:
The sorbet can be made in advance.

INGREDIENTS

sweet pastry tart case:

125g	butter
75g	icing sugar
2	egg yolks
250g	plain flour
25ml	iced water

passion fruit custard:

4	eggs
150g	caster sugar
190g	passion fruit purée
125ml	double cream

lime leaf panna cotta:

250ml	double cream
40g	caster sugar
6	lime leaves
1¾	leaves gelatine
100ml	mango purée
4tsp	diced fresh mango

coconut sorbet:

200ml	unsweetened coconut milk
75ml	water
125g	caster sugar
juice of ½ lemon	

to serve:

demerara sugar, for glazing

GLAZED PASSION FRUIT CREAM, COCONUT, MANGO & LIME LEAF
BY HYWEL JONES

METHOD

sweet pastry tart case:
Preheat the oven to 180°C.

Cream the butter and sugar together. Add the egg yolks. Fold in the flour and gently mix to a smooth dough, adding the water if required. Allow to rest before rolling out and lining a 200ml tart ring. Blind bake for 10-12 minutes or until golden.

passion fruit custard:
Whisk together the eggs and sugar and mix in the remaining ingredients. Pour the mix into the blind baked pastry case and cook at 130°C for 35 minutes or until just set.

lime leaf panna cotta:
Bring the cream, sugar and lime leaves to a simmer. Cover and allow to infuse and cool. Dissolve the ¾ leaf gelatine into the cream and then decant. Mix into shot glasses and leave to set in the fridge. Mix the mango purée with the diced mango and one leaf of gelatine and again decant on top of the set panna cotta mix.

coconut sorbet:
Mix the ingredients together and churn in an ice-cream machine according to the manufacturer's instructions.

to serve:
Cut the passion fruit tart into four even oblong rectangles, dust with demerara sugar and caramelise with a blow torch. Sit next to a ball of coconut sorbet and serve a panna cotta/mango shot separately.

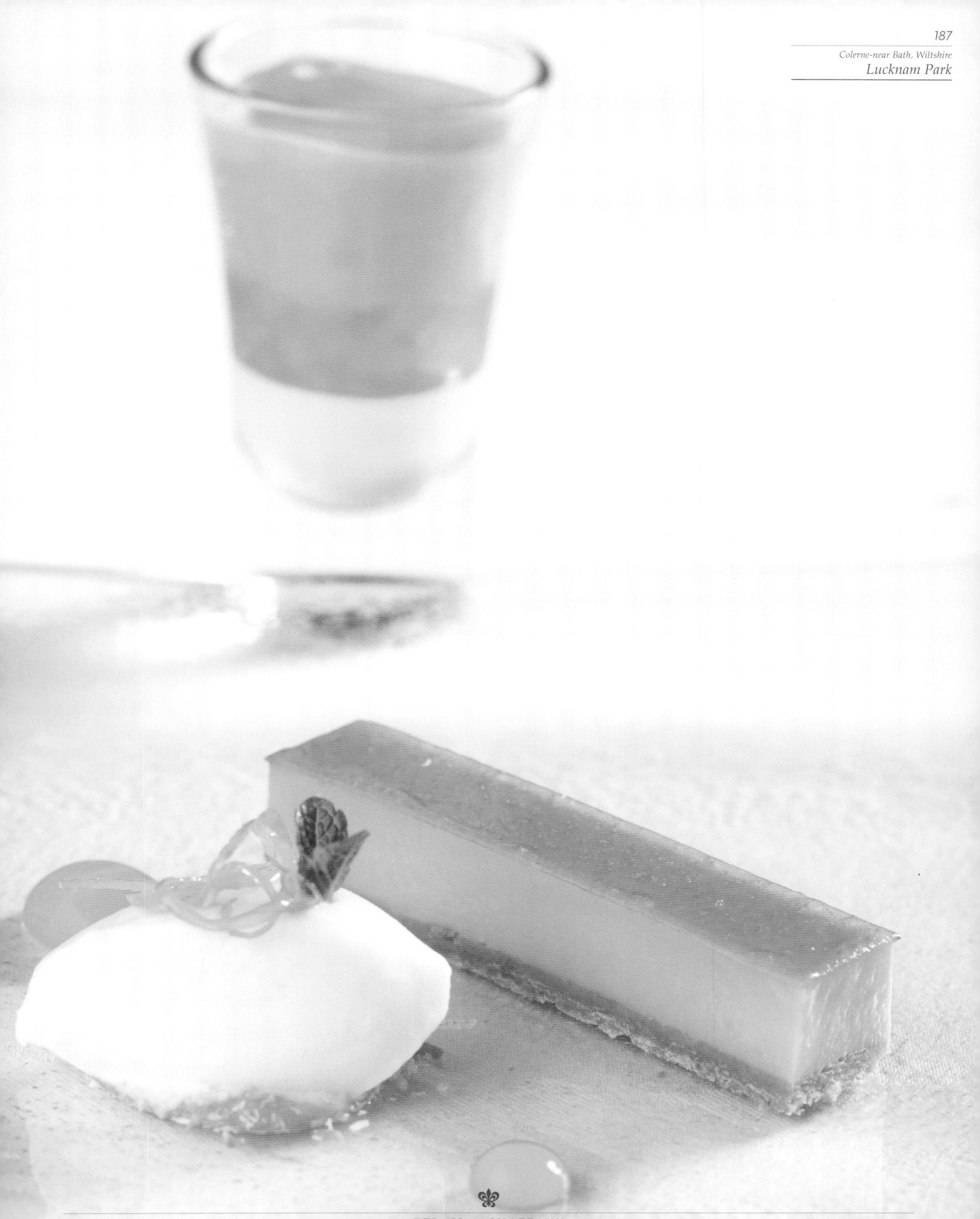

Somerset

Georgian majesty and mellow Cotswolds

Somerset, situated in the heart of south-west England, is known as a perfect holiday destination boasting scenes of epic beauty, dramatic coastline and wonderful seaside resorts. Bath, situated in the ceremonial county of Somerset, remains the most complete and best preserved Georgian city in Britain, its status confirmed by it being granted the coveted World Heritage Site status. The formality of Bath is in complete contrast to the villages and towns of the Cotswold Hills whose character defines rural England for many visitors. In terms of food and drink the county is best known for its cider as well as being the home of Cheddar cheese and the unique Exmoor blue cheese. Sampling a West Country cream tea or Ploughman's lunch is also a necessity while in the area, as well as experiencing some of the finest ice cream made from clotted cream. A secret of Somerset is the fact that there are a number of vineyards producing a variety of English wines with an array of flavours.

Sam Moody

Sam started his career as a chef at the age of 16, working part-time in a local hotel, while also studying catering at college. At 17 he started his first full-time job in the kitchens of Ockenden Manor Hotel, when after a year's hard work under the direction of Head Chef Steve Crane, the team won a Michelin star.

At the age of 20 Sam decided it was time for a new challenge. This ambition and desire to expand his knowledge took Sam to the famous two Michelin-star kitchen at Gidleigh Park. For the four years Sam was there he worked his way around all the sections of the kitchen, learning the importance of every little detail and the basis of what makes great food.

In early 2009 a new challenge arrived for Sam when Michael Caines MBE, Executive Head Chef at Gidleigh Park, also took over the kitchens at sister hotel The Bath Priory and appointed Sam as his Sous Chef. In September 2009 Sam was promoted to Head Chef.

The Bath Priory

Hotel

{ *The Bath Priory offers a serene base from which to explore the city of Bath.*

Proud of a long-held reputation offering genuinely warm hospitality, reminiscent of a wonderful country home where you would be welcomed by the gentleman host. Linger in the delightful gardens and muse over our fascinating Art Collection. Under the direction of Michael Caines MBE, the culinary experience is a truly memorable part of your stay. Why not spend some time unwinding in our contemporary Spa, enjoying totally relaxing and sumptuous treatments.

PLATE OF ROAST & CONFIT RABBIT, CRISPY HAM HOCK, PEASE PUDDING, MUSTARD JUS ROTI

BY SAM MOODY

This dish can be served as a complex starter or a light main course — the ham hock and smokiness of the pease pudding along with the rich jus roti really are brilliant together.

Serves 8
Preparation time: 20 minutes
Cooking time: 2-3 hours

Special equipment:
Fine mesh chinoise, deep fryer.

Planning ahead:
The early stages of the crispy ham hock, rabbit preparation and pease pudding can be made in advance.

INGREDIENTS

crispy ham hock:

1	large smoked ham hock
1	carrot
1	onion
1	leek
½	clove garlic
sprigs of thyme	
parsley stalks	
black peppercorns	

rabbit:

2	large tame rabbits, or 4 wild
100g	coarse sea salt
sprigs of thyme	
garlic	
black pepper, to taste	
duck fat, as required	
olive oil, as required	
1kg	chicken wings
non-scented oil, as required	
1	pinch salt
½	onion, cut into rings
1	sprig of thyme
1	sprig of tarragon
2 litres	chicken stock
veal glace, as required	
water, as required	

pease pudding:

200g	split yellow peas
1	bouquet garni

batter:

50g	cornflour
50g	plain flour
150ml	sparkling water

to serve:

salt and pepper, to taste	
1 tbsp	whole-grain mustard
non-scented oil, as required	
1	knob butter
Young salad leaves, kale, celery, mustard	

METHOD

crispy ham hock:

Place the ham hock into a large pan and cover with cold water, bring to a simmer, then pour away the water. Cover the hock with fresh cold water and add the carrot, onion, leek, celery, garlic, thyme, rosemary, parsley stalks and a few black peppercorns. Bring to a simmer and cook over a gentle heat for 2-3 hours. Once soft and falling away from the bone allow to cool in the liquid. Remove the cooked ham hock and pick over the meat, removing any fat. Reserve for later use. Pass the stock through a fine mesh chinoise and reserve.

rabbit:

Take your rabbits, remove the legs and shoulder and marinate these in the sea salt, thyme, garlic and black pepper for 8 hours, then confit in duck fat until falling away from the bone. Cool, then pick the meat away from the bones, removing any tendons, and reserve.

Now with the body of the rabbits, remove the head and discard, carefully pull out the offal, keep the kidney and liver, separately, covered with a little olive oil. Discard the heart and lungs. With the rabbit on its back find the last two ribs and cut in-between them — you are going to split the rabbit's body into two parts, the rack (rib cage) and the loin. Firstly, remove the loins by carefully cutting down between each loin, using the tip of a sharp knife and keeping as close to the bone as possible. Remove the loins, trim well so you are just left with a neat and clean loin. For the racks, with a sharp knife scrape the inside of the rib cage, then with a pair of scissors trim the ribs to about 20mm — you should then be able to pull away the skin and have the rib bone exposed. Repeat on the other side, then cut the ribs away from the back bone, giving you two rabbit racks.

Chop the rabbit carcass and chicken wings into small, even pieces. Heat a large heavy-bottomed pan, add a little non-scented oil and as it starts to haze add the carcass along with a pinch of salt. Cook over a medium-high heat until evenly golden brown, reduce the heat and add the onion rings, cook for 5 minutes. Add the thyme and tarragon, then add the stock, veal glace and enough water to cover. Simmer over a gentle heat for 2 hours, pass through a colander and then a fine mesh chinoise. Reduce to your desired consistency. Reserve this sauce for later use.

pease pudding:

Place the split yellow peas into a saucepan and cover with the reserved ham stock, add a boquet garni, cover with a cartouche (greaseproof or parchment paper lid) and simmer slowly until cooked. Reserve.

batter:

Sieve the cornflour and flour together and make your batter with the sparkling water. Lightly flour the pieces of flaked ham hock and dip into the batter. Deep fry at 180°C until golden and crispy. Reserve.

to serve:

Heat the pease pudding with a little more stock if the consistency is too thick and adjust the seasoning. Heat the sauce and the grain mustard, adjust the seasoning and split between two pans: in one pan add the confit leg meat, cover both and keep warm. Heat a wide heavy-based pan and add some oil, season the rabbit meat well, add the loins to the pan first, and then a knob of butter, then the racks. Roast well, remove and allow to rest, flash fry the liver and kidney at the last second. Refry the ham hock.

Assemble all the elements on a warm plate, pour over the sauce, add the salad leaves and serve.

BRIXHAM TURBOT ROASTED ON THE BONE, POTATO PUREE, RED WINE JUS

BY SAM MOODY

Cooking a piece of turbot on the bone will give you fantastic results as the bones hold so much flavour. If turbot is unavailable a large brill will give you the same results.

Serves 8
Preparation time: 30 minutes
Cooking time: 2 hours

Special equipment:
Chinoise, drum sieve.

Planning ahead:
The jus can be made in advance and freezes well.

INGREDIENTS

red wine jus:

70g	unsalted butter
50g	shallots, thinly sliced
1	pinch salt
90g	button mushrooms, thinly sliced
750ml	Cabernet sauvignon
1kg	turbot bones
25ml	double cream
	Dried orange peel
1	star anise
1	sprig thyme
1	bay leaf
5g	caster sugar
150ml	good veal glaze
1	knob butter, to finish
	salt and pepper, to finish
	double cream, to finish

turbot:

8 x 160g turbot pieces
coarse sea salt, as required
pepper, to taste
olive oil, as required
1   knob butter

potato purée:

3	baking potatoes
200ml	milk
100g	butter
	salt and pepper

vegetables:

24	baby leeks
24	florets purple sprouting broccoli
	baby spinach
200g	mixed wild mushrooms
	butter, as required

to serve:

coarse sea salt
good olive oil

METHOD

red wine jus:

In a wide heavy-based pan melt the butter, add the shallots and sweat for 5 minutes with a good pinch of salt, then add the mushrooms and sweat for a further 5 minutes. Add half of the red wine to this pan, and reduce to one-fifth. In a separate pan reduce the other remaining red wine by one-fifth. Now add all the ingredients together except for the finishing ingredients, bring to the boil, skim well and cook for 30 minutes. Pass through a fine chinoise, then reduce to 250ml. To finish melt a knob of butter and cook to a nutty golden brown, add the sauce to the pan, adjust the seasoning with salt and pepper to taste and the acidity with a little double cream.

turbot:

Lightly cover both sides of the turbot portions with salt and leave for 20 minutes, then wash in cold running water, dry on kitchen paper and refrigerate for later use.

Preheat the oven to 180°C.

When ready to cook remove the fish from the fridge and allow to come to room temperature, season with pepper, heat a non-stick pan and add a little olive oil and a good knob of butter. Just as the butter starts to turn golden add the fish, with the thickest fillet down, cook until golden and then turn, repeat on the other side, place in the oven for 2 minutes, then remove from the pan and rest in a warm place for 2 minutes before serving.

potato purée:

Preheat the oven to 180°C.

Cook the potatoes in the oven for 1 hour or until cooked, remove the skins and push the flesh through a fine sieve — it's very important to do this while the potato is still piping hot, otherwise you end up with starchy potatoes. Place the potatoes into a large pan, bring the milk and butter to the boil and whisk into the potatoes. Adjust the seasoning with salt and pepper and whisk again until creamy and smooth.

vegetables:

Blanch the baby leeks in boiling salted water for 3 minutes or until tender, then refresh in iced water. Repeat for the broccoli. Trim the leeks to 8cm with an angle on the end of each leek and trim the broccoli florets so they are all the same size. Pick and wash the spinach. Sort the

mushrooms, trim away any excess stalk, cut into medium pieces and wash well.

Sauté the mushrooms in butter and then cook the spinach. Keep both warm.

to serve:

Heat the jus and potato purée. Reheat the vegetables in boiling water, season with a little salt and olive oil. Take a hot plate and drag the potato purée down the middle, forming a base. Put the spinach in the middle with the mushrooms and broccoli around the outside. Place the fish on top of the spinach, add the leeks around and on top, drizzle with olive oil, then generously sauce the plate with the jus.

COCONUT RICE PUDDING BEIGNET, SPICED POACHED PINEAPPLE, MANGO SORBET

BY SAM MOODY

A sweet version of aranchini of sorts, watch out for the crispy rice pudding – it's incredibly moreish – then all together it's a wonderfully fun and fresh dessert.

Serves 8
Preparation time: 15 minutes
Cooking time: 2 hours

Special equipment:
Ice-cream machine, fryer set to 160°C.

Planning ahead:
The sorbet can be made in advance.

INGREDIENTS

mango sorbet:

75g	water
75g	caster sugar
500ml	Alphonso mango purée

rice pudding:

100g	pudding rice
1 litre	full-fat milk
1	vanilla pod
200g	caster sugar
50g	desiccated coconut

coating:

50g	demerara sugar
100g	coconut
200g	breadcrumbs
3	eggs
Plain flour, as required	

spiced pineapple:

1	large pineapple
200g	caster sugar
250ml	water
1	vanilla pod
5	star anise
1 tsp	fennel seeds
½ tsp	cumin seeds
2	cardamom pod

to serve:

1	large mango

METHOD

mango sorbet:

Bring the water and sugar to the boil, then pour onto the mango purée. Churn in an ice-cream machine and freeze.

rice pudding:

Bring the rice to the boil in water, then refresh under cold running water. Place the rice and all the other ingredients into a wide pan and cook over a medium heat until the rice is cooked and the liquid has nearly all been absorbed by the rice. Remove the vanilla pod, spread onto a tray, cover with cling film and leave to cool.

coating:

In a food processor grind the demerara sugar to a fine powder, do the same with the coconut, then mix both with the breadcrumbs. Whisk the eggs and place the flour into a deep tray.

Quenelle (make an oval shape) the rice pudding using two dessertspoons onto silicone paper. Place in the freezer for 10 minutes to firm up a little, then dip into the flour. Brush off any excess, then place into the eggs and finally into the breadcrumbs mix. Put back into the egg and breadcrumbs twice more, then refrigerate.

spiced pineapple:

Peel the pineapple, cut in half through the middle across the core, then cut each half down through the centre of the core. Cut each quarter into

three – you should finish with 12 wedges of pineapple. Using a sharp knife carve each wedge into a barrel, removing all the core.

Place all of the ingredients and 50ml water into a pan, make a caramel, stop the cooking with the remaining 200ml water, bring to a simmer then add the pineapple and cook gently for 20 minutes.

to serve:

Peel and dice the mango into small dice. Deep fry the rice pudding beignets until golden brown, then allow to cool a little. Scatter the diced mango onto a plate and place a scoop of sorbet onto some of the dice. Put three halves of poached pineapple onto the plate, add a beignet and some caramel.

Gordon Jones

Gordon trained at Birmingham College of Food and gained the first Gordon Ramsay scholarship before going on to work with Martin Wishart and Martin Blunos. Five years ago he joined the Royal Crescent Hotel as Demi-Chef progressing to Sous Chef and then to Head Chef. Gordon is always striving for excellence both in producing inspiring dishes for the menu and by using only the best produce and suppliers available, using local businesses wherever possible.

'Food that is innovative without being gimmicky'

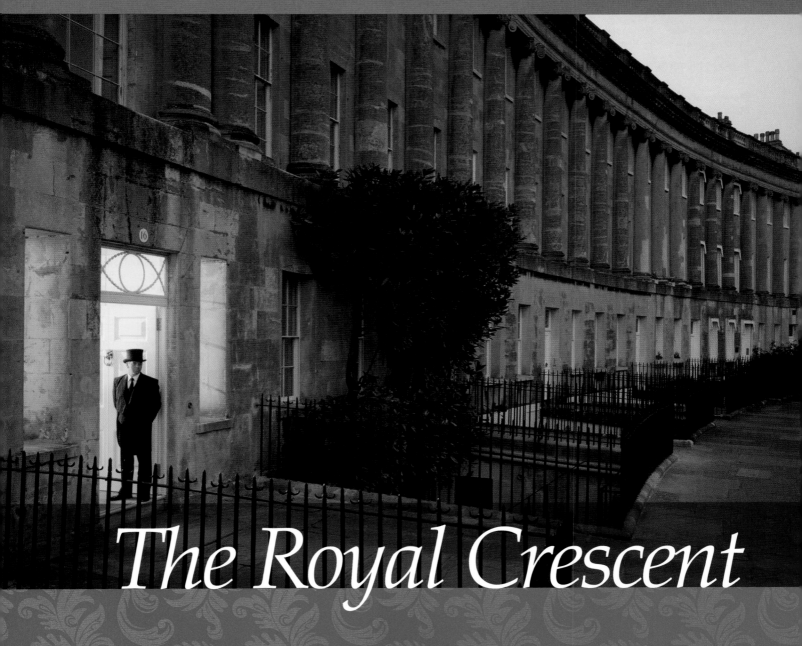

The Royal Crescent

{ *Renowned for its hot spring baths dating back to Roman times, Bath is undoubtedly one of the most fascinating towns in Europe.*

The equally impressive Royal Crescent Hotel invites you on a journey back in time to the 18th century. The majestic residence is one of the major works of the architect John Wood, who, at that time, was commissioned by the Queen to give the medieval town a facelift. With its splendid manicured gardens and its chic, opulent interiors, staying at The Royal Crescent Hotel is like stepping straight into the pages of a novel by the famous local writer Jane Austen. The hotel has its own river launch, a highly reputed spa of its own and charming, supremely elegant rooms. Venture out and explore this fascinating Georgian town, with marvels like the fan vaulting in the Bath Abbey, the temple of the Goddess Sulis Minerva, the arcades of the Union Passage, and the typical charm of George Street, Milsom Street and Queen Street. On your return, retire to The Bath House spa for the very best in pampering and relaxation!

ROAST LOIN OF FALLOW DEER, CEP RISOTTO, ICE WINE VINEGAR JELLY, PARSLEY PUREE
BY GORDON JONES

The venison is a really robust dish which combines sweet, sour, savoury, hot and cold and all of these flavours come together to form one of my favourite venison dishes.

Serves 4
Preparation time: 20 minutes
Cooking time: 20 minutes

Special equipment:
N/A

Planning ahead:
N/A

INGREDIENTS

1	loin of fallow deer

risotto:

250g	Arborio rice
1 litre	venison stock
2	banana shallots
1	clove of garlic
100ml	Madeira
50g	cep powder
50g	parmesan
25g	butter
Trimmings from ceps	

jelly:

250ml	ice wine vinegar
15g	powdered vegetable gelatine
bunch of flat leaf parsley	
salt and pepper to taste	

garnish:

mustard frills	
parsley purée	
250g	whole ceps
100g	crosne

METHOD

venison:

Portion the venison and season in chopped tarragon, salt and pepper and a little ground coffee beans, wrap in clingfilm and poach at 55.5°C for 25 minutes. Once cooked remove from the clingfilm and seal in a very hot pan and leave to rest.

risotto:

For the risotto finely chop one shallot and half a clove of garlic and sweat off with the diced stalks of the ceps and cep powder made from all the trimmings, add rice and cook for two minutes then deglaze with Madeira and carry on cooking slowly adding the venison stock a bit at a time until the rice is tender. Finish the risotto with parmesan and butter to give a creamy finish.

jelly:

For the jelly heat the ice wine vinegar up 65°C then add the vegetable gelatine, and cook out for a further 3 minutes then cool on a flat tray.

to assemble:

Pan fry the ceps. Place the risotto in a neat line on the plate and finely slice the venison and place on the risotto, then arrange the pan fried ceps and sweet pickled crosne on the venison. Cut the ice wine vinegar jelly into a long strip and pipe five dots of parsley purée. Garnish with the mustard cress and then sauce.

CIGAR POACHED PLUMS, OAT CAKES & BALVENIE ICE CREAM
BY GORDON JONES

This is a good autumnal dish that reminds me of Scotland so I had to include it to be true to my roots.

Serves 4
Preparation time: 40 minutes
Cooking time: 1-1 ½ hours

INGREDIENTS

poached plums:

4	mirabelle plums.
5g	mixed spice
fresh grated nutmeg	
1	vanilla pod
1	lemon, juiced
¼	of a Griffin cigar
250ml	stock syrup

oat cakes:

375g	oats
375g	plain white flour
9oz	butter
5g	salt
10g	bicarbonate of soda
75g	soft brown sugar
Balvenie whiskey, matured in port wood	

ice cream:

200ml	milk
250ml	double cream
50g	chestnuts
a splash of Balvenie whiskey	
100g	caster sugar
125g	egg yolk
50g	glucose syrup

METHOD

poached plums:

First infuse ¼ of the cigar in a little hot water, after 10 minutes remove the cigar from the water and squeeze out any excess liquid. Blanch the plums in water for 20 seconds then plunge into cold water to stop the cooking process; you should then be able to peel the plums. Place the peeled plums into a vacuum pack bag and add mixed spice, vanilla, nutmeg, stock syrup, the cigar water and a splash of lemon juice. Seal the bag and poach at 55.5°C for 35 minutes.

oat cakes:

For the oat cakes cream sugar and butter and then add all the dry ingredients and bind with a splash of whiskey. Chill the mix in the fridge for 20 minutes then roll out to the desired thickness and bake for 40 minutes at 140°C. As soon as the oat cakes are cooked remove them from the oven and cut into diamonds and cool on a cooling wire.

ice cream:

To make the ice cream heat milk and cream together with the glucose syrup, then mix the sugar and egg yolks and slowly pour the hot liquid over. Cook the custard until it coats the back of a spoon. Pass the mix through a fine sieve and chill over night. Add the whiskey to taste just before churning. Once the ice cream is churned add some of the chestnuts to the ice cream and mix being careful not to break the chestnuts up too much.

to serve:

Warm the poached plums in some of the poaching liquid, then arrange between the oat cakes and a little of the whiskey ice cream and some fresh blackberries. Blitz all the trimmings from the oat cakes with a little soft brown sugar until it resembles breadcrumbs, sprinkle a little of the crumbs on the plate and place a scoop of the ice cream onto the crumbs. To garnish use a few blackberries, blackberry purée and quince purée.

Worcestershire

Worcestershire... a county of contrasts

Worcestershire, lying between the ancient Malvern Hills and the mellow Cotswolds, plays host to small charming villages such as Broadway as well as bustling towns and the vibrant cathedral city of Worcester. All this is set in a variety of backgrounds ranging from beautiful, mature woodland to meandering river valleys where visitors have the opportunity to participate in a number of outdoor pursuits or if they prefer to simply admire the stunning landscape. With fine churches, historic buildings, Britain's premier steam railway, a thriving arts scene with internationally acclaimed festivals and events, a superb range of retail outlets and continental restaurants, the county has a lot to offer, giving visitors the chance to experience the very essence of England. Worcester is renowned for its tangy Worcestershire sauce, a near universal condiment that is most definitely a British food legend but is also the place to enjoy delicious plums at Pershore during August and asparagus throughout the county in spring.

William Guthrie

William started his career as a commis at Llangoed Hall in Wales. He slowly moved east and found himself as chef de partie at Mallory Court hotel in 2001. Five years later as senior sous chef he left Mallory Court to set up a new restaurant with rooms in Wiltshire. As head chef he quickly gained accolades from the AA and Michelin and was voted in the top 100 restaurants in the UK. William joined Buckland Manor in February of this year (2011) and is looking forward to achieving greater national recognition in the near future.

Buckland Manor

{ *One of the finest Manor houses in the Cotswolds, set next to a 13th century church, amidst beautiful, mature gardens which create an oasis of tranquility.*

Perfect for relaxation with horseback riding, golf, tennis, hunting and walks. Crackling log fires warm the cosy lounges. Bedrooms with ample bathrooms have a country house feel; you will have the impression that you're spending some quiet, relaxing days in your home.

Serves 2
Preparation time: 30 hours
Cooking time: 10 minutes

Special equipment:
N/A

Planning ahead:
The pigeon, foie gras and crumbs need to be
prepared the day before. The pigeon and foie gras
need to be pressed for 3 hours before serving.

INGREDIENTS

pigeon and foie gras:

1	whole pigeon
100ml	Madeira
Peel of 1 orange	
20g	salt
10g	sugar
5g	pepper
100g	foie gras

ruby wine jelly:

500ml	ruby port
150g	caster sugar
4	gelatine leaves

pain d'épices crumb:

1 x 100g loaf sliced bread

balsamic gel:

350ml	balsamic vinegar
100g	brown sugar
2½ tbsp	honey
6oz	agar agar

to serve:

micro leaves

PRESSING OF PIGEON & FOIE GRAS, RUBY WINE JELLY, PAIN D'EPICES CRUMB & BALSAMIC GEL
BY WILLIAM GUTHRIE

The combination of foie gras and wood pigeon really works for me. With ruby wine and spiced bread it all marries together to make a lovely salad fit for any winter.

METHOD

pigeon and foie gras:
Prepare the pigeon by taking off the breasts from the whole pigeon and marinate in the Madeira and orange peel overnight.

Mix together the salt, sugar and pepper. Devein the foie gras, sprinkle with the salt mix and leave overnight.

ruby wine jelly:
Bring the port to a simmer with the sugar, add the gelatine leaves then place into the port. Whisk and let it set in a piping bag.

pain d'épices crumb:
Dry out the pain d'épice (slices of bread) for 24 hours before blitzing in a blender to make crumbs.

balsamic gel:
Bring the vinegar, sugar and honey up to a simmer, whisk in the agar agar and let it set. Once set, blitz in a blender and place the gel in a squeezy bottle.

pressing of pigeon and foie gras:
Pan fry the pigeon breast for about 1½ minutes on both sides.

Place the foie gras in the oven at 160°C for 4½ minutes until cooked. Place on a tray to let any excess fat drain off.

Slice the pigeon in half; place the foie gras in-between the two pieces of pigeon. Wrap in cling film and gently press for 3 hours in a fridge.

to serve:
Plate up by slicing the pigeon/foie gras into five slices lengthways. In-between the slices pipe the ruby wine jelly and sprinkle the crumbs over. Add two dots of balsamic gel to the plate and garnish with the micro leaves.

Chef's tip:
Use the leftovers from the pigeon to make a pigeon stock for a winter soup.

HERB-CRUSTED LOIN OF COTSWOLD LAMB, BRAISED SHOULDER, HONEY-ROASTED SWEETBREADS, SMOKED AUBERGINE PUREE & BLACK OLIVES

BY WILLIAM GUTHRIE

Spring lamb has to be one of the highlights on the food calendar. Using the three types of lamb really showcases this wonderful product.

Serves 4
Preparation time: 48 hours
Cooking time: 20 minutes

Special equipment:
N/A

Planning ahead:
The shoulder of lamb needs to be prepared a day in advance and then it takes 8 hours to cook in the oven. The herb crust should be prepared the day before. The sweetbreads need to be soaked in milk for 4-6 hours.

INGREDIENTS

lamb:

1	shoulder of lamb approximately 600-800g
100g	salt
1	pinch pepper
50g	sugar
2	shallots, sliced
1 x 750ml bottle red wine	
water, as required	
1	sprig of thyme
½	bulb garlic
1	loin of lamb approximately 300g
100g	chives
2	shallots
3	sunblushed tomatoes
25g	grain mustard
salt and pepper	

herb crust:

1 x 400g loaf bread, diced	
150g	parsley
salt, to taste	
1 tbsp	olive oil

aubergine purée:

2	aubergines

sweetbreads:

150g	sweetbreads
milk, as required	
1 tbsp	local honey

black olive crumbs:

100g	black olives

red pepper coulis:

4	red peppers
1	pinch salt
1	pinch sugar

to serve:

1	knob butter
spinach, as desired	
red wine jus, as desired	

METHOD

lamb:

Salt down and de-bone the shoulder of lamb with the salt, a pinch of pepper and sugar. Add the two sliced shallots and leave for 24 hours.

The next day wash the shoulder and place in a braising pot. Cover with the red wine, water, thyme and garlic. Then place in the oven at 120°C for 8 hours.

Prepare the loin of lamb by taking off the sinew and fat and place to one side.

Take the shoulder of lamb and strip the meat off into a bowl. Cut the chives, dice two shallots, chop the tomatoes and add with the mustard to the bowl. Season then mix.

Roll with cling film into a 5cm diameter-sized sausage and let it set. To warm it up place it back into the braising liquid.

herb crust:

Dry out the diced bread overnight then blitz with the parsley until green. Add salt and the olive oil.

aubergine purée:

Cut the aubergines in half then colour the top flesh on a hot, solid top until dark. Then cook, covered, in an oven for 1 hour at 160°C. Once cooked take off the skin and blitz the flesh in a blender until smooth.

sweetbreads:

Let the sweetbreads soak in milk for 4-6 hours in a fridge to draw out the blood. Then wash through with cold water. To cook, blanch in boiling water for 1 minute. Place into iced water then remove the outer skin and fat. Place in a hot pan with the honey until golden.

black olive crumbs:

Stone the olives, cut in half and dry out over 2 days at 60°C. Blitz in a food processor then dry again for 1 day before serving.

red pepper coulis:

Peel and deseed the peppers, cook in the oven at 160°C until soft, then blitz in a blender with a

pinch of salt and sugar. Put through a sieve and store in a fridge.

to serve:

Pan fry the loin in a hot pan and colour on the outside. Place a knob of butter in the pan and roast for 3 minutes at 160°C. Take out of the oven and let it rest for 5-6 minutes.

Plate up by placing a drag of red pepper coulis and a quenelle of aubergine purée on the plate and add some black olive crumbs. Sweat some spinach and place in a ring. Remove the ring and place the shoulder on the spinach. Roll the cooked loin in the herb crust then slice. Place on the plate with the sweetbreads. Finally sauce with a red wine jus.

DARK CHOCOLATE CANNELLONI, PASSION FRUIT CURD & COCOA ICE CREAM

BY WILLIAM GUTHRIE

Dark chocolate with passion fruit is a fine balance to bring together, done so in this case by a rich velvety ice cream and a sweet passion fruit curd. I think this is a great dessert to finish a meal.

Serves 4
Preparation time: 4 hours
Cooking time: 1 hour

Special equipment:
½ litre iSi canister, ice-cream machine.

Planning ahead:
The chocolate foam needs to be refrigerated for 3 hours before use.

INGREDIENTS

chocolate pasta:

100g	isomalt
200g	fondant
50	cocoa paste

chocolate foam:

200ml	double cream
4	tbsp cocoa powder
1	shot brandy
50g	icing sugar
1 tsp	Camp Coffee

passion fruit curd:

126g	passion fruit juice
4	egg yolks
100g	sugar
2	eggs
84g	butter

cocoa ice cream:

450ml	full-fat milk
300ml	double cream
9	egg yolks
1 tbsp	glucose
400g	caster sugar
100g	cocoa paste
1	shot chocolate liquor

passion fruit jelly (optional):

200ml	passion fruit juice
3	leaves gelatine
50g	caster sugar

to serve:

melted chocolate
chocolate crumbs

METHOD

chocolate pasta:

Mix together the isomalt and fondant and bring to 160°C, then add the paste. Turn down to 125°C. Let it set and blitz to a powder in a blender.

chocolate foam:

Warm the cream up, add all the other ingredients and let it cool. Then place in a ½ litre iSi canister. Add one charge of gas and refrigerate for 3 hours before use.

passion fruit curd:

Bring the juice to the boil. Mix the egg yolks and sugar together. Whisk the eggs and juice together, then add the yolk/sugar mix and cook out until thick. Whisk in the butter and put in the fridge.

cocoa ice cream:

Make a crème Anglaise (light pouring custard) with the milk, cream, egg yolks, glucose and sugar. Then add the cocoa paste and alcohol to taste. Churn in an ice-cream machine according to the manufacturer's instructions.

cannelloni:

Sieve the chocolate powder onto a mat and cook in the oven at 160°C until melted. Take out and let it set slightly. Cut into 10cm lengths and wrap around a cylinder to form the cannelloni shape, then cool until crisp.

passion fruit jelly:

Combine all the ingredients, place in a mould and allow to set in the fridge.

to serve:

Place some melted chocolate on the plate. Take the cannelloni and slowly fill with chocolate foam, then place on the plate. With a spoon take the passion fruit curd and gently make a couple of drags across the plate. Make balls with the ice cream and place on a chocolate crumb mix base. Then drizzle the plate with a blitz of passion fruit for the finished result and add the jelly, if using.

Warwickshire

Following Shakespeare's footsteps in the heart of England

Despite its wealth of history, the county of Warwickshire is dominated by William Shakespeare and the town of his birth, Stratford-upon-Avon, a literary shrine to England's greatest playwright and home to the Royal Shakespeare Company. Stratford remains the most visited tourist destination outside the capital with its fine Tudor buildings, including the Bard's birthplace, and its origins beside the River Avon almost certainly date back to Roman times. Sharing the same river and just a few miles away is Warwick, dominated by the mighty castle, which is renowned for being the finest medieval fortress in England. Some fine medieval and Jacobean buildings survive here in a town that possesses a real sense of history at every turn. The county showcases a range of of food from English teas to baltis, fine gourmet experiences to a snack at the bar of a traditional English Country pub.

Mallory Court

Simon Haigh

Simon joined Mallory Court Hotel as Head Chef in December 2001, was made Executive Head Chef in 2006 and was recently appointed Executive Head Chef of the Eden Hotel Collection. Prior to his move to Mallory, Simon spent seven years at Inverlochy Castle in Scotland, where he gained a Michelin star, followed by Seaham Hall in Northumberland. In January 2003 Simon and his team successfully regained a Michelin star which has been retained for the last seven years.

'Luxury country house hotel surroundings, fine food and wines are always at the forefront of your Mallory dining experience'

Mallory Court

{ *Not far from Stratford-upon-Avon, the birthplace of William Shakespeare, Mallory Court will charm you with its understated beauty and the dedication of its staff.*

This country manor house cultivates British elegance down to the slightest detail, as you will immediately notice on seeing the perfectly cut lawns. This is an ideal place to recharge your batteries among games of croquet. Another must is a visit to the house where Shakespeare was born. And you never know, perhaps a woodland creature will even whisper into your ear a verse composed by the great man himself — "With this field-dew consecrate, Every fairy take his gait" — so that your time here will forever remain in your mind like a midsummer night's dream.

BREAST OF QUAIL, CELERIAC MOUSSE, COMPRESSED APPLE
BY SIMON HAIGH

A combination of ingredients that work well together, each complementing each other – a dish of subtle flavours.

Serves 4
Preparation time: 3 hours
Cooking time: ½ hour

Special equipment:
Vacuum bags,. dariole moulds, deep-fat fryer.

Planning ahead:
The compressed apple needs to marinate for 12 hours.

INGREDIENTS

quail:

4	quail
1	chicken breast
salt and pepper	
2	field mushrooms, diced and cooked
1	sprig tarragon, chopped
100g	breadcrumbs

compressed apple:

200ml	stock syrup
200ml	sweet wine
Zest of 1 lemon	
Zest of 1 lime	
2	Granny Smith apples
50g	caster sugar

quail eggs:

4	quail eggs

celeriac Bavarois:

225g	celeriac
water, as required	
1	sprig thyme
1	clove garlic
salt and pepper	
75g	double cream
50ml	full-fat milk
125g	crème fraîche
3	leaves gelatine
10ml	full-fat milk
150g	whipped cream

candied hazelnuts:

18	hazelnuts
200ml	stock syrup
oil, as required	
salt	

METHOD

quail:

Remove the breast and legs from the quail carcasses, then take out the bone from the legs. Blitz the chicken, season and gradually add the cream, being careful not to split the mousse. Mix the mushrooms and tarragon together, check the seasoning then fill the legs with the mixture and sandwich two together with some mousse. Roll in cling film to form a cylinder. Cover the rolled quail with cold water and bring to the boil then cool. Once cooled place to one side until later, French trim the leg then remove the cling film and coat with the breadcrumbs.

compressed apple:

Make the liquid with the syrup and sweet wine, add the citrus zests to the heat to 37°C. Peel and core the apples then cut into triangles, keep the apple trimmings to one side, vacuum pack the apples and leave to marinate for 12 hours. With the trimmings cook down with the sugar and then blitz to make a purée.

quail eggs:

Cook in boiling water for 2 minutes and then refresh in iced water. Once cooled peel and place to one side. Allow 1 per person.

celeriac Bavarois:

Dice the celeriac, cover with water, add the thyme, garlic and seasoning (salt and pepper) then cook until soft. Once cooked blitz in a Thermomix with the cream, 50ml milk and crème fraîche. Soak the gelatine in cold water for 5 minutes, remove from the water and melt over a low heat with 10ml milk. Once melted add to the celeriac mix. Season and pass the mix through a sieve then leave to cool. Once cold fold in the whipped cream, place in dariole moulds and leave to set for 3 hours.

candied hazelnuts:

Cover the nuts with syrup and heat to 120°C. Once this temperature is reached place the nuts on a silpat mat without the syrup to cool. When the nuts are cold place in a deep fat fryer set at 170°C and cook until golden, remove and season with salt.

to serve:

Roast the quail breasts in a pan and leave to rest. While they are resting dress the plates: start with a swipe of the apple purée, add the turned out Bavarois and place five apple pieces around. Deep fry the quail legs, cut the quail eggs in half, carve the breast in half and also place on the plate. Garnish with the hazelnuts.

Serves 4
Preparation time: 2 days
Cooking time: 1 hour for the shoulder but
                     dependent on the quality it
                     may take longer

Special equipment:
Thermomix.

Planning ahead:
The shoulder of lamb needs to be cured
24 hours in advance.

INGREDIENTS

shoulder of lamb:

1	shoulder of lamb
20g	pepper
100g	pink salt
1	sprig thyme
1	large shallot
2	cloves garlic
1	onion, diced
1	leek, diced
1	carrot, diced
100ml	white wine
400g	plum tomatoes
	chicken stock, as required
1	sprig rosemary
½	chicken breast
200ml	cream
1	carrot
200g	celeriac
200g	swede
2 tbsp	baby capers
2 tbsp	grain mustard
1	lamb fillet
	butter, as required

Alexander purée:

500g	Alexander leaves or spinach
1	shallot
2	cloves garlic
100ml	cream

garnish:

4	black olives
1	courgette
24	salfrino potatoes (small balls formed using a parisienne scoop) from approximately 6 maris piper potatoes
	saffron stock, as required
12	cherry tomato halves
	balsamic vinegar, as required
	olive oil, as required
	garlic, to taste
	basil, to taste
12	green beans
12	baby onions
	chicken stock, as required
1	sprig of thyme
	sherry vinegar, as required

BRAISED SHOULDER, ROASTED FILLET OF LIGHTHORNE LAMB; PUREE OF ALEXANDERS
BY SIMON HAIGH

This recipe was devised for use through the early spring months when the new season lamb isn't quite ready to use, but the general public see Easter approaching and start to think of lamb. It uses two meats, one marinated then braised and the other basically flash fried using the tenderest of cuts, but one which never really develops a deep lamby flavour due to its lack of fat. The other is enhanced by the marination then the long slow cooking process which really complement each other.

METHOD

shoulder of lamb:
Cure the shoulder with the pepper, pink salt, thyme, sliced shallot and cloves garlic for 24 hours.

Wash off, re-tie and seal off in a hot pan with a little oil and colour all how but do not season then and add to a pan of roasted mirepoix (onion, leek and carrot), deglaze with the white wine and add the tomatoes. Cover with chicken stock and rosemary, and braise for 45 minutes, then leave to cool in the stock.

Blitz the chicken breast with salt in a food processor, adding the cream slowly to make a mousse.

Dice the carrot, celeriac and swede and cook in individual pans till tender and cool.

Pick off choice pieces, discarding any fat or grizzle (reserve the stock to use as a lamb sauce) and add the cooked vegetables, capers, mustard and chicken mousse. Cook a small amount to check the seasoning. Roll into ballotines using cling film and tin foil then poach by bringing to a simmer and cooking for approximately 10 minutes or until the core temperature reaches 75°C. Place in the refrigerator. When chilled cut into portions, remove the tin foil and reheat in the lamb sauce till hot and glazed.

Pan fry the lamb fillet for 20 seconds each side, season and finish with butter.

Alexander purée:
Pick and blanch the Alexander leaves, drain and squeeze out any excess water. Sweat the shallot and garlic till tender, add the cream and reduce, then add the Alexanders and liquidise in a Thermomix till smooth. Pass through a chinoise and correct the seasoning.

garnish:
Dice the courgette and sauté in butter.

Cook the salfrino of maris piper potatoes in a saffron stock.

Cut the cherry tomatoes in half, season, add the balsamic, olive oil, garlic and basil, then place on a tray cut side up and semi dry in a hot place or a low oven.

Cut the green beans into 3cm pieces and blanch in salted water.

Peel the baby onions, cook in the chicken stock, thyme and garlic till tender, drain off and sauté in butter till golden. Deglaze with sherry vinegar.

to serve:
Plate up as pictured.

CARAMELISED POACHED PEAR, EUCALYPTUS MOUSSE, CHICORY ICE CREAM

BY SIMON HAIGH

These pears have the stalks dipped in red wax, the theory being the wax stops them ripening too quickly, creating a longer shelf life and being able to use them at their peak.

Serves 4
Preparation time: 4 hours
Cooking time: 30 minutes

Special equipment:
Parisienne scoop, ice-cream machine, deep-fat fryer.

Planning ahead:
The chicory essence, pear crisp, chicory ice cream and candied hazelnuts need to be prepared in advance.

INGREDIENTS

poached pears:

4	wax-tipped pears
100g	caster sugar
2	lemons
200ml	sweet white wine
1	vanilla pod
1	cinnamon stick
2	star anise

hazelnut cannelloni:

200g	white fondant
100g	glucose
100g	isomalt
10g	hazelnuts

eucalyptus mousse:

9	egg yolks
210g	caster sugar
105ml	sweet wine
juice of ½ lemon	
6	drops eucalyptus essence
2	sheets gelatine
650ml	double cream

chicory essence:

1	bottle chicory essence (Camp Coffee)
30g	caster sugar

pear crisp:

1	pear — any type, under-ripe
acidulated stock syrup, as required	

chicory ice cream:

658g	full-fat milk
116g	double cream
160g	caster sugar
70g	egg yolks
chicory essence, to taste	

candied hazelnuts:

40g	hazelnuts
stock syrup, to cover	
oil, as required	

METHOD

poached pears:

Peel the pears and core using a parisienne scoop, then set aside in acidulated water (water and juice of one lemon). Make a caramel with the sugar in a large pan and deglaze with the juice of the other lemon, add wine, enough to just cover the pears. Sweeten again to taste and flavour the liquor with 1 vanilla pod, the cinnamon stick and star anise. Simmer the pears for 15-20 minutes or until soft (place a sharp-tipped knife through the tip to check).

hazelnut cannelloni:

Bring the white fondant, glucose and isomalt up to 160°C. Meanwhile roast the hazelnuts and blitz to a powder. When the sugars have reached 160°C cool down to 120°C and whisk in the hazelnut powder. Pour out onto parchment paper and leave to set. When set liquidise in a food processor to a fine powder. Sieve onto a greased baking tray and melt under a grill, being careful not to let it burn. Using a knife and a cylinder you can then mould this into your desired shape, such as a tall tube.

eucalyptus mousse:

In a large mixing bowl add the egg yolks, sugar, wine, lemon juice and eucalyptus essence. Soak the gelatine and set aside. Place the large mixing bowl over a warm bain marie and whisk until the sabayon is at a really thick ribbon stage. At this point add the gelatine, mix well and chill over an ice bath. When three-quarters set, whisk the cream and fold the two mixtures together. Allow to set fully and reserve in the fridge for at least 3 hours to set fully.

chicory essence:

Reduce the chicory essence to a thick syrup and add sugar to taste. Leave at room temperature so it is easier to paint across the plate.

pear crisp:

Thinly slice the pear on a slicer machine, dip into acidulated stock syrup, then dehydrate at 63°C for 12 hours. Store in an air-tight container.

chicory ice cream:

Bring the milk and cream to the boil. Meanwhile whisk together the sugar and egg yolks, then pour the millk/cream mix onto the eggs, whisking constantly. Return to the pan and cook out until it reaches 80°C. Flavour with chicory essence. Churn in an ice-cream machine according to the manufacturer's instructions.

candied hazelnuts:

Bring the hazelnuts up to 118°C in the stock syrup, drain onto baking parchment and leave to cool. When cool deep fry the hazelnuts at 170°C until golden.

to serve:

Plate up as pictured.

RELAIS & CHATEAUX

Rutland

Stately splendour and England's smallest county

{ The eastern counties of the Midlands, long recognised as the hunting shires, remain something of a microcosm of an England of yesteryear. Old market towns sit comfortably alongside some of the country's finest stately homes, the open countryside remains pleasantly unspoiled and the area is still largely untouched by mass tourism. Belvoir Castle, with its dominant position giving views of the Leicestershire Wolds, lent its name to a noted Foxhound breed in the 18th century. The region is the home of Stilton cheese, which takes its name from the town where it was first served to stagecoach travellers, although it was never made there, and Melton Mowbray pork pies, another regional speciality. The greatest change to the region was the opening of Rutland Water in the 1970s, which has now become the region's most popular tourist attraction with its balance of sport, leisure and wildlife conservation. Rutland itself is the smallest county in England with the old Norman market town of Oakham at its centre.

Aaron Patterson

Aaron Patterson is a youthful genius who started at Hambleton in 1984 and gained useful experience with Raymond Blanc, Anton Mosimann and others before returning to Hambleton as Head Chef in 1992. He may be lured from time to time to caper about in the television studio for such shows as Here's One I Made Earlier or MasterChef but his heart remains in the kitchen with his team of over 15 like-minded enthusiasts. Aaron is also an advocate of seasonal and locally sourced produce where possible – herbs, salads and berries from the kitchen garden and top-quality seafood and game dishes of all kinds (in season) are specialities.

Hambleton Hall

{ *Hambleton Hall is situated in a spectacular lakeside setting overlooking Rutland Water in the charming county of Rutland some 100 miles north of London.*

Owners Tim and Stefa Hart have acquired a loyal following for 30 years thanks to a number of special qualities. There is a calm and confident atmosphere created by a team of experienced staff who are genuinely pleased to see you. Stefa Hart's interiors are comfortable and practical as well as very stylish. Lastly, Aaron Patterson's exuberant cooking ensures that dinner is the big event of the day, even if you have seen Burghley House and sailed twice around the lake.

SALAD OF CRAB & AVOCADO WITH BROWN MEAT ICE CREAM

BY AARON PATTERSON

Serves 4
Preparation time: 24 hours
Cooking time: N/A

Special equipment:
Ice-cream machine, ice-cream scoop, mandoline, set of cutters.

Planning ahead:
The ice cream, the potato gallette, and the apple and walnut garnishes can be prepared the day before.

INGREDIENTS

apple crisp:

1	Granny Smith apple
100g	sugar
100ml	water
juice of 1 lemon	
icing sugar, as required	

crab salad:

100g	salt
1	large 2kg cock crab
2	ripe avocados
2	Granny Smith apples
2 tbsp	mayonnaise
1 tbsp	tomato ketchup
juice of 1 lime	
salt and pepper	
1	dash Tabasco sauce

potato gallette:

2	large Maris Piper potatoes
2 tbsp	vegetable oil
1	pinch salt

crab ice cream:

150g	brown crab meat (from inside the large cooked crab)
280ml	full-fat milk
1200ml	whipping cream
165g	maltodextrin
4g	salt
1.5g	umami paste
2.5g	silk gel (food stabiliser)
2g	fresh ginger
1	stick lemongrass

garnish:

1	Granny Smith apple cut into large cubes (10mm)
12	halves of walnut, lightly salted
12	slices celery cut on an angle thinly

METHOD

crab salad:

Bring a large pan of water to a rolling boil, add 100g salt and bring back to the boil. Cook the crab for 14 minutes. Remove and place in a large bowl of iced water to halt the cooking. When cool, break off the legs and claws, crack open and carefully pick all the white meat into a bowl. Pull the rounded body of the crab away from the shell, taking care to discard the Dead Men's fingers which look like grey feathery fronds. Spoon the brown meat from the shell into another bowl and purée for the ice cream. Pick over the white meat to check for bits of shell. You should be left with about 300g-450g of white crab meat. Remove the skin and stones from the avocados, dice roughly and mix through the white meat with the Granny Smith apples that have been peeled and grated on a cheese grater. Add the mayonnaise, ketchup, lime juice, salt, pepper and a dash of Tabasco sauce. Gently mix together and adjust the seasoning to taste. It is best to assemble this dish on a tray before moving it to a serving plate as it can be a bit messy. Place four ring moulds or cutters (8cm diameter and 4cm deep) on a tray and fill almost to the top with the crab and avocado mix.

crab ice cream:

Mix all the ingredients together, blend in a food processor and push through a fine sieve, then churn in an ice-cream machine until thick and glossy. Remove from the machine and freeze for at least 4 hours before you need it.

potato gallette:

Peel the potatoes then slice thinly to about 2mm thick, then cut these potato slices into thin strips with a sharp knife. Mix the strips with a little vegetable oil and a pinch of salt. In a cold non-stick pan put in a 100mm cutter and add some of the potato mix and form a lattice (shredded effect) to make a very thin potato gallette. If you have room in the pan repeat this process four times, then cook over a medium heat until lightly browned on one side, then, using a palette knife, turn each one over and cook the other side but be careful not to over colour. When they are golden put them on a tray until you are ready to use them.

apple crisp:

Slice the Granny Smith apple as thinly as you can on a mandoline. Put the sugar and water into a pan with the lemon juice and bring to the boil, then take off the heat and put the slices of apple into the liquid for 1 minute, until they have wilted. Cling film a metal baking tray and

dust it with icing sugar. Put the slices of apple on top of the cling film. Put them into an oven on pilot light temperature overnight until they become crisp.

to serve:

To assemble this dish you will need a small plate and an ice-cream scoop. Put the diced apple, walnuts and celery around the outside of the plate. The crab mix goes in the middle of the plate, then remove the cutter. Next add the potato gallette, followed by a scoop of ice cream and lastly the apple crisp.

FILLET OF HAMBLETON LONGHORN BEEF WITH FONDANT ROOT VEGETABLES & A RED WINE SAUCE

BY AARON PATTERSON

Serves 4
Preparation time: 1 hour
Cooking time: 30 minutes

Special equipment:
Mandoline.

Planning ahead:
All elements, apart from the cooking of the beef fillets, can be done 5 hours before you need them.

INGREDIENTS

beef fillet steaks:

vegetable oil, as required
4 x 8oz fillet steaks
salt and pepper

red wine sauce:

570ml	red wine
140ml	port
285ml	veal glace
5	sprigs tarragon
salt and pepper	

pommes Anna:

2	large Maris Piper potatoes
1	pinch salt
100ml	vegetable oil

carrot purée:

6	large carrots
570ml	chicken stock
140ml	double cream
1	clove garlic
115g	unsalted butter
3	sprigs tarragon
salt and pepper	

to serve:

1	swede
1	celeriac
4	cantonnay carrots
4	baby beetroots
4	baby turnips
4	baby onions

METHOD

beef fillet steaks:

In a large frying pan, heat up a small ladle of vegetable oil and sear the fillet steak all over until well coloured, then season with salt and pepper. Put in a hot oven at 200°C for approximately 2 minutes either side, then take out of the oven and put onto a metal tray and allow to rest for a further 3 minutes before you need them.

red wine sauce:

In a large deep-sided pan, pour in the red wine and port and bring to the boil. Allow to boil for 4 minutes, then add the veal glace and boil for approximately another 10-15 minutes until the liquid has reduced down to a sauce consistency. Add the tarragon sprigs, season with salt and pepper then push the sauce through a fine sieve

pommes Anna:

Peel the potatoes, then slice off both sides so you are left with two flat sides. Season with the salt. Using a 40mm cutter, cut out as many small round discs as possible, then slice the discs on a mandoline very thinly to about 2mm in thickness. Using a 100mm non-stick Yorkshire pudding mould, start to overlap the thin discs until a rosette has been formed. You need four of these. Then ladle in a little vegetable oil and cook them on the solid top of your stove until golden brown. If you haven't got a solid top, put your Yorkshire pudding tins inside a large flat-bottomed pan and put that onto gas and brown accordingly. When ready to use carefully turn the little Yorkshire pudding tins onto a plate and you will be left with crispy pommes Anna.

carrot purée:

Peel the carrots and chop them into even-sized pieces. Put them into a deep-sided pan and add the stock, cream and garlic. Cook until the carrots are soft (no bite). Strain the carrots from the liquid. Blend the carrots in a food processor, adding back a little of the liquid, approximately 400ml until a smooth purée forms, then add the butter and tarragon, and season with salt and pepper.

to serve:

Peel and chop the vegetables, but not the onions, as desired and cooked in boiling salted until tender. Keep warm.

Warm up the sauce, onions, carrot purée and pommes Anna. When hot put your fillets of beef back in the oven at 200°C for no longer than 4 minutes for medium rare. Then, on large white plates, arrange the root vegetables in a straight line two-thirds down the plate. Just above the vegetables put one of the pommes Anna potatoes on top of each beef fillet and the onions. Spoon on three little pools of carrot purée either side of the beef fillet and serve the red wine sauce on the side.

PAVE OF CHOCOLATE WITH HONEYCOMB PARFAIT & LIME CURD, LIME LEAF ICE CREAM

BY AARON PATTERSON

Serves 4
Preparation time: 1 hour
Cooking time: 30 minutes

Special equipment:
Ice-cream machine, 20 x 15cm containers (2),
20cm sheets of acetate (4), 50mm cutter.

Planning ahead:
The ice cream can be made in advance. The lime curd needs 4 hours in the fridge and the chocolate jelly 3 hours. The pavés take 5 hours in total to freeze.

INGREDIENTS

lime curd lime leaf ice cream:

200ml	double cream
225ml	full-fat milk
4	lime leaves
150g	caster sugar
14	egg yolks

chocolate jelly:

½	tbsp olive oil
8	leaves of gelatine
120g	caster sugar
40g	cocoa powder
300ml	water + extra for soaking the gelatine
100ml	crème de cacao

salted and caramelised macadamias:

100g	caster sugar
75g	macadamia nuts
1	pinch salt

lime curd:

265ml	lime juice
265g	caster sugar
5g	agar agar
3	eggs
350g	butter

chocolate glaze:

115ml	water
90g	caster sugar
40g	cocoa powder
85g	whipping cream
75g	50% dark chocolate

chocolate oil:

50g	50% dark chocolate
100g	olive oil

lime zest:

1	lime
25g	caster sugar
100ml	water

honeycomb:

150g	caster sugar
50ml	water
½	tbsp. bicarbonate of soda

pavé shell:

100g	50% dark chocolate

honeycomb parfait:

75ml	water
200g	caster sugar
4	egg yolks
2	egg whites
100ml	double cream
75g	honeycomb (see above)

METHOD

lime curd lime leaf ice cream:

In a thick bottom pan add the double cream, milk and lime leaves and bring to a simmer. Whisk the caster sugar and egg yolks until they turn pale. Add the yolk mixture to the pan, whisking all the time. Immediately take off the heat. Keep stirring the mix until the egg is cooked out. Pass through a sieve and churn in an ice-cream machine according to the manufacturer's instructions.

chocolate jelly:

Pour the olive oil inside a 20 x 15 cm container. Soak the gelatine in cold water for 10 minutes. Add the caster sugar, cocoa powder and 300ml water to a small pan and bring to the boil. Add the soaked gelatine and crème de cacao. Pour the mix into the container and refrigerate for 3 hours.

salted and caramelised macadamias:

In a small pan, heat the sugar until it forms a light caramel. Add the macadamia nuts and salt and pour onto a piece of greaseproof paper. Once cooled, crush into small pieces.

lime curd:

Line a 20 x 15cm container with cling film. In a thick-bottomed pan add the lime juice, caster sugar and agar agar. Bring to the boil. Crack the eggs into a bowl and beat lightly. Dice the butter. Once the mixture has boiled take it off the heat and add the eggs, whisking continuously. Once mixed, slowly melt in the butter and pour into the container. Leave to set in the fridge for 4 hours.

chocolate glaze:

In a thick-bottomed pan, add the water, caster sugar, cocoa powder and cream. Boil for 10 minutes, stirring occasionally. After the 10 minutes take the pan off the heat and add the chocolate. Pour into a suitable container and refrigerate. When pouring on top of the pavé, the mix must be reheated, so that it can be poured.

chocolate oil:

Melt the chocolate in a bowl over a bain marie. Slowly whisk in the olive oil.

lime zest:

Peel the lime and cut into thin slices. Place in a

small pan with the water and sugar, and bring to the boil.

honeycomb:

In a small pan, boil the caster sugar and water until it becomes a light caramel. Constantly whisking, add the bicarbonate of soda. Whisk for a few seconds in the pan and pour onto a sheet of greaseproof paper to cool.

pavé shell:

Melt the chocolate in a bowl over a bain marie. Once melted, pour a tablespoon of chocolate over a 20cm piece of acetate and spread to a 3mm thickness. Wrap the chocolate and acetate

around the inside of a 50mm cutter. Leave to set in the fridge for 20 minutes.

honeycomb parfait:

Firstly add the water and 100g of the caster sugar to a small pan and take to 121°C to make the pate bomb. Whisk the egg yolks in a mixer until they go light in colour. Slowly pour the sugar mixture onto the yolks, whisking continuously to make the pate bomb and leave to go cold. In a separate bowl whisk the remaining 100g of sugar and the egg whites until they form stiff peaks. Fold the egg whites through the pate bomb. Whisk the cream to soft peaks and fold through the rest of the mixture. Finally crush the honeycomb up into

small pieces and fold through the mixture. Pour into the chocolate rings (½ cm off the top) and freeze. After 2 hours take out the pavés and pour on the chocolate glaze to the top and freeze for 3 hours.

to serve:

Put one of the chocolate shells onto the centre of the plate, making sure that you have removed the acetate. Put the chocolate jellies down one side of the plate and a spoonful of the macadamia nuts on the other with a scoop of lime leaf ice cream. Then place a cube of lime curd on top of the pavé, dress with the chocolate oil and lime zest, and serve.

Cumbria

Lakeland glory and Border legends

A predominantly rural county, described by the painter John Constable as having "the finest scenery that ever was", Cumbria is home to the Lake District, one of England's most popular tourist destinations. Yet despite the influx of 18 million visitors annually, there still remains dramatic and tranquil beauty away from the bustling Windermere and quieter Ullswater. Lake trips and hill walking are popular summer pursuits, but the spring of Wordsworth's golden daffodils and the glorious shades of autumn are when the region is seen at its best. Away from Lakeland is the border city of Carlisle, a reminder of the years of Anglo-Scottish conflict. The World Heritage Site of Hadrian's Wall, the 73-mile long defence built on the orders of the eponymous Emperor to mark and defend the northern limits of the British province of the Roman Empire, is remarkably preserved. When it comes to food, it appears traditions have evolved from the land itself: farm-raised lambs for meat dishes, pigs for sausage and ham, and cattle for dairy products. The moors and mountains provide wild game such as duck and deer and the seas allow for herring, char, shrimp, trout and salmon.

Barry Quinion

After college Barry started in the kitchen at The Bell at Aston Clinton, one of the founder members of Relais & Châteaux in the UK. From there he moved to a Relais in Switzerland and then back to the UK to The Waterside Inn at Bray under Pierre Koffmann. This was followed by a change to front of house, as by then the family's plan was to have their own hotel. He has been happily in charge of his own kitchen since the move to Farlam Hall in 1975 and now runs the hotel with his wife Lynne and sister Helen.

A meal to delight the tastes and also satisfy the inner man – or woman

LEMON MOUSSE WITH BLUEBERRIES, RASPBERRIES & A RASPBERRY COULIS

BY BARRY QUINION

A zesty and refreshing dessert.

Serves 6 or 4 if you are greedy!
Preparation time: 20 minutes
Cooking time: N/A

Special equipment:
6 rings or moulds

Planning ahead:
N/A

INGREDIENTS

200g   crème fraîche
50g   caster sugar
2   lemons, juice and zest
1½   gelatine leaves, soaked in the lemon juice
200ml   whipping cream

to serve:

blueberries, as desired
raspberries, as desired
raspberry coulis, as desired

METHOD

In a bowl, mix together the crème fraîche, sugar and lemon zest.

Heat the lemon juice to dissolve the gelatine, cool slightly and strain onto the crème fraîche mix.

Whisk the cream to soft peaks and fold into the crème fraîche.

Pour into the rings and refrigerate.

to serve:

Put a ring on a large plate, run a hot wet knife around the edge and lift it off. Decorate with the fruit and coulis.

Chef's tip:

This mousse goes well with many types of fruit and berries. You can stay with the seasons by changing these.

Russell Plowman

Russell trained for three years at the Relais & Châteaux, three Michelin-starred Waterside Inn at Bray and two years at the Michelin-starred L'Ortolan before joining Gilpin in January 2009. With very seasonal menus and a particular interest in butchery, he makes the most of fantastic local suppliers, "Cumbria and the Lake District are at the forefront of supplying some of the top restaurants and we're so lucky to have these on our doorstep – and of course we get the pick of the bunch before it go elsewhere."

'Warm smiles, fresh flowers, real fires and friendly, unpretentious service.
Classically based yet thoroughly modern'

Gilpin Lodge
Country House

{ *Animated by the hospitality of the Cunliffe family, Gilpin Lodge exerts its natural charms in an extraordinary setting: the Lake District National Park, close to Windermere — the country's largest natural lake.*

Drop your bags in the modern suites — some with their own private garden and open-air cedarwood hot tub — and make time for the simple pleasures in stunning surroundings. With a distinct absence of weddings, conferences and children under the age of seven, there is a sense of tranquility as you enjoy soothing body treatments, invigorating sporting activities, and sample culinary delights with an abundance of produce from within the National Park.

TWICE-BAKED STICHELTON CHEESE SOUFFLE, WALDORF SALAD, RED WINE REDUCTION
BY RUSSELL PLOWMAN

The great British cheeseboard, soufflé style.

Serves 4
Preparation time: 2 hours
Cooking time: 30 minutes

Special equipment:
6 ramekins.

Planning ahead:
The Waldorf salad needs to marinate for 24 hours.

INGREDIENTS

soufflé:

125g	butter
125g	plain flour
700ml	semi-skimmed milk
125g	mild cheddar, grated
125g	Stichelton cheese (or other medium-strength blue cheese), grated
½ tsp	Dijon mustard
	salt and pepper, to taste
	crushed walnuts, as required
250g	egg whites

red wine reduction:

250ml	red wine
25ml	ruby port
½	cinnamon stick
½	star anise
2	cloves

Waldorf salad:

125ml	red wine
25g	sugar
½	star anise
½	cinnamon stick
1	clove
50g	green seedless grapes, peeled
2	large shallots, sliced

to serve:

½	head of celery, sliced
½	Granny Smith apple, peeled and sliced
5	shelled walnut halves
	celery cress to garnish

METHOD

soufflé:

Preheat the oven to 180°C .

Melt the butter in a saucepan and add the flour. Cook out the flour for 5 minutes before adding the milk. Cook the mix for 20 minutes and take off the heat. In a food processor, mix the sauce with the cheeses and add the Dijon mustard, salt and pepper. Blend until it becomes a smooth mix. Butter the 4 ramekins and line with some crushed walnuts. Whisk the egg whites into soft peaks and fold into the cheese mix. Fill the lined ramekins with the soufflé base and bake in the oven for 7 minutes, then turn the ramekins and cook for a further 7 minutes. Leave to cool before removing the ramekins.

red wine reduction:

Bring the alcohol and spices to the boil and slowly reduce until syrupy. Strain the syrup.

Waldorf salad:

Make a syrup by bringing the red wine, sugar and spices to the boil; pour over the grapes and shallots and leave to marinate for 24 hours to absorb the flavour of the marinade and colour.

to serve:

Arrange the celery on the plate, top with the apple slices, walnut halves and Waldorf salad. Meanwhile reheat the soufflés in the oven (preheated to 180°C) for 7 minutes; add to the plate, dress with the red wine reduction and celery cress, and serve immediately.

PAN-FRIED FILLET OF ORGANIC SEA TROUT, FENNEL, CARROT & ORANGE PUREE, STAR ANISE NAGE

BY RUSSELL PLOWMAN

Summer flavours of fennel and orange married with a great organic fish.

Serves 4
Preparation time: 2 hours
Cooking time: 10 minutes

Special equipment:
N/A

Planning ahead:
N/A

INGREDIENTS

sea trout:

| 4 | sea trout fillets |

toasted orange couscous:

| 200g | couscous |
| 400g | fresh orange juice |
| Salt, pepper and olive oil |

star anise nage:

| 1 | shallot, sliced |
| 100g | button mushrooms, sliced |
| butter, as required |
1	sprig thyme
1	bay leaf
3	star anise
250ml	dry white wine
1 litre	fish stock
500ml	whipping cream
salt, to taste
1	squeeze lemon juice

carrot and orange purée:

| 350g | carrots |
| 50g | shallots |
| olive oil, as required |
250ml	orange juice
250ml	water
1	orange zest
5g	fennel seeds
1	star anise
1	bay leave
5	sprigs thyme
salt, to taste

fennel flames:

2	fennel bulbs, sliced lengthways into fennel flames (1cm pieces through the heart of the vegetable)
100ml	white wine
200ml	chicken stock
juice of 1 lemon
1	sprig thyme

1	bay leaf
1	star anise
10	fennel seeds

fennel salad:

| 1 | bulb fennel, very thinly sliced |
| salt, to taste |
| lemon juice, to taste |
| orange segments, as required |

to serve:

| olive oil, butter, lemon juice as required |
| 8 | baby carrots |
| orange juice, as required |

METHOD

toasted orange couscous:

In a saucepan toast the couscous in olive oil until a dark nut-brown golden colour. Add the orange juice, cover with a tight-fitting lid and allow to steam; remove from the heat. Once all the juice has been absorbed, leave to cool. Gently reheat the couscous with a little orange juice and olive oil to achieve a perfect consistency. Season and serve.

star anise nage:

Soften the shallot with the mushrooms in butter until soft. Add the thyme, bay leaf, star anise and white wine. Reduce by two-thirds and add the fish stock. Reduce again by two-thirds. Pass through a fine sieve and add the cream. Reduce by one-third and season with salt and a squeeze of lemon juice.

carrot and orange purée:

Finely slice the carrots and shallots and sweat in olive oil. Add the orange juice, water and spices and cook until the carrots are very soft. Remove the spices and blend to a fine purée. Season with salt and adjust the consistency with fresh orange juice.

fennel flames:

Place all the ingredients in a pot and bring to a boil, braising the fennel until tender.

fennel salad:

Season the fennel with salt and lemon juice and add a few orange segments.

to serve:

Pan-fry the sea trout first in olive oil and finish with butter and lemon juice. Blanch the baby

carrots in boiling salted water then glaze them in fresh butter and a little orange juice.

Reheat the orange and carrot purée and couscous. Fry the fennel flame in olive oil and baste with butter.

Drag a spoonful of the carrot purée across the middle of the plate. Sit the roasted fennel flames on top. Lay the couscous on the plate in two mounds (one at each end of the fennel flame). On top of each mound place two slices of the fennel salad rolled up, to add height.

Then nestle a baby carrot in each of the fennel salad mounds. Lay the cooked piece of sea trout on top of the fennel flame. Froth the nage with a hand blender and spoon next to the fish.

Serves 4
Preparation time: 2 hours
Cooking time: 1 hour

Special equipment:
Sugar thermometer.

Planning ahead:
The caramelised pistachios, white chocolate powder and rhubarb parfait can be made in advance.

INGREDIENTS

pistachio crumb:

200g	whole shelled pistachios

caramelised pistachios:

200g	water
200g	caster sugar
150g	whole shelled pistachios

pistachio Anglaise:

40g	caster sugar
3	egg yolks
125g	semi-skimmed milk
125g	double cream
20g	pistachio paste
1	vanilla pod

white chocolate powder:

95g	white chocolate
40g	cacao (cocoa) butter
300g	water
90g	double cream
25g	caster sugar

crispy oats:

200g	oats
100g	crushed hazelnuts
100g	crushed pecans
2	egg whites
100g	honey

poached rhubarb:

500ml	stock syrup (50% water and 50% sugar)
20	crushed juniper berries
2	sprigs thyme
2	sprigs rosemary
2	lime juice
1 tsp	citric acid
4	rhubarb sticks

rhubarb purée:

1kg	rhubarb (washed and finely sliced)
100g	caster sugar
50g	water

rhubarb parfait:

5	egg yolks
150g	caster sugar
100ml	water
200g	rhubarb purée
300ml	double cream

POACHED RHUBARB, PISTACHIO & WHITE CHOCOLATE POWDER
BY RUSSELL PLOWMAN

Rhubarb and custard sweetened with white chocolate and pistachios.

METHOD

pistachio crumb:
Using a blender, blitz the pistachios into a fine powder.

caramelised pistachios:
Make a stock syrup with the water and sugar. Bring to the boil, add the pistachios, bring back to the boil for 30 seconds, then drain. Deep fry at 150°C until the nuts begin to colour slightly, drain and cool immediately on a metal tray. Once completely cold, store in an air-tight container before use. They will keep for 3-4 days.

pistachio Anglaise:
Whisk the sugar and yolks until pale. Bring the milk, cream, pistachio paste and vanilla to the boil, pour over the egg mix, continually whisking until smooth. Return to the pan and cook on a low heat until the cream thickens. Pass through a fine sieve and chill.

white chocolate powder:
Melt the chocolate and the butter, add the water and cream. Bring to the boil, then add the sugar. Pass through a fine sieve and freeze. This will keep for 1 month. Grate just before dressing the plate.

crispy oats:
Mix all the ingredients together and lay out on baking parchment. Bake at 160°C until golden brown.

poached rhubarb:
Bring all the ingredients except the rhubarb to the boil and allow to infuse for 30 minutes before using. Prepare the rhubarb in 10cm long batons, poach in the liquor at 80°C for 10 minutes or until tender. Chill in an ice bath immediately.

rhubarb purée:
Sweat down the rhubarb with the sugar very quickly in a pan without colour. Add the water and simmer until tender. Blitz in a blender, pass through a sieve and chill.

rhubarb parfait:
Beat the yolks and 25g caster sugar until pale and thick, then set aside. Put the remaining caster sugar and the water in a pan, bring to the boil. Place a thermometer inside; when the sugar reaches 118°C, pour over the egg mix while beating vigorously with an electric whisk. When the sugar mix is incorporated continue to beat vigorously until the mix is cooled, fold in the rhubarb purée and set aside. Whip the cream to soft peaks and fold through the rhubarb base. Pipe into moulds and freeze. It will keep for 1 month.

to serve:
First put the frozen white chocolate powder mix through a blender – the result should be a fine powder. Next spoon a small amount of the powder into the middle of a chilled plate. Roll the parfait in pistachio crumb to coat and place on top of the powder. Now top and tail two pieces of the poached rhubarb on a diagonal and place either side of the parfait. With the rhubarb purée in a squeezy bottle, place two large dots either side of the parfait next to the poached rhubarb. Do the same with the pistachio Anglaise. Finish by scattering a few crushed caramelised pistachios and crispy oats around the plate.

Colin Akrigg

Colin Akrigg began his career when he joined Sharrow Bay in 1968 as a 15-year-old kitchen porter from a nearby farm. Even as a 13 year old Colin was hugely ambitious: 'I knew exactly what I wanted, I wanted to be the Head Chef at Sharrow Bay'. His talents were quickly recognised and under the guidance of the late Francis Coulson, Colin became Head Chef in 1997 and achieved a Michelin star the following year, a feat that has remarkably been achieved for the last 13 consecutive years. Over the years Colin has trained some of the industry's top chefs such as Paul Heathcote and continues, alongside his highly-talented young team, to develop the world-famous cuisine at Sharrow Bay.

'An experience to be shared and cherished with magnificent views of the lake and fells'

Sharrow Bay
Country House

{ *Sharrow Bay Country House was originally a little fisherman's house but since it was converted into a hotel, it is one of the most sought after and welcoming addresses around.*

The hotel celebrated its 60th anniversary in 2009 and even has its own food range. Nestled on the banks of Lake Ullswater, this pioneering English countryside hotel will offer you many a delightful hour of escapism whether you choose the "champagne cruise" on a Vintage Steamer or, for those who prefer livelier waters, rock climbing in the surrounding mountains or canoeing. Horseback riding, fishing, golf and cooking lessons complete this relaxation programme for the mind and body.

PRESSED TERRINE OF HAM HOCK & FOIE GRAS
BY COLIN AKRIGG

Serves 6
Preparation time: 1 hour
Cooking time: 6 hours 30 minutes

Special equipment:
Terrine mould.

Planning ahead:
The ham hock for the terrine takes approximately 6 hours to cook. The terrine needs to be placed in the fridge overnight.

INGREDIENTS

ham hock:

1	ham hock
1	small onion
1	orange, halved
4 tbsp	white port
6	cloves
2	bay leaves
6	black peppercorns
2	white peppercorns

½ tsp salt and ½ tsp sugar blitzed to a powder

foie gras:

1	lobe foie gras

braised leeks:

leeks, as required
salt and pepper, to taste
butter, as required

terrine assembly:

100g	creamed potatoes
150g	wild mushrooms, washed then cooked

in butter, chicken stock and seasoned
12   baby carrots cooked until tender in a little water with butter to glaze, and sugar and salt added to taste

to serve:

mixed salad leaves

METHOD

ham hock:

Cover the ham hock with plenty of water, add the other ingredients and bring to a simmer for 6 hours or until tender and falling cleanly from the bone. Remove the meat and discard the fat. Carefully tear the meat into bite-sized pieces.

foie gras:

Sauté the foie gras in a moderate to hot pan until golden and soft. Set aside.

braised leeks:

Trim away the dark leaves from the leeks, cut through and wash well. Cut into 6mm dice, wash well, season and cook in a little butter.

terrine assembly:

In a large bowl bring together the hock, leeks, creamed potatoes and wild mushrooms and gently mix together. Lightly oil your terrine and line with cling film, allowing an excess to fold over the top. Layer the hock mixture randomly with the foie gras and baby carrots until full. Fold over the cling film and prick it with a cocktail stick. You will require a large flat-based pan filled with water to press down on the terrine then place it in the fridge overnight.

to serve:

Remove the terrine from the mould, slice and serve with some mixed salad leaves.

BELLY PORK, PIG CHEEKS & SWEETBREAD BLACK PUDDING

BY COLIN AKRIGG

Serves 6
Preparation time: 45 minutes.
Cooking time: 24 hours for the belly pork,
                      4 hours for the pig cheeks.

Special equipment:
Cast casserole pan, 2.5cm round cutter.

Planning ahead:
The belly pork needs to marinate overnight. It then takes 1 day to cook. The lamb sweetbreads need to soak in water overnight. The pig cheeks need to braise for 4 hours.

INGREDIENTS

belly pork:

900g	belly pork
flavourless oil, as required	
coarse sea salt	
10	black peppercorns
1	bunch of sage
4	strips of lemon peel
duck fat, as required	

sweetbread black pudding:

1	onion
200ml	cider vinegar
150g	caster sugar
2	fresh bay leaves, finely chopped
1	sprig of thyme
1	sprig of rosemary
200g	back fat, finely diced
250g	sultanas
1½kg	lamb sweetbreads, soaked overnight in plenty of cold water
500g	dried pig's blood

pig cheeks:

6	pig cheeks
1	onion
1	carrot
2	sticks celery
oil, as required	
55g	plain flour
570ml	chicken stock
6	black peppercorns
2	sprigs of sage
salt and pepper	

fondant potatoes:

3	baking potatoes
salted butter, as required	
1	sprig of thyme

creamed savoury cabbage:

1	Savoy cabbage
1	medium onion
1	carrot
½	celeriac
a little cream	
salt and pepper	

buttered baby spinach:

spinach, as required	
butter, as required	
salt and pepper	
1	pinch of nutmeg

glazed apples:

icing sugar, as required	
2	Granny Smith apples, quartered and turned into barrels
1	knob of butter
Calvados, optional	

METHOD

belly pork:

Remove the nipples and bone from the belly. Moisten with the oil. Marinate with the salt, peppercorns, sage and lemon peel and leave overnight in the fridge. Remove from the marinade and submerge in duck fat in a roasting tray. Cover in foil and cook at 90°C for 1 day or until tender. Remove and press between two cling filmed trays weighed down with a flat-based and water-filled pan.

sweetbread black pudding:

In a pan add the onion, vinegar, sugar, herbs, back fat and sultanas. Cook over a moderate heat until lightly caramelised and thickened. In another pan cover the sweetbreads in cold water and bring to the boil. Drain and peel off the skins. In a large bowl mix together the pig's blood with warm water until it becomes a dropping consistency. Add in the components from the other pan and the sweetbreads. Lay out a sheet of cling film on a flat work surface. Spoon the mixture down one side of the film and roll up the mixture into a cylinder. Do this again with another piece of cling film to reinforce it. Then finish with foil in the same way and finally twist the two ends to tighten. Poach in a tray of simmering water for 20 minutes.

pig cheeks:

Preheat the oven to 110°C. Trim the fat and skin from the cheeks. Colour in a hot pan. Roughly chop the onion, carrot and celery and colour them using a little oil in a cast casserole pan. Add the flour and mix until incorporated into the fat. Gradually add the stock to create a gravy. Add the cheeks, peppercorns and sage, and season to taste. Braise for 4 hours.

fondant potatoes:

Slice the potatoes 4cm thick then cut out with a 2.5cm round cutter. Cover a thick-bottomed pan with a thick layer of butter. Place the potatoes on top and submerge with water until just covered. Add the thyme. Cover with a disc of greaseproof paper and cook until nearly tender. Remove the paper and reduce down the water, allowing the butter to caramelise the potato bases. Leave to cool in the pan then remove carefully.

creamed savoury cabbage:

Peel away the cabbage leaves individually and discard any dark, tough leaves. Add to boiling, salted water and cook for 3 minutes. Refresh in iced water. Cut out the thick veins and finely shred. Finely dice the onion, carrot and celeriac. Sweat off the onion followed by the carrot and celeriac. When soft add the cream and reduce until thickened. Mix in the cabbage, season and serve.

buttered baby spinach:

Pick the spinach off the stems, wash well and cook in a hot pan with butter, seasoning and the nutmeg. Serve immediately.

glazed apples:

Sprinkle a pan with icing sugar and allow it to caramelise on a moderate heat. Add the apples and butter and cook until al dente. Finish with a splash of Calvados, if using.

to serve:

Chop the belly pork into squares. Remove the black pudding from the water and slice into portions. Place a small amount of cabbage on the plate and top with the belly pork. Place a small amount of spinach on the plate and top with a pig's cheek. Add a slice of black pudding and a glazed apple. Pour over some gravy from the pig cheeks and serve.

BANANAS IN CARAMEL SYRUP WITH CINDER TOFFEE, VANILLA & CASHEW NUT PARFAIT

BY COLIN AKRIGG

Serves 6
Preparation time: 40 minutes
Cooking time: 50 minutes

Special equipment:
Sugar thermometer.

Planning ahead:
The cinder toffee tuile can be made in advance and stored in an air-tight container. The parfait needs to be put in the freezer overnight.

INGREDIENTS

bananas:

150g	caster sugar
230ml	water
2-3 tbsp	rum and crème de banana
1	vanilla pod
3	bananas

caramel sauce:

115g	caster sugar
115g	double cream

cinder toffee tuile:

35.5g	clear honey
70g	glucose
200g	caster sugar
3 tbsp	water
10g	bicarbonate of soda

vanilla and cashew nut parfait:

1	whole egg
2	egg yolks
100g	caster sugar
water, as required	
350g	double cream, whipped
1	vanilla bean, scraped
crushed praline, to taste (see below)	

praline:

115g	caster sugar
water, as required	
140g	toasted cashew nuts

METHOD

bananas:

Put the sugar and 5 tbsp water into a large shallow pan over a gentle heat, stirring once or twice until dissolved. When this sugar syrup is clear, raise the heat and cook until it becomes a light caramel, for about 5 minutes. Remove from the heat immediately and stir in the rum, crème de banana and remaining water. Split the vanilla pod lengthways and add to the pan. Peel the bananas and halve lengthways. Place in a single layer in the pan and spoon over the caramel to coat them completely. When they are golden take off the heat.

caramel sauce:

Place the sugar into a pan, lightly cover with water and bring up to a caramel, then slowly pour the cream into the pan and stir until all is dissolved. Leave to cool.

cinder toffee tuile:

Line a shallow tray with parchment paper. Place all the ingredients except the bicarbonate of soda into a pan on a low heat, stirring occasionally until the sugar dissolves, then increase the heat to medium and cook until the syrup starts to turn to a light golden caramel: it should read 150°C on a sugar thermometer. Mix in the bicarbonate of soda — this will highly foam. Immediately pour onto the prepared baking tray. Set aside to cool for about 1 hour until firm and crisp. Put into a freezer bag and bash to a powder.

To make the tuile, preheat the oven to 150°C fan. Prepare a tray with parchment paper and grease lightly. Place the cinder toffee into a sieve and lightly sieve onto the tray until evenly covered. Place into the oven for approximately 3 minutes until it is all dissolved. Remove from the oven — it should look flat and glossy. Leave to cool for 30 seconds and cut into the required shapes and store in an air-tight container.

vanilla and cashew nut parfait:

Place the egg and egg yolks into a bowl. Whisk until you have reached a sabayon. Place the sugar and enough water to cover it into a pan and cook out until it reaches 118°C on a sugar thermometer. Pour the mixture slowly onto the sabayon and leave to cool. When cooled fold through the cream and vanilla. Add the crushed praline and place into a mould. Put into a freezer and leave overnight.

praline:

Lightly cover the sugar with water in a pan, place onto the heat and cook until caramelised. When caramelised place the nuts onto parchment paper on a metal tray and pour the caramel over the top of the nuts. Allow to cool then place into a freezer bag and batter with a rolling pin into fine pieces.

to serve:

Place the bananas on the plate, unmould the parfait and add to the plate, resting a tuile against it. Spoon around any spare caramel.

RELAIS & CHATEAUX

Scotland

A country of immense contrast, history, tradition and innovation

Scotland is a constant surprise to its visitors from all over the world. The remote wilderness scenery of the Highlands and Islands contrasts with the peaceful Trossachs and the rich farmlands of the Borders, while the great lowland cities of Glasgow and the nation's capital, Edinburgh, remain its commercial and cultural heartbeat. Never far away are the reminders of a turbulent past, while stepping back further in time to the islands of the Western Isles, Orkneys, Shetlands and Skye there is evidence of ancient and prehistoric civilisations. Scotland is justifiably proud of its cuisine that can rival that to be found anywhere in the world. The country's renowned beef, venison, lamb, game and salmon, trout and oysters have long been the inspiration for chefs and hoteliers alike, while the traditional haggis with neeps and tatties remains the definitive Scottish dish, eaten to celebrate Burns' Night every January.

Robert MacPherson, Head Chef at The Airds Hotel, Port Appin, Argyll, began his career in his home town of Fort William, where his genuine talent was very quickly spotted. At the age of 22 he was awarded three rosettes by the AA for food and has worked consistently at this level ever since. Robert has been a Master Chef of Great Britain for many years and was honoured to be made a 'fellow' in 2005.

Airds Hotel

{
Breathtaking landscapes, incredible views down towards the loch… For all of those who want to soak up the beauty of Scotland, Airds Hotel is the perfect spot.

This remote and peaceful setting epitomises classic west coast scenery. This exquisite lochside 18th century inn with charmingly decorated rooms exhibits the very best of Scottish elegance and sophistication. The quality of service is combined with the finest cuisine, reputed to be among the best in Scotland with a wine list as impressive. The area is famous for its highland game and west coast seafood, not matched anywhere else. A highlight of any stay at the Airds Hotel is to enjoy lunch or dinner in the restaurant while admiring the spectacular views of the atmospheric loch and iconic mountains behind. The Airds is the perfect base from which to explore the Hebrides, a group of Islands accessible by ferry, starting with Lismore, only a five-minute trip away, a remote and wild paradise.

WILD MUSHROOM RISOTTO WITH WILTED SPINACH & PARMESAN

On the West Coast of Scotland we have such an abundance of wonderful wild mushrooms which give real depth of flavour to this simple dish.

Serves 4
Preparation time: 30-40 minutes
Cooking time: 30-40 minutes

Special equipment:

N/A

Planning ahead:

The fresh chicken stock needs to be prepared the day before or purchased ready made.

INGREDIENTS

1 litre	chicken stock
50ml	olive oil
2	shallots, finely chopped
½	clove garlic
200g	wild mushrooms, chopped
200g	carnaroli rice
4 tbsp	white wine
75g	butter
50g	parmesan cheese, grated
150g	spinach
2 tbsp	chopped parsley
salt and pepper	
½	squeezed lemon

to serve:

parmesan cheese, grated
herbs, as desired

METHOD

In a saucepan, simmer the chicken stock. In a separate pan, heat the oil and sweat the shallots, garlic and mushrooms in it for about 3 minutes. Add the rice and sweat for a further 2 minutes. Pour in the wine and simmer until it has reduced to a glaze. Begin pouring in the stock gently, about 50ml at a time, and bring to the boil each time. It is important to allow the stock to evaporate stirring continuously. Repeat several times until the rice is cooked but not chalky to the bite. In total this should take around 20-25 minutes.

Add the butter, parmesan and spinach and stir to an emulsion, adding the parsley, salt and pepper and lemon juice. If it becomes too thick add a little more stock, or if too thin simmer for a little longer.

to serve:

Place the risotto in warm serving bowls with extra cheese on top as required and herbs to garnish.

ROASTED HIGHLAND VENISON WITH RED CABBAGE, BEETROOT & A BERRY VINEGAR REDUCTION

Truly Scottish!

Serves 4
Preparation time: 50-60 minutes
Cooking time: 20-30 minutes

Special equipment:
N/A

Planning ahead:
The red cabbage can be cooked the day before.

INGREDIENTS

venison and sauce:

4 x 120g venison loins	
salt and pepper	
olive oil	
125g	unsalted butter
100g	chopped shallots
100ml	raspberry vinegar
200ml	red wine
1 tsp	redcurrant jelly
300ml	chicken stock

red cabbage:

900g	cabbage (roughly ½ a cabbage)
1	apple
100ml	red wine
1	pinch nutmeg
1	pinch allspice
1	clove garlic
2 tbsp	wine vinegar
1	medium red onion
1	orange (juice and rind)
1 tbsp	brown sugar
1	pinch cinnamon
4	sprigs thyme

to serve:

50g	beetroot (diced and cooked)
knob of butter	

METHOD

venison:

Preheat the oven to 180°C.

Season the loins with salt and pepper. Heat a frying pan and add a few drops of oil and a knob of butter. Fry the venison quickly until coloured on both sides and then place in the oven for 4-7 minutes, depending upon how you like it cooked. Remove from the oven and place on a warm plate to rest for 5 minutes.

sauce:

Use the pan you fried the venison in, pouring off the old fat. Add the shallots and fry quickly. Deglaze with the vinegar and reduce by half. Add the wine and reduce by half or until it has gradually thickened in texture. Add the jelly and stock and reduce by two-thirds in order to create the sauce. Using either a very fine sieve or muslin, sieve the sauce through and keep warm.

red cabbage:

Shred the cabbage and dice the apple and onion into small pieces. Create layers of cabbage, apple and onion and sprinkle with salt and pepper. Pour the remaining ingredients into a jug. Mix well and pour over the layers of cabbage. Cover and bake in a medium 180°C oven for approximately 40 minutes. When ready keep hot or cool and reheat when required.

to serve:

Heat up the cabbage and maintain the heat. Simmer the sauce and add the diced beetroot, simmer then add a knob of butter. Stir until melted and keep hot. Arrange the cabbage on the plate. Carve the venison and arrange on top of the cabbage. Drizzle over the hot sauce and serve.

Chef's tip:

Other vegetables may be added to this dish depending upon your own preference.

PRUNE & ARMAGNAC SOUFFLE

This has always been a favourite with guests and is such a light dessert, with the prunes and Armagnac perfectly suited to providing a blend of subtlety and zest, an ideal way to finish a meal.

Serves 4 (possibly more depending on the size of the ramekins used)

Preparation time: 20-30 minutes
Cooking time: 7-10 minutes

Special equipment:
4 ramekins.

Planning ahead:
The prunes must be soaked a week or two in advance.

INGREDIENTS

prunes:

300g	prunes, stoned
120ml	Armagnac
100ml	dark rum
150ml	stock syrup

soufflé paste:

25g	cornflour
1	splash Armagnac

soufflé:

4	egg whites*
150g	caster sugar* + extra for dusting the ramekins
100g	soft butter

to serve:

ice cream or crème Anglaise
* 1   egg white + 25g caster sugar = 1 soufflé

METHOD

prunes:

Soak the prunes in the Armagnac, dark rum and 50ml of the stock syrup. Lightly warm then store in the fridge for up to 2 weeks.

Reserve some of the prunes for the centre of the soufflé and then blitz the rest with stock syrup until smooth to make a purée. Set aside a spoonful for the soufflé.

soufflé paste:

Place half the prune purée in a small pan and cook vigorously with the cornflour mixed with a splash of Armagnac. Cook for 3 minutes then allow to cool. When cooled, mix in the remaining prune purée, which then becomes the paste for the soufflé.

soufflé:

Preheat the oven to 180°C.

Butter and dust the ramekins with caster sugar.

Whip one egg white with 25g caster sugar until stiff. Fold in the reserved spoonful of prune purée and a spoonful of the prune paste. Fold together. Place half the mixture in the ramekin and add half a prune, then top up with the mixture. Wipe round the ramekin with your thumb. Repeat for the remaining soufflés depending on how many you are making. Bake in the oven for 7-10 minutes.

to serve:

Serve with ice cream or crème Anglaise.

Andrew Fairlie

Andrew's appetite for cooking was evident early on and at 15 he began a classical four-year apprenticeship in his hometown of Perth. At 20, Andrew become the first recipient of the prestigious Roux Scholarship and remains to this day its youngest scholar. The scholarship radically altered Andrew's perception of both his life and his craft, and with it came an unprecedented honour for a British chef – to work in the kitchen of Michael Guerard, one of the great masters of French culinary tradition. Guerard's approach to cooking was inspirational and Andrew still adheres to his mentor's ethos of 'simple food, brilliantly done'.

Positions followed at the Hotel de Crillon in Paris, the luxurious 5-star Royal Scotsman train, the Ritz Hotel in London and the opening of Euro-Disney, specifically to take advantage of, what Andrew believes to be, the best management training in the world.

In 1995 he became Executive Chef at Glasgow's One Devonshire Gardens Hotel and received acceptance into the esteemed Academie Culinaire de France and his first Michelin star. In 2001 Andrew opened his eponymous restaurant at the legendary Gleneagles Hotel and Resort. Within its first year the restaurant was awarded a Michelin star and a stream of awards followed. In 2006 the restaurant was awarded a second Michelin star and Andrew himself was voted AA UK Chefs Chef of the Year.

Restaurant Andrew Fairlie

{ *Restaurant Andrew Fairlie is an entirely independent entity based inside the world-famous Gleneagles.*

Set within a backdrop of rolling Perthshire hills, this palatial five-star luxury hotel and resort offers outstanding hospitality with amazing facilities, including three championship golf courses. A beautifully manicured 850-acre resort in one of Scotland's most stunning settings, yet easily accessible by rail or car, and within an hour of Glasgow or Edinburgh.

Serves 4
Preparation time: 30 minutes
Cooking time: Approximately 1 hour

Special equipment:
Vac pac machine and bags, water bath, muslin, hand blender, Thermomix (blender), silpat, dehydrator, deep fryer, mandoline, griddle.

Planning ahead:
The jelly can be made in advance.

INGREDIENTS

shellfish:

4	large scallops
12	squat lobsters
4	spoots
400ml	water

dashi broth:

900ml	mineral water
60g	dried kelp
6g	shaved bonito flakes
soy sauce and mirin, to taste	

dashi jelly:

230g	dashi broth (see recipe above)
2.1g	agar agar
0.3g	gellan gum

lemon gel:

100g	lemon juice
100g	water
30g	sugar
3g	agar agar

potato crisp:

1	large rooster potato
200g	water
2	sheets dried nori

sea vegetables:

sea lettuce, as required
aster, as required
dulse, as required
purslane, as required
sea blyte, as required
radishes, as required

SEARED SCALLOPS, SPOOTS, SQUAT LOBSTERS & SEA VEGETABLES
BY ANDREW FAIRLIE

Diver-caught scallops and squat lobsters from Mull together with 'spoots', more commonly known as razor clams, combined with sea vegetables from the Isle of Bute make this dish the essence of Scotland's coastline.

METHOD

shellfish:

Open the scallops, remove their roe and skirts, wash quickly under running water, cut in half and keep refrigerated till needed. With the lobsters, remove the tails from the body and shell. Skewer the tails with a cocktail stick and refrigerate till needed. Wash the spoots thoroughly and place into a vac pac bag with the water. Seal and place into a water bath at 62°C and cook for 11 minutes. Remove from the bath and leave to cool. Remove from the bag and slice the clam meat on the bias and reserve till needed in a little of the cooking juices.

dashi broth:

Add the water and kelp to a vac pac bag, seal and cook in a water bath at 60°C for 1 hour. Pour the water into a clean saucepan, bring the temperature up to 85°C and remove from the heat. Add the bonito, count to 10 and immediately strain through muslin into a clean bowl. Season the broth with soy and mirin. Reserve till needed.

dashi jelly:

Warm the dashi broth to 85°C, add the agar agar and gellan gum to dissolve. Pour the liquid onto a clean tray to set about 2mm thick. Once the jelly has set cut out squares 5 x 5cm and reserve till needed.

lemon gel:

Place all the ingredients into a small pan and whisk to a boil. Pour into a small bowl to set. When set use a hand blender to form a very smooth gel.

potato crisp:

Peel, dice and cook the potato in salted water till just overcooked. Grind the nori to a powder. Add the potatoes to the Thermomix with the water and powdered nori and mix at number 3 setting for 1 minute (or use a blender). Spread the mix onto a silpat mat, place into the dehydrator or in a low oven at 60°C overnight till crisp. Deep fry at 180°C till crisp and reserve till needed.

sea vegetables:

Tear the sea lettuce into small pieces, blanch in boiling water for 30 seconds and refresh in iced water. Drain and reserve till needed. Pick and wash the remaining leaves and wash three times in cold water. Drain, mix with the sea lettuce and reserve till needed. Thinly slice the radishes on a mandoline, place into iced water and reserve till needed.

to serve:

In a small saucepan warm the sea vegetables in a few spoonfuls of dashi broth and keep warm. Season the scallops and squat lobsters, oil the plancha (griddle) and sear the scallops and lobsters. Add the sliced clams to the vegetables and warm gently. Spoon the vegetables into warmed bowls and cover with a piece of dashi jelly. Place a few dots of lemon gel around the vegetables. Place the scallops and lobsters into the bowls. Garnish with a few slices of radish and crisp potato. Pour a little dashi into the bowls and serve immediately.

Serves 4
Preparation time: 30 minutes
Cooking time: 1 hour 30 minutes
                      (squabs and confit legs
                      simultaneously) plus
                      finishing time

Special equipment:
Blowtorch, vac pac machine and bags, water
bath, spice grinder.

Planning ahead:
N/A

INGREDIENTS

squabs:

4 x 450g Anjou squab

confit marinade:

2	cloves garlic, peeled and sliced
8	black peppercorns, crushed
½ tsp	fresh thyme leaves
4	plump juniper berries, crushed
1	bay leaf, shredded
1 tbsp	coarse sea salt
1	pinch sugar
300g	duck fat, melted

ground spices:

¼	cinnamon stick
1 tbsp	coriander seeds
1 tbsp	cloves
1 tbsp	4 spice (available in jars)
2 tbsp	black peppercorns
1 tbsp	coarse sea salt

to serve:

4 tbsp	groundnut oil
50g	unsalted butter

ROASTED BREAST & CONFIT LEG OF SPICED ANJOU SQUAB
BY ANDREW FAIRLIE

Squab refers to a young pigeon reared especially for the table. Most of the meat comes from the breasts; the legs are usually used to make stocks or sauces but here I have cooked them very slowly in duck fat. Although the legs are small I love the contrast between the tender breasts and the crispy legs.

METHOD

squabs:

Remove the legs from the squabs and set aside. Carefully remove the wishbones from the birds, break the backbone and remove, leaving the crown intact. Use a blowtorch to singe off any remaining feathers from the crowns. Place the crowns into individual vac pac bags and seal tightly. Set the water bath to 55°C and cook in the bath for 1 hour 30 minutes.

confit marinade:

Mix all the ingredients for the marinade together except the duck fat. Spread half the marinade onto a shallow dish, place the squab legs on top and cover with the remaining mixture. Leave to marinate for at least 3 hours and up to 4 hours. Wash all the marinade off the legs and pat dry with kitchen paper. Place the legs in a single layer into a shallow pan, pour over the duck fat and poach very gently for 1 hour 30 minutes or until the legs are meltingly tender. Allow the legs to cool in the fat until they can be handled safely. Take out of the fat and remove the thighbone with a small sharp knife.

ground spices:

Place all the ingredients onto a small tray and toast very gently till they just start to release their aroma. Place into a spice grinder, pulverise then sieve, keeping the fine spice.

to serve:

Place the squab legs skin-side down in a dry non-stick pan, place onto a medium heat till the skin crisps up then keep warm. Remove the crowns from the vac bags; dry the birds using kitchen paper and season with the spice mixture. Heat a sauté pan over a medium high heat, Add the oil and when hot caramelise the skin on the breasts, add the butter, allow it to foam then baste the birds for 1 minute. Remove the birds from the pan; place onto a wire rack and re-season with the spice mix. Remove the breasts from the crowns, place onto warmed plates and serve the crisp legs on top.

PEACH, ALMOND & BASIL
BY ANDREW FAIRLIE

This is a dessert using classical as well as very modern techniques. We have also used proven combinations of peach and almond, which marries beautifully with the quite pungent yet floral taste of my all-time favourite herb, basil.

Serves 6

Preparation time: 1 hour 30 minutes
Cooking time: 6 hours for the peach crisps

Special equipment:
Mixer, sugar thermometer, piping bags, 2cm and 5mm plain nozzles, vac pac machine and bags, water bath, Pacojet, silpat mat, dehydrator, blender, off-set palate knife, blowtorch.

Planning ahead:
The sorbet needs to freeze overnight. The jelly can be made in advance.

INGREDIENTS

peach parfait:

120g	egg yolks
300g	peach purée
120g	caster sugar
110g	egg whites
90g	caster sugar
600g	double cream

poached peaches:

2	yellow peaches
100g	peach juice

peach and basil jelly:

200g	peach juice
10g	Greek basil leaves, torn
1g	agar agar

almond cream:

80g	egg yolks
120g	almond syrup
80g	cornflour
500g	full-fat milk
3	leaves gelatine, soaked
120g	double cream, whipped to soft peaks

peach meringue:

300g	caster sugar
80g	crème de peche
110g	egg whites

sorbet syrup:

525g	caster sugar
8g	sorbet stabiliser
225g	glucose powder
500g	water

peach sorbet:

1 litre	yellow peach purée
800g	sorbet syrup (see recipe above)
280g	water
citric acid, to taste	

peach crisps:

250g	yellow peach purée
100g	anti-humidity sugar

nougatine:

240g	fondant
160g	glucose
120g	flaked almonds, toasted and cooled
4g	ground sea salt

to serve:

green basil cress or sorrel
fresh or toasted almonds

METHOD

peach parfait:

Place the egg yolks into a mixing bowl with the whisk attachment. Mix together the peach purée and 120g sugar in a saucepan and bring to the boil. Starting on a low to medium speed pour the peach purée mixture onto the yolks, increase the speed to medium high and continue to whisk till the mixture is cool, pale, light and fluffy. Transfer this mixture to a clean bowl. Pour the egg whites into a clean mixing bowl with the whisk attachment. Boil the remaining 90g sugar till 121°C. Start whisking the whites on a medium speed till they form light peaks, pour the hot sugar onto the whites and continue to whisk till cold. Fold the meringue into the yolk mix. Finally whip the cream to soft peaks and fold into the mix.

Spread a long sheet of cling film onto a clean surface. Place the peach mixture into a piping bag fitted with the 2cm plain nozzle. Pipe a line of the parfait mix onto the cling film and roll into a sausage, tie the cling film at each end and place in the freezer to set.

poached peaches:

Halve the peaches, remove the stone and portion into eight wedges.

Place the peach segments into a vac pac bag so they sit flat. Add the peach juice and sous vide: place the bag in the water bath to poach for 14 minutes at 62°C. Remove from the bath and plunge into iced water to chill.

peach and basil jelly:

Warm the peach juice in a saucepan, add the basil, pour into a clean bowl, cover with cling film and leave to infuse for 1 hour at room temperature. Pass through a sieve back into a

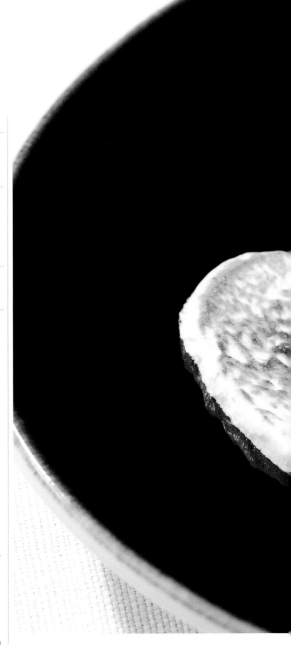

clean saucepan, bring to the boil and add the agar agar. Pour into a small tray till it is 5mm thick and refrigerate till set. When set cut into cubes of 1cm.

almond cream:

Whisk together the yolks, syrup and cornflour. Bring the milk to the boil in a saucepan and pour half of it onto the yolks, whisk together then return to the saucepan with the remaining milk. Bring back to the boil, whisking all the time, then add the gelatine. Pour the mix into a bowl to chill. Put the cold almond mix into a mixer bowl and whisk vigorously till smooth, then fold in the whipped cream. Place into a piping bag fitted with a 5mm plain nozzle and chill in the fridge.

peach meringue:

Add the sugar and crème de peche to a pan and boil to 121°C. Start whisking the egg whites in a mixer on a low speed, then add the peach syrup slowly and whisk at full speed till the mix is cool. Place in a piping bag with a 2cm plain nozzle.

sorbet syrup:

Mix all the dry ingredients together. Pour the water into a saucepan, heat to 85°C and whisk in all the dry ingredients. Chill.

peach sorbet:

Mix the peach purée, sorbet syrup and water, then add the citric acid to taste. Pour the mix into Pacojet containers and freeze overnight. Turn as needed.

peach crisps:

Blend the purée with the sugar, spread a very thin layer on a silpat mat and place in the dehydrator for 6 hours at 60°C or a low oven at 60°C overnight.

nougatine:

In a pan add the fondant and glucose cook to 160°C then mix in the almonds. Pour onto a tray and leave to cool. Break into pieces and blend to a powder with the salt.

to serve:

Dip a thin-bladed knife into hot water and cut the frozen parfait into 4cm lengths, remove the cling film from each piece and roll in the powdered nougatine. Place back into the freezer. On a round plate pipe a little amount of the meringue, then swipe with an off-set palette knife, then heat with a blowtorch till golden brown. Sprinkle a little pile of nougatine in the middle of the swipe. On the other side of the plate place two pieces of the peach parfait. Place two pieces of the poached peaches around the parfait. Randomly pipe small piles of the almond cream around the peaches and parfait. Place three pieces of the jelly around the almond cream. Quenelle the sorbet onto the meringue and finish with a piece of broken peach crisp. Garnish with green basil cress or sorrel and fresh or toasted almonds.

Adam Stokes

Adam Stokes grew up in Lincolnshire and joined Glenapp Castle following seven years in the kitchen brigade at fellow Relais & Châteaux Hambleton Hall. Following culinary experiences in London and Paris he has created an individual and stylish blend which incorporates traditional flavour marriages and modern inventive twists. Adam uses the finest Scottish and local ingredients, such as South Ayrshire spring lamb, Ballantrae Bay lobster and crab and locally foraged herbs and leaves such as wild garlic and wood sorrel. These ingredients feature on the daily changing six-course menu which was awarded 'Gourmet Menu of the Year' at the Scottish Chef awards and the restaurant is Catering in Scotland Excellence 2011 Restaurant of the Year.

RELAIS & CHATEAUX

Glenapp Castle

{ *Standing high above a dramatic coastline overlooking the Irish Sea, in the south west of Scotland's historic lowlands, Glenapp is the perfect example of a Scottish Baronial Castle set in an area of outstanding and unspoiled natural beauty.*

Its fairytale turrets and towers shelter a timeless world of oak-panelled rooms, rich fabrics and fine antiques, as well as the modern luxuries of fine cuisine and service. The castle is hidden from the rugged landscape by 36 acres of magical gardens filled with specimen trees and plants, including a fine collection of rare and unusual rhododendrons.

WILD HALIBUT WITH CHERVIL ROOT, CAPERS, COCKLES, PARMA HAM & YELLOW MUSTARD SEED

BY ADAM STOKES

I love this dish because the flavours are so clean and pure. The key to the whole dish is the freshness of the halibut and cockles. The chervil root complements the sweet flavour of the cockles, also the crucial nutty note from the beurre noisette sauce helping with the depth of the dish.

Serves 4
Preparation time: 1 hour
Cooking time: 20 minutes

Special equipment:
Fryer, meat slicer (optional)

Planning ahead:
You will need to soak the mustard seeds overnight. The crispy capers can be made a few hours beforehand and stored in an air-tight container. To save preparation time you can buy Parma ham already sliced.

INGREDIENTS

beurre noisette sauce:

20g	dried yellow mustard seeds
100g	butter
juice of 1 lemon	
1 tsp	chives, chopped

crispy capers:

30	baby capers

chervil root purée:

500g	chervil root
500g	milk
1	clove garlic, finely chopped
1	sprig of thyme

crispy Parma ham:

100g	Parma ham

halibut and cockles:

240g	wild halibut
100g	butter
8	cockles
50g	Sauternes wine
20g	olive oil
juice of 1 lemon	

to serve:

small bunch baby wood sorrel

METHOD

beurre noisette sauce:

The night before, place the mustard seeds into a pan of water and bring to the boil, remove from the heat and leave to soak overnight. The sauce is made to order. Heat the butter in a pan to a nut brown colour and then add a squeeze of lemon juice to stop the cooking procedure. Add a teaspoon of the soaked mustard seeds and a teaspoon of chives.

crispy capers:

Drop the capers into the fryer at 180°C until they are open, then remove and place on kitchen towel to dry. These can be stored in an air-tight container for a few hours.

chervil root purée:

Peel the chervil root. Put the peeled pieces of root into an ascorbic acid water solution (10g ascorbic acid, 3 litres water) as you go along to prevent the root from turning brown. Remove and put into a pan of milk with the garlic and thyme and bring to the boil. Cook until the root is soft. Place into a food processor and purée.

crispy Parma ham:

Thinly slice the Parma ham on a meat slicer if not already sliced. Julienne the slices into thin 4cm long strips and deep fry until crispy.

halibut and cockles:

Portion the halibut into four 60g pieces, then poach in the butter for approximately 3-4 minutes, turning continually until opaque.

Thoroughly rinse the cockles in cold water. Heat a deep-sided pan. Add the cockles (still in the shell) and the wine to the pan. Remove the cockles from the pan as soon as they open, de-shell and drizzle with olive oil and lemon juice.

to serve:

Place three dots of chervil root purée onto warm plates and garnish with baby wood sorrel. Place the halibut slightly off centre. Place cockles around the fish, a pile of crispy Parma ham on the top of the fish and crispy capers around the plate as in the photograph. Pour the sauce around the plate.

LOIN OF HARE WITH RED CABBAGE, BRUSSELS SPROUTS, PURPLE SPROUTING BROCCOLI & SEA PURSLANE

BY ADAM STOKES

This dish is a stylish modern twist on some traditional marriages. The richness of the hare is offset by the sweet and sour red cabbage purée, also a slight bitterness of the Brussels sprouts and flashes of salt from the sea purslane bring the dish together.

Serves 4
Preparation time: 2 hours
Cooking time: 45 minutes

Special equipment:
Vacuum packer (optional), water bath (optional), muslin.

Planning ahead:
The red cabbage needs to marinate 24 hours in advance. The prunes and chestnuts can be prepared in advance.

INGREDIENTS

hare:

2	hare saddles (large)
butter, as required	
4	juniper berries
salt, to taste	
4	sprigs of thyme

red cabbage purée:

½	red cabbage
200g	port
600g	red wine
300g	cider
10g	balsamic vinegar
1	spicy bouquet garni (cinnamon, star anise, cardamom)
50g	redcurrant purée
50g	blackberry purée
50g	blueberry purée
salt, to taste	
lime juice, to taste	
5.5g	gellan gum type F

prunes:

4	pitted Agen prunes
50g	sorbet syrup
2g	lemon juice
zest of ½ lemon	
zest of ½ orange	
¼	vanilla pod
1	star anise

chestnuts:

4	chestnuts
130g	chicken stock
10g	honey
5g	lime juice
3g	salt

20g	butter
20g	balsamic vinegar
5g	soy sauce

hare sauce:

hare bones, reserved from the hare	
500g	chicken stock
1	clove garlic
1	sprig of thyme
1	juniper berry
1	bay leaf
1	splash Armagnac
2	puréed prunes

to serve:

12	sprigs of purple sprouting broccoli
8	small Brussels sprouts
bunch of sea purslane	
small loaf of pain d'épice	
olive oil	

METHOD

hare:
Remove the loins from the saddle and keep the bones for the sauce. Each portion of hare should be approximately 90g. Place each piece in a vacuum bag with a knob of butter, one juniper berry, salt and a sprig of thyme. Seal the bag using a vacuum packer. Cook in a water bath at 54.5°C for 25 minutes. Alternatively the hare can be pan cooked to order if a vacuum packer is not available.

red cabbage purée:
Slice and marinade the cabbage for 24 hours in the port, wine, cider, vinegar and bouquet garni. Slowly cook the cabbage with the liquid for 1 hour and add the berry purées, some salt and lime juice to taste. Blitz the red cabbage with a hand-held food processor and pass through muslin. Thicken 600g red cabbage juice with the gellan gum by heating up to 90°C for 2 minutes, then allow to cool and purée.

hare sauce:
Roast the hare bones and add to the stock along with the garlic, thyme, juniper berry and bay leaf. Add the prunes and the Armagnac. Reduce and pass through muslin.

prunes and chestnuts:
Poach the prunes in a pan with the ingredients listed and steep for 1 minute, then remove from the liquid and allow to cool.

Seal the chestnuts in a vacuum bag with the ingredients listed and cook in a water bath for 40 minutes at 95°C. Alternatively the chestnuts can be slowly braised in a pan on the stove for approximately 30 minutes. Both these ingredients can be prepared in advance.

to serve:

Cut the purple sprouting broccoli into small florets with a centimetre of stalk. Place in boiling salted water (180g salt to 2 litres water) and leave until tender. Place the sprouts in boiling salted water until tender. Peel off the individual Brussels sprout leaves.

Wash the sea purslane thoroughly and blanch for 30 seconds in boiling water. Remove and glaze with olive oil. Place as shown in the photograph.

Slice the pain d'épice into thin strips and toast.

Heat the red cabbage purée, place into a piping bag and pipe onto a warm plate. Slice the hare into three equal-sized pieces and stand up on the plate, sprinkling the loin with broccoli and Brussels sprout leaves. Warm the prunes and chestnuts and place on the dish as pictured. Lean the pain d'épice up against the loin and finish with the hare sauce.

LIQUID DARK CHOCOLATE TART WITH PEANUTS & A GRANNY SMITH APPLE SORBET

BY ADAM STOKES

Everybody enjoys a chocolate fondant and this dish has taken it a step further. The peanut influences add to the richness of the dish for a really decadent finish.

Serves 4
Preparation time: 3 hours
Cooking time: 45 minutes

Special equipment:
Thermomix, muslin, Pacojet (or ice-cream machine), micro scales.

Planning ahead:
Much of this dessert can be prepared in advance. Have some reliable, air-tight containers to hand for storing each component.

INGREDIENTS

malted barley ice cream:

62½g	pearl barley
125g	double cream
250g	full-fat milk
50g	egg yolks
25g	caster sugar
37½g	malt extract

apple sorbet:

250g	Granny Smith apple pulp
25g	pro-sorbet powder (sugar stabiliser)
12.5g	caster sugar

sweet paste tart case:

165g	plain soft flour
50g	icing sugar
1	egg yolk
zest of ½ lemon	
½	vanilla pod
83g	melted butter
1 tsp	cold water

dark chocolate fondant:

77g	70% dark chocolate
75g	butter
83g	caster sugar
70g	egg whites
40g	plain soft flour

chocolate crumble:

94g	soft butter
30g	cocoa
94g	plain soft flour
87g	caster sugar
1g	salt

peanut cookie:

45g	soft butter
0.65g	salt
60g	plain soft flour
30g	granulated sugar
30g	light brown sugar
1g	baking powder
24g	eggs
15g	peanut paste

to serve:

15g	liquid chocolate
16	oven-roasted peanuts
16	candied lemon zest strips

METHOD

malted barley ice cream:

Preheat the oven to 180°C and toast the pearl barley for 5 minutes until golden. Add this to a pan containing the cream and milk, bring to the boil, remove from the heat and leave to infuse for 45 minutes. Whisk together the egg yolks, sugar and malt extract along with half of the milk mixture. Slowly add the remaining half while continuing to whisk. Warm to 80°C in a Thermomix, pass through muslin and then cool. Refrigerate the mixture for a day and then freeze. This must be made in advance and will keep for a couple of weeks and can then be processed by a Pacojet before use. If a Pacojet is not available follow an ice-cream machine manufacturer's instructions.

apple sorbet:

Blitz all the ingredients thoroughly together. Pass through muslin and refrigerate for a day and then freeze. This must be made in advance and will keep for a couple of weeks and can then be processed by a Pacojet before use. If a Pacojet is not available follow an ice-cream machine manufacturer's instructions.

sweet paste tart case:

Preheat the oven to 180°C. Mix the flour, sugar, egg yolk, lemon zest and vanilla pod together. Add the softened butter to the mix, and then add cold water. Roll out the pastry, cut to size and fill small tart case moulds. Do not overwork the mixture. Bake the cases in the oven for 7 minutes and once cooled, store in an air-tight container. Use on the same day.

dark chocolate fondant:

Preheat the oven to 200°C. Melt the chocolate and butter together and add the sugar. Lightly whisk the egg whites and add them to the melted mixture. Add the flour to make a chocolate paste. Put the paste into a piping bag,

refrigerate and cool for a couple of hours. Just before serving, pipe into the pastry cases and bake in the oven for 4-5 minutes.

chocolate crumble:

Preheat the oven to 175°C. Using the paddle attachment on a food processor mix together the butter, cocoa, flour, sugar and salt together. Spread the mixture on a sheet of silicone and

bake in the oven for 20 minutes. Allow to cool and then blitz. The crumble can be made 2 days in advance and kept in an air-tight container.

peanut cookie:

Preheat the oven to 170°C. Mix the butter and salt together. Add the flour, sugars and baking powder. Fold in the eggs and add the peanut paste. Spread onto a silicone sheet and bake in

the oven for 12 minutes. Once cooled, roughly break into 2.5cm-sized pieces and store in an air-tight container. This can be done the day before.

to serve:

Use a brush to paint a line of chocolate down the plate. Place the hot chocolate fondant tart in the middle of the plate. Spoon a small pile of chocolate crumble onto one side of the tart

and then place a scoop of apple sorbet on top. Arrange some roasted peanuts and the candied lemon around the sorbet as shown in the picture. On the other side of the tart place small pieces of broken peanut butter cookie with a quenelle of malted barley ice cream on top.

Derek Johnstone

The inaugural winner of BBC 'MasterChef: the Professionals', Derek Johnstone is the dedicated and talented head chef at Greywalls Hotel and Chez Roux Restaurant in Muirfield.

He studied at Glasgow's Food and Technology College before securing an apprenticeship with the Lodge on Loch Lomond Hotel. Derek went on to win bronze at the 2007 Knorr Scottish Chef of the Year as well as being a finalist at the Martin Wishart Scholarship in the same year.

His triumph on the popular television show 'MasterChef' in 2008 opened the door for him to work at the famous Le Gavroche in London and he spent two years learning from world-renowned chef Michel Roux Jnr.

Derek was part of the team that re-opened Greywalls in 2010 and within a year he was promoted to Head Chef at the hotel's Chez Roux Restaurant.

The 2011 Scottish Hotel Awards saw him picking up the Restaurant of the Year Award as well as the highly coveted Medaille D'Or.

Greywalls Hotel
& Chez Roux Restaurant

{

Greywalls Hotel is uniquely situated on the edge of Muirfield championship golf course with stunning views over East Lothian and the Firth of Forth.

Overlooking the world famous greens of the 9th and 18th holes, it has earned itself a reputation as 'a golfers' paradise'! Offering one of the very best country house accommodations in Scotland, Greywalls' stylish Edwardian splendour makes an ideal retreat for individuals, golfing holidays, family gatherings, weddings and corporate entertainment.

Designed by the celebrated Edwardian architect Sir Edwin Lutyens as a 'dignified holiday home' Greywalls was built in 1901 and still retains the charm and character for which it is renowned. A haven of peaceful tranquillity it enjoys a reputation for the excellence of its food and service. As well as the elegant drawing rooms and delightful dining areas the house has 23 en-suite bedrooms. The splendid walled gardens are attributed to Gertrude Jekyll and contain a hard and grass tennis court, croquet lawn and putting green as well as borders filled with herbaceous plants.

WARM TARTINE OF PIGS' HEAD WITH OX TONGUE, SHALLOT PUREE, APPLE & HAZELNUT SALAD, SHERRY & ARRAN MUSTARD VINAIGRETTE

BY DEREK JOHNSTONE

During my time at Le Gavroche I was taught to cook a lot of less sought-after cuts of meat. The one I enjoyed preparing the most was 'Tete du Porc'. This really is quite a remarkable piece of meat which is extremely flavoursome and cost effective.

Serves 6-8

Preparation time:	1 hour 40 minutes
Cooking time:	3 hours for the chicken stock, 7 hours for the pig's head terrine, 40 minutes for the remainder

Special equipment:
Robot Coupe/food processor or blender, fine sieve, mixer with dough hook attachment.

Planning ahead:
The stock can be made in advance and frozen. Allow plenty of time for the pigs' heads.

INGREDIENTS

white chicken stock: (makes approximately 12 litres)

10kg	chicken bones
1kg	carrots
1.5kg	onions
800g	celery
500g	leeks
80g	garlic
20 litres	water
5g	black peppercorns

pigs' head terrine: (serves 20 people)

200g	leeks
300g	carrots
300g	onions
200g	celery
500ml	Madeira
4 litres	white chicken stock (see recipe above)
2	pigs' heads
1.1kg	ox tongue
30ml	sherry vinegar
salt, to taste	

shallot purée:

1kg	banana shallots
60ml	pomace oil
75g	unsalted butter
150ml	double cream
10g	cooking salt

white bread base: (2kg white bread)

2.4kg	T55 flour
100g	milk powder
100g	unsalted butter
1400ml	water

64g	yeast
464g	cooking salt
egg wash, as required	

croutons:

200g	white bread
30ml	olive oil
50g	garlic

mixed salad leaves:

lollo rosso lettuce
curly frisee lettuce
oak leaf lettuce
radicchio

sherry vinaigrette:

50ml	sherry vinegar
200ml	pomace oil
10g	Arran mustard
1g	cooking salt

to serve:

150g	pigs' head terrine (see above)
40g	croutons (see above)
50g	shallot purée (see above)
10g	mixed salad leaves (see above)
10ml	sherry vinaigrette (see above)
15g	Granny Smith apples
10g	blanched and roasted hazelnuts

METHOD

white chicken stock:

Place all the ingredients into a saucepan, bring to a simmer and skim the surface. Reduce the heat and cook for 3 hours. Strain the stock and blast chill (freeze).

pigs' head terrine:

Cut all the vegetables into a mirepoix and roast in a large gastronome tray. Once caramelised deglaze with the Madeira and reduce, add the stock, pigs' heads and ox tongue and bring to the boil. Cover and slowly braise in the oven for 7 hours until tender. Scrape the flesh off the pigs' heads, leaving the skin behind. In a flat gastronome tray lay the skin down evenly, making sure there are no gaps, press with a smilar-size mould with a few heavy tins on top and leave in the fridge to set. Meanwhile pick the pigs' heads down and season with the

vinegar and salt and cut the tongue into long strips. Take the tray with the skin and place in it just under half of the pigs' head mixture, again allow to set in fridge. After 10 minutes lay the tongue lengthways and cover with the remaining pigs' head mix. Cover with a layer of cling film and replace the mould on top and place the tins on again to weigh down and to press the pigs' head mix together.

shallot purée:

Thinly slice the shallots. Heat the oil and butter in a saucepan and add the shallots, cook until tender and caramelised, then add the cream. Blitz in a food processor, pass through a fine sieve and season.

white bread base:

Place the flour, milk powder and butter into a mixer with a dough hook attachment. Mix together the water and yeast and pour onto the flour mix. Place on speed 2 for 5 minutes. Add the salt and work for another 5 minutes. Leave to prove in a warm place for 5 minutes. Once proved, knock back and roll into the required shapes. Place onto a tray lined with greaseproof or a silpat and prove for a further 10 minutes in a warm place. Brush with egg wash and bake in an oven preheated to 190°C for 10 minutes.

croutons:

Preheat the oven to 180°C. Slice the bread into long rectangular croutons and brush generously with the oil. Crush the garlic and rub onto

the croutons. Place onto a tray lined with greaseproof or a silpat and bake in the oven for 6 minutes.

mixed salad leaves:

Pick the outside leaves off each lettuce and discard. With the remaining leaves pick out the small ones or tear into small pieces, wash and dry.

sherry vinaigrette:

Mix all the ingredients together, check the seasoning and use when required.

to serve:

Slice the terrine the same size as the croutons and lightly grill to warm. Meanwhile heat up the purée, dress the salad with the vinaigrette and

slice the apples into batons. Swipe the purée onto the place, mix the hazelnuts and apples into the salad and place on the plate. Add the warm terrine and croutons, then serve.

Chef's tips:

When preparing the pigs' heads make sure to fillet carefully the cheeks and the temples as this is where most of the meat is. Blowtorch the heads carefully as they tend to have unwanted hairs. Prove the bread in a warm place for maximum results and ensure you egg wash all the visible dough for a better looking bread roll. Sprinkle a little finely chopped rosemary on top of the croutons for a fuller flavour.

Serves 4
Preparation time: 12 minutes
Cooking time: 9 minutes

Special equipment:
N/A

Planning ahead:
N/A

INGREDIENTS

lobster:

4 x 450g native lobsters from North Berwick

sauce bois boudran:

20g	banana shallots
5g	tomato ketchup
5ml	sherry vinegar
3ml	Worcestershire sauce
3g	chives
6g	chervil
10g	fresh tarragon
30ml	vegetable oil
15ml	extra virgin olive oil
1g	cooking salt
3	drops green tabasco
3ml	sesame oil

leek and shallot filling:

12g	banana shallots, diced
oil, as required	
400g	fresh young leeks
1g	unsalted butter
20ml	saice bois boudran (see recipe above)

to serve:

60g	seasonal potatoes (I like to use Jersey royals, charlotte or maris peer), cooked
200g	butter, unsalted
5g	flat leaf parsley, chopped
4g	fresh chervil
30g	per person mixed seasonal salad leaves

ROASTED NORTH BERWICK LOBSTER BOIS BOUDRAN WITH BUTTERED NEW POTATOES & SEASONAL SALAD

BY DEREK JOHNSTONE

Lobster Bois Boudran is a Chez Roux favourite. We serve it with lobsters that have been pulled from the water that very day and seasonal salad picked from our own garden. We also dress up the salad with edible flowers.

METHOD

lobster:
Cook the lobster in a court bouillon for 9 minutes, remove and allow to rest for 10 minutes.

sauce bois boudran:
Lightly mix all the ingredients together.

leek and shallot filling:
Add the shallots to the oil and slowly confit. Meanwhile dice and wash the leeks then blanch and refresh in ice water. Strain and squeeze out all excess water and mix with the butter, shallots and a spoonful of bois boudran dressing.

to serve:
Dress the cooked potatoes with the butter and parsley then add the chervil. Crack the lobster in two, head to tail, and remove the sack that runs down the tail. Place back in the shell and put the leek and shallot filling inside the head. Dress the lobster with the sauce and serve with the potatoes and mixed leaf salad.

Chef's tip:
Allow the lobster to rest but not cool too much as it's best served warm. Once the sauce is made keep it slightly warm to maximise the flavour – do not put it in the fridge. For the salad I like to use leaves that are slightly bitter. Dandelion leaves and radicchio work well with the sweet lobster.

SABLE BRETON, KIRSCH PARFAIT, RED WINE POACHED CHERRIES & PISTACHIO ICE CREAM

BY DEREK JOHNSTONE

What makes this simple dessert so great is that the cherries are handpicked from the Greywalls' garden. This dessert always gets great reviews from our guests at Chez Roux.

Serves 4-6

Preparation time:	2 hours
Cooking time:	20 minutes

Special equipment:
Mixer, non-stick baking tray 20 x 30cm, sugar thermometer, ice-cream machine.

Planning ahead:
The cherries need to macerate in the fridge for 24 hours.

INGREDIENTS

sable Breton:

450g	butter, softened
320g	caster sugar
10g	salt
160g	egg yolks
450g	plain T55 flour
30g	baking powder

Kirsch parfait:

175g	caster sugar
175g	water
500g	egg yolks
1kg	double cream
100g	Kirsch

red wine poached cherries:

1kg	cherries
500g	red table wine
zest of 1 orange	
zest of 1 lemon	
150g	caster sugar
2	pink peppercorns

pistachio ice cream: (makes 1200ml/15-20 portions)

6g	stabiliser
300g	caster sugar
1605g	milk
89g	milk powder
125g	trimoline
143g	butter
225g	pistachio paste

to serve:

reduced red wine syrup, as required
confit orange zest julienne, as required

5g	per person green pistachios

METHOD

sable Breton:

Preheat the oven to 180°C. Beat the butter, sugar and salt with the whisk attachment. After 5 minutes when the butter is foamy add the yolks and continue mixing for 5-10 minutes. Sift the flour and baking powder together. Change to the paddle attachment and add the flour. Mix for 30 seconds. Spread onto the non-stick baking tray and bake in the oven for 12 minutes.

Kirsch parfait:

Boil the sugar and water to 84°C. Start whipping the yolks and pour over the sugar syrup while whipping. Whip till cold. Whip the cream to medium peaks and fold in. Add the Kirsch last.

red wine poached cherries:

Halve and stone the cherries. Boil the wine, zests, sugar and peppercorns. Pour over the cherries and leave to macerate in the fridge for 24 hours.

pistachio ice cream:

Mix the stabiliser with 30g sugar. Bring the milk, milk powder and remaining sugar to the boil, add the trimoline and allow to cool to 84°C (check with a sugar thermometer). Add the stabiliser and-sugar mixture with the butter. This is the base ice cream. Pass and add the pistachio paste.

to serve:

Cut a rectangle of sable Breton and place to one side of the plate. Top with a small slab of parfait. Place cherries along one side of the parfait. Paint a line of reduced red wine syrup along the plate. Place a quenelle of ice cream opposite the parfait on top of some orange confit zest. Sprinkle with the pistachios for colour and texture.

Chef's tip:

The ice cream recipe can be used as a basic ice cream base. You can add whatever flavouring you like after the base is made.

Philip Carnegie

Philip Carnegie grew up in the tiny hamlet of O'Neill Corse, near Alford. His career began at Shelly Leigh's Restaurant in Aberdeen, followed by the Waterwheel Inn, Bieldside and then onto the Lairhillock Inn, Stonehaven. He spent around five years there before moving to Germany to work in the Villa Hammerschimede, an upmarket hotel on the edge of the Black Forest. Moving quickly through the ranks, Philip worked at a variety of hotels in the UK and Europe before joining Inverlochy Castle hotel in 2010 as Sous Chef and now Head Chef. He has helped Inverlochy retain its Michelin-star status through creating dishes that are elegant and innovative, and which show off his superb technical skills, flair and imagination. Philip uses all of Scotland as a larder, picking the very best of Scottish seasonal produce to feature in his daily changing menus.

Inverlochy Castle

{ *The mysterious waters of the lochs surrounded by the misty mountains that rise out of the earth in this part of Scotland never fail to plunge the visitor into a gentle dreaminess and an atmosphere of deep restfulness.*

With its very own loch, Inverlochy Castle offers one of the most stunning Scottish panoramas. Queen Victoria used to come here and she described it as "one of the loveliest and most romantic spots" that she had ever seen. At the foot of Ben Nevis – the highest peak in the United Kingdom – this charming castle with its snooker room and its princely interiors is also a great place for sport. Try water skiing on Loch Ness for a unique blend of pleasure and beauty.

ROASTED LANGOUSTINE WITH TRUFFLE, PEARL BARLEY & PIG'S HEAD
BY PHILIP CARNEGIE

Serves 4

Preparation time: 30 minutes
Cooking time: 15 minutes

Planning ahead:
N/A

Special equipment:
N/A

INGREDIENTS

1 tbsp	olive oil + more for the langoustines
1 tbsp	shallots, finely chopped
1	small sprig thyme
4 tbsp	pearl barley
salt and pepper	
50ml	white wine
50ml	Noilly Pratt
400ml	chicken stock
1 tbsp	parmesan, grated
1 tbsp	vegetable brunoise (carrot, courgette, celeriac), blanched
2 tbsp	pig's head — equal quantities of cheek, tongue, head — diced
1 tbsp	butter + a little for the leeks
8	extra large langoustines, shelled and de-veined
16	baby leeks, blanched and refreshed
vegetable stock, as required	
fresh truffle, 3 slices per person and shaved	
shellfish jus, as required	

METHOD

Warm the tablespoon of olive oil in a wide deep pan, then add the shallots and thyme and cook for 3 minutes. Add the pearl barley and season, then deglaze with the wine and Noilly Pratt. Reduce until dry then add the stock and cook until soft. Add the parmesan, vegetable brunoise, pig's head and the tablespoon of butter, warm through and season.

Season both sides of the langoustines and roast in a pan with hot olive oil for 1 minute on each side.

Warm the baby leeks in a little butter and vegetable stock.

to serve:

Place the pearl barley mix onto warmed plates. Place the baby leeks around the barley, put the langoustines on top and then garnish with the truffle and shellfish jus.

Serves 4
Preparation time: 10 minutes
Cooking time: 45 minutes

Planning ahead:
The chickpeas need to be soaked overnight.

Special equipment:
N/A

INGREDIENTS

2   shallots, finely chopped
2   sprigs thyme
2   sprigs rosemary
1   clove garlic, crushed
olive oil, as required
120g   chickpeas, soaked overnight
400ml   chicken stock
salt and pepper
1   lemon, juice
4 x 120g   pieces of lamb loin
butter, as required
12   dried tomato fillets
1 tsp   pesto
80g   Golden Cross goat's cheese
140g   spinach

to serve:

6   violet artichokes, cooked
pesto, as required
lamb jus (reserved from cooking the lamb)

LOIN OF LAMB WITH CHICKPEAS, TOMATO, GOAT'S CHEESE & A SIMPLE LAMB JUS
BY PHILIP CARNEGIE

METHOD

Preheat the oven to 200°C.

Sauté the shallots, 1 sprig each of thyme and rosemary. and garlic in olive oil until the shallots are translucent then add the chickpeas and stock. Cook for about 30 minutes then remove and discard the thyme and rosemary. Take out 4 tablespoons of the chickpeas with some stock to cover. Put the rest of the chickpeas with 3 tablespons of olive oil and the rest of the stock into a liquidiser and blitz to a fine purée. Pass the purée through a fine sieve, season with salt, pepper and lemon juice and keep warm.

Season the lamb loins and seal on all sides then add butter, the remaining thyme and rosemary, and place in the oven for 3 minutes each side. Remove from the oven and leave to rest on a warm plate for 10 minutes. Reserve the juices (jus).

Take the dried tomato fillets and rub with a little pesto. Stuff with the goat's cheese and then roll together – place in the oven (still at 200°C) to warm through.

Cook the spinach in butter for 1 minute then season.

to serve:

Place the spinach in the middle of the plate then place the lamb on top. At one side of the lamb put some of the purée and at the other side the chickpeas, tomatoes and violet artichoke. Finish by drizzling some pesto and lamb jus around.

RUM ROASTED PINEAPPLE WITH A CHOCOLATE BEIGNET & COCONUT SORBET

BY PHILIP CARNEGIE

Serves 4
Preparation time: 10 minutes
Cooking time: 25 minutes

Planning ahead:
The sorbet can be made in advance. The beignet mix needs to be frozen before use.

Special equipment:
Ice-cream machine

INGREDIENTS

beignet mix:

90g	full-fat milk
80g	double cream
160g	70% Valrhona dark chocolate + 150g of praline paste, melted together
1	egg white
45g	almonds, ground

batter mix:

40g	butter
260ml	Champagne
2	eggs
pinch of salt	
50g	caster sugar
200g	plain flour
50g	cocoa powder

coconut sorbet:

1	400g tin coconut milk
110g	caster sugar
50ml	coconut liqueur
juice of ½ lemon	
200g	coconut purée

pineapple:

1	pineapple
150g	caster sugar
100ml	rum
25g	butter

METHOD

beignet mix:

Boil the milk and cream together, add the melted chocolate and praline mix then allow to cool. When cold roll into 25g balls, dip into the egg white and coat with the almonds, then freeze.

batter mix:

Preheat the oven to 200°C.

Melt the butter then mix it with the Champagne, eggs, salt and sugar. Stir in the flour and cocoa powder.

Slide a cocktail stick into each beignet ball then coat them in batter and deep fry for 3 minutes at 180°C. Remove and place on a tray, then bake in the oven for 5 minutes.

coconut sorbet:

Boil all the ingredients together, cool then place into an ice-cream machine. Churn according to the manufacturer's instructions.

pineapple:

Cut the pineapple into slices 2cm thick, core each slice and trim into a neat circle. Caramelise the sugar to a light golden colour, add the pineapple and deglaze with the rum. Add the butter and cook until soft and golden, then turn and colour on the other side.

to serve:

Place a pineapple ring on each plate, put a beignet on top and finish with a scoop of sorbet beside that.

Simon McKenzie

Simon has recently moved to the West Coast of Scotland and the shores of Loch Creran and the picturesque Isle of Eriska to take charge of the kitchen where he hopes to transform the food into his own comfortable polished style. Utilising the very best the West Coast has to offer Simon, using his knowledge of the latest culinary science coupled with his honed skill set gained from working in some of the UK's leading kitchens, subtly transforms the wonderful ingredients into elegant, sophisticated dishes executed in such a way that guests are not alienated nor left confused by their complexity.

Simon, a Northern lad by birth, swapped Sunderland for London three days after completing his college exams and caught the train after securing a position in the prominent Lanesborough hotel under Paul Gayler. After this Simon held stints in Gordon Ramsay's eponymous restaurant, Aubergine and Les Saveurs under Marco Pierre White. More recently Simon held a senior position under John Campbell when he was at his two Michelin-starred kitchen, the Vineyard at Stockcross, and opened the New Forest's gem, Lime Wood as Head Chef, rubber stamping its standards before handing over to Luke Holder.

Image courtesy of Dennis Hardley Photography www.scotphoto.com

Isle of Eriska

Hotel, Spa & Island

{

The Eriska Hotel and Spa offers luxurious 5-star accommodation with a view to match.

Enjoy a traditional Scottish breakfast while taking in 300 acres of lush landscapes all from the comfort of your own bed. Carefully blending the old with the new the designer rooms and luxury suites offer the finest bed linen, rich fabrics and warm, contemporary décor. Your every need is anticipated with a wide range of in-room facilities and guest services. Guests can also relax and enjoy a quiet reprieve with their favourite tipple next to the fireplace in the hotel lounge.

Since 1997 the Restaurant at Eriska has held the award of 3 AA Rosettes and a mark in the Good Food Guide. In March 2011 it was the 'Hotel Restaurant of the Year' at the Scottish Restaurant Awards and in 2010 the restaurant won the 'Taste of Scotland Award' at the Scottish Thistle Awards.

SMOKED & CONFIT BELLY OF LAMB, ROAST SCALLOP, ARTICHOKE, PINE NUT & BROAD BEAN SALAD, SHERRY DRESSING

BY SIMON MCKENZIE

I am a huge fan of mixing meat and fish — this dish in particular is a fantastic combination especially when you take into account our location on the Scottish West Coast, and arguably the best scallops in the world are dived for here.

Serves 4
Preparation time: 2 hours
Cooking time: 3 hours

Special equipment:
Vac pac machine/bags, water bath, blender, fine sieve, muslin cloth.

Planning ahead:
The day before prepare and salt the lamb, then cook overnight. Press in the morning. A lot of the preparation for this dish can be completed a day or two in advance, such as the dressing, purée and sauce.

INGREDIENTS

lamb belly:

1kg	lamb belly
100g	Maldon salt
1	sprig rosemary
200g	vegetable oil

sherry dressing:

150g	sherry vinegar
1	pinch salt
50g	vegetable oil
50g	olive oil
100g	walnut oil

artichoke purée:

500g	peeled Jerusalem artichokes
100g	full-fat milk
50g	unsalted butter
2g	salt
50g	double cream

globe artichoke:

1	globe artichoke
100g	vegetable oil
5	coriander seeds
1	clove garlic, peeled and sliced
1	banana shallot, peeled and sliced
1	sprig thyme
100g	white wine

lamb jus:

100g	shallots, peeled and sliced
3	cloves garlic, peeled and sliced
50g	button mushrooms, sliced
100g	unsalted butter
200g	red wine
150g	lamb stock
400g	chicken stock
100g	fresh tomatoes, chopped
400g	lamb bones, chopped small
	vegetable oil, for frying
150g	Cabernet Sauvignon vinegar
	salt, to taste

to serve:

	vegetable oil, for frying
	unsalted butter, for frying
20g	broad beans, podded and blanched
5g	toasted pine nuts
	salt, to taste
4	scallops
	coriander cress, as required

METHOD

lamb belly:

Trim the belly of any sinew or excess fat. Cover with the salt and wrap tightly in cling film. Chill for 6 hours. Remove from the cling film and wash under cold running water for 10 minutes, then dry in a clean cloth. Place the belly in a suitable vac pac bag along with the rosemary and the vegetable oil and seal tightly. Cook in a water bath set at 82°C for 10 hours. Remove from the water bath and open the bag. Place the belly on a suitable tray, place another tray on top of the belly and a weight on top of the tray and chill for 4 hours. Remove the belly from the tray and score the fat with a sharp knife in a diagonal pattern, cut into rectangles 7 x 2cm.

sherry dressing:

Place the vinegar and salt in a bowl and whisk. Gradually add the oils while continuously whisking.

artichoke purée:

Cut the artichokes into 1cm pieces and place in a vac pac bag along with the milk, butter and salt. Seal tightly and place in a steamer for 45 minutes. Place all ingredients from the vac pac bag into a blender along with the cream and purée for 5 minutes. Pour through a fine sieve. Check the seasoning.

globe artichoke:

Remove the stalk and outer leaves of the artichoke. Trim away any green. Heat the oil in a pan and add the coriander seeds, garlic, shallot and thyme, then gently fry for 2 minutes. Add the artichoke and gently fry for a further 2 minutes, turning often. Add the wine and simmer until the artichoke is tender. Cool in the cooking liquor. Remove the artichoke and, using a spoon, remove the fibres from the centre. Cut in half lengthways then into wedges, six from each half.

lamb jus:

Fry the shallots, garlic and mushrooms in foaming butter until golden brown. Reduce the wine by half in a pan, drain the shallots, garlic

and mushrooms and add to the wine. Reduce the stocks by half and add to the wine mixture along with the tomatoes. Fry the lamb bones in the oil until golden brown, drain the fat and deglaze with the vinegar. Add to the wine mixture. Place the pan on the stove and bring to the boil, reduce to a simmer and skim. Cook the sauce for 1 hour then pass through a fine sieve and muslin cloth. Place in a clean pan and reduce to a sauce consistency. Season with salt.

to serve:

Roast the artichoke pieces in a little vegetable oil and foaming butter. Mix the broad beans and

pine nuts together with a little of the dressing and season with salt. Heat the jus and whisk in the dressing until the jus takes on a light brown colour and thickens. The flavour should be meaty and zingy, like vinaigrette. Heat the purée and season with salt. Caramelise the lamb belly by frying in a hot pan with a little oil fat-side down and keep hot. Roast the scallop in a hot pan with a little oil and butter and rest for 2 minutes, keep hot. Warm the plates. Place two spoons of purée down at opposite ends and, using a spoon, 'swipe' one from left to right and the other right from left. Place the lamb belly on the left-hand swipe. Place the scallop on the right-hand swipe. Scatter the artichoke pieces

around. Scatter the broad bean salad around. Drizzle the sherry dressing over and around the dish. Place a little coriander cress on top of the scallop. Serve.

Chef's tip:

Source good stocks as these are imperative to the quality of the jus. Try to only use diver-caught scallops and avoid dredged scallops. When you are buying your scallops try and find them in the shell; if they are open tap the shell and they should close, if they don't they are probably dead and should not be eaten.

LOIN OF RABBIT & TORTELLINI, ROAST LANGOUSTINE, ASPARAGUS BAVOISE, CHARRED SHALLOT, ALMOND & TRUFFLE

BY SIMON MCKENZIE

This is a cracking dish with delicate flavours. The rabbit is poached but the flavour is pulled back by the sweet roast langoustine, the asparagus adds a new 'mouth feel' and lightens the dish while the almond foam bridges the contrasting flavours.

Serves 4
Preparation time: 3 hours
Cooking time: 2 hours

Special equipment:
Vac pac machine and bags, water bath, hand blender, pasta machine, food processor.

Planning ahead:
The tortellini filling and asparagus bavoise should be made 1 or 2 days beforehand.

INGREDIENTS

rabbit:

1	whole rabbit
1	sprig thyme
20g	olive oil
20g	unsalted butter
20g	chicken stock
salt	

chicken mousse:

200g	raw chicken breast, skin removed
3g	salt
200g	double cream

tortellini mix:

legs from the rabbit	
100g	Maldon salt
100g	vegetable oil
50g	chicken mousse (see recipe above)
10g	golden raisins
2g	chopped chervil
1 tsp	sherry vinegar

pasta dough:

250g	'00' pasta flour
2	whole eggs
3	egg yolks

asparagus bavoise:

4	bunches asparagus, sliced with the tips kept for use later
1	clove garlic, peeled and sliced
100g	finely sliced shallots
10g	unsalted butter
400g	chicken stock
150g	double cream
salt	
50g	Vege-Gel

charred shallot layers:

2	banana shallots
salt	

2	sprigs thyme
balsamic vinegar	

almond foam:

300g	toasted flaked almonds
500g	semi-skimmed milk
10g	almond oil
10g	soya lecithin
salt	

thyme jus:

100g	rabbit bones, chopped small
vegetable oil, for frying	
100g	shallots, peeled and sliced
3	cloves garlic, peeled and sliced
50g	button mushrooms, sliced
100g	unsalted butter
150g	sherry vinegar
200g	red wine
400g	chicken stock
150g	lamb stock
10g	thyme
salt, to taste	

truffle dressing:

1	whole egg
20g	muscatel vinegar
salt	
20g	truffle oil
80g	vegetable oil
15g	chopped truffle

to serve:

8	langoustine, blanched and peeled
vegetable oil, for frying	
unsalted butter, for cooking	
Maldon salt, to taste	
50g	pousse (baby spinach), picked and washed
zest of 1 lemon	
1	frisee, picked and washed
12	asparagus tips, blanched
8	sprigs picked chervil
4	slices truffle (optional)

METHOD

rabbit:

Remove the loins and legs from the rabbit. Trim the loins and remove the belly. Place the loins in a suitable vac pac bag along with all the remaining ingredients, seal tightly in a vac pac machine. Place in a water bath set at 54°C for 45 minutes.

chicken mousse:

Place the chicken breast and salt into a blender and purée. Scrape down the sides and add the cream. Blitz briefly. Pass through a fine sieve.

tortellini mix:

Place the rabbit legs in a container and cover with the salt, leave overnight in the fridge. Remove the legs from the salt and wash under cold running water, place in a vac pac bag along with the vegetable oil and seal tightly. Place in a water bath set on 85°C for 12 hours. Remove the legs from the oil, pick the meat from the bones and allow to cool. Mix with the mousse, raisins and chervil. Add the vinegar and season with salt. Roll into 25g balls and chill.

pasta dough:

Place the flour into the food processor and turn on. Add the eggs and as soon as a sandy texture is achieved stop the machine and empty the contents onto the bench. Knead to make dough. Roll out the pasta thinly and cut into 6cm discs. Cover.

tortellini:

Roll the discs through the pasta machine. Brush half with cold water then place a ball of the tortellini mix in the centre of the disc. Fold the pasta over and seal around the mix, removing all of the air. Cut with a 4cm round cutter to form a neat semi circle. Fold around your little finger and seal. Blanch in boiling water for 3 minutes.

asparagus bavoise:

Sweat the asparagus, garlic and shallots with the butter in a hot saucepan until the shallots are opaque. Add the stock and cream then simmer until the asparagus is tender. Pour into the blender and purée. Pass through a fine sieve and season. Allow to cool. Weigh 500g of the purée into a clean saucepan and add the Vege-Gel. Place on a high heat and whisk continuously until it boils, pour into a container and allow to set.

charred shallot layers:

Preheat the oven to 180°C. Place the shallots on a large sheet of foil along with a little salt and the thyme, wrap up into a parcel and place in the oven. Cook until the shallots are tender, around 1 hour. Remove from the foil and cool. Peel the shallots and cut in half lengthways. Heat a pan and place the shallot cut-side down until charred. Remove and turn over, drizzle the vinegar onto the layers. Remove the stalk and allow the layers to fall apart.

almond foam:

Place the almonds, milk and oil in a pan and bring to the boil. Remove from the heat and infuse for 20 minutes. Place in a blender and blitz. Pass the contents through a fine sieve and place into a clean pan. Add the soya lecithin and season with salt. Reheat but do not boil. Using a hand blender pulse the liquid to make foam.

thyme jus:

Roast the bones in a frying pan with a little vegetable oil. Drain and place in a clean saucepan. Fry the shallots, garlic and mushrooms in the butter until golden brown, drain and deglaze with the vinegar. Add to the bones. Reduce the wine by half in a clean pan and add to the bones. Reduce the stocks in a clean pan by half and add to the bones. Place the saucepan with all of the ingredients in it on the stove and bring to the boil, skim and reduce to a simmer. Simmer for 45 minutes. Pass through a fine sieve and add the thyme, then reduce to a sauce consistency. Pass through a fine sieve once again. Season with salt.

truffle dressing:

Boil the egg for 3 minutes and refresh in ice water. Remove the yolk and place in a round-bottomed bowl. Add the vinegar and a pinch of salt. Whisk continuously while slowly pouring the oils onto the egg to form a mayonnaise consistency. Add the truffle and check the flavour. Add more vinegar if required or more oil if slightly too acidic. Season with salt.

to serve:

Roast the langoustine in a hot pan with a little vegetable oil and butter. Season with salt. Heat a plate. Wilt the pousse in a clean pan and season with salt, then add the zest. Place the frisee and asparagus in a bowl and season with salt, then dress with the truffle dressing. Place the drained pousse to the left of the plate. Slice the rabbit loin into four rounds on an angle. Arrange neatly on the pousse. Place the tortellini to the right of the plate. Arrange the langoustine around the tortellini and the asparagus on top of the langoustine. Using a dessert spoon scoop out three pieces of bavoise and arrange around the plate. Arrange two shallot layers neatly next to the rabbit loin. Spoon a little of the jus over and around the dish. Neatly arrange the frisee around the dish with the chervil and truffle. Spoon a little foam over and around the dish. Serve.

Chef's tip:

When you make the tortellini filling roll a little in cling film and tie the ends. Cook in boiling water and remove the mix. Taste to check the seasoning and correct as necessary. This prevents you making the tortellini to find that the mousse is not correctly seasoned!

BITTER CHOCOLATE PARFAIT, RUM & RAISIN, BANANA & CORIANDER

BY SIMON MCKENZIE

I am a fan of using sponges in my desserts. I think it is a great way of adding a texture as well as a flavour and it is there to soak up any sauces, foams or ices that melt like the bread on a main course!

Serves 4
Preparation time: 2 hours 30 minutes
Cooking time: 1 hour

Special equipment:
30 x 20cm cake tin, sugar thermometer, mixer, 10 x 20cm tray, blender, fine sieve, ice-cream machine, hand blender, squeezy bottle.

Planning ahead:
The parfait and tuile mix need to be made at least a day in advance. The ice cream and foam need to chill overnight. The chocolate ganache and panna cotta will need to be in the fridge for at least 4 hours to set.

INGREDIENTS

muscovado sponge:

100g	muscovado sugar
100g	butter
100g	eggs, beaten
100g	soft plain flour
5g	baking powder

parfait:

150g	caster sugar
125ml	water
5	large free-range egg yolks
150g	72% dark chocolate
300ml	double cream
	cocoa powder, for dusting

chocolate tuile:

10g	butter
16g	water
8g	glucose
30g	caster sugar
0.5g	pectin
100g	Valrhona 100% chocolate
20g	cocoa powder

coriander ice cream:

150g	coriander, picked and washed
4	egg yolks
270g	sugar
50g	glucose
500g	milk
200g	crème fraîche
300ml	yoghurt

banana foam:

100g	caster sugar
50g	butter
3	bananas, sliced

150ml	Malibu
500ml	full-fat milk
10g	soya lecithin

white chocolate ganache:

200g	Philadelphia cream cheese
325g	double cream
200g	white chocolate
2	vanilla pods, seeds only

rum and raisin panna cotta:

50g	raisins
100ml	rum
75ml	full-fat milk
225ml	double cream
1	vanilla pod
35g	caster sugar
2	leaves gelatine

caramelised banana:

100g	caster sugar
1	banana, halved
10g	Malibu

treacle oil:

150g	hazelnut oil
50g	black treacle

METHOD

muscovado sponge:

Preheat the oven to 180°C. Place the sugar and butter in a mixing bowl with a paddle attachment and beat until the mixture changes to a light brown colour, around 5 minutes. Gradually add the eggs. Sieve the flour and baking powder together and fold into the cake mixture by hand. Pour into the cake tin and bake in the oven for 20-30 minutes. Remove from the tin and cool. Cut into slices 1cm thick then into rectangles 9 x 1cm.

parfait:

To make a sugar syrup place the sugar and water into a pan and bring to the boil. Using the thermometer boil until it reaches 118°C. Place the yolks in the mixer bowl and place on the machine with a whisk attachment. Turn onto full speed and pour the sugar syrup over the yolks slowly. Melt the chocolate in a bowl over a pan of hot water. Semi whip the cream in a bowl until it thickens. Mix the chocolate and cream together with a spatula and add the yolks. Line the tray, pour in the mixture and freeze. Remove the parfait from the tray and, using a hot knife, cut into rectangles 9 x 1cm. Dust with cocoa powder.

chocolate tuile:

Preheat the oven to 120°C. Boil the butter, water and glucose in a saucepan. Mix the sugar and pectin together and add to the boiling liquids, then bring back to the boil. Add the remaining ingredients and cool. Spread thinly onto a non-stick tray. Bake in the oven until the mixture starts to bubble. Remove and cool. Break into random shards.

coriander ice cream:

Blanch the coriander in boiling water for 3 minutes and refresh in iced water. Drain and dry in a clean cloth. Mix the yolks, sugar and glucose together. In a clean pan bring the milk to the boil, pour over the yolks and return to the pan. Place on a gentle heat and stir continuously until the mixture coats the back of a spoon. Pour into the blender and add the remaining ingredients. Turn the blender on full for 5 minutes. Pass through a fine sieve and place in a container. Cover and chill overnight in the fridge. Pour into an ice-cream machine and churn according to the manufacturer's instructions.

banana foam:

Place the sugar and butter into a saucepan and place on the stove. Cook until it becomes a caramel then add the bananas and Malibu. Keep on the stove until the bananas are caramelised, then add the milk. Bring to the boil then remove from the heat and cool. Leave covered in the fridge overnight. Place the foam into the blender and turn onto full speed for 5 minutes. Pour through a fine sieve into a clean pan and add the soya lecithin. Reheat the foam but do not boil; using a hand blender pulse the liquid to create foam.

white chocolate ganache:

Whisk the cream cheese in a mixer until it thickens. Separately semi whip the cream. Melt the chocolate in a bowl over a pan of hot water with the scraped-out vanilla pod seeds. Add the cream to the cream cheese by hand with a spatula then add the chocolate. Place into a piping bag. Chill until the mixture sets.

rum and raisin panna cotta:

Soak the raisins in the rum for 1 hour. Meanwhile, bring the milk and cream to the boil; infuse with the vanilla pod and sugar. Soak the gelatine in cold water. Pass the liquid and add the soaked gelatine to the milk and cream. Drain the raisins and add the rum to the milk and cream. Stir over ice until the mixture is semi-thick. Chop the raisins into 2mm dice approximately. Add them right at the end, just before setting. Pour into a container and chill.

caramelised banana:

Place the sugar in a clean frying pan and place on the stove. Heat until it forms a caramel. Carefully place the bananas cut-side down in the caramel then add the Malibu. Cook on the heat until the bananas are caramelised. Turn over and remove from the pan.

treacle oil:

Warm the oil and add the treacle. Place in a squeezy bottle and keep in a warm area.

to serve:

Place one piece of sponge to the left and slightly down on a plate and another piece of sponge to the right and slightly up. Place a piece of parfait on top of each piece of sponge. Using a dessert spoon scoop out three pieces of panna cotta and place in between the parfait. Pipe two dollops of ganache against the parfait, one at the top and one at the bottom. Using a dessert spoon scoop out four pieces of banana and place in between the parfait. Using a dessert spoon dipped in cold water form two quenelles of the ice cream and place in between the parfait. Spoon the banana foam over the elements in between the parfaits. Place three shards of tuille sticking up out of the elements in between the parfaits. Shake the treacle oil bottle and drizzle around the plate. Serve.

Chef's tip:

The majority of this dish can be made in advance; the sponge and the parfait could even be made up to a month in advance and stored in the freezer.

Steven MacCallum

Steven was born in Argyll and raised on a hill farm. Later he moved to Shropshire where he began his training before moving back to Scotland.

His career has taken him to various locations around the world including stints in Sydney and Melbourne as well as two years working alongside Bryan Webb at Hilaire Restaurant in London.

The abundant game, wild foods and soft fruits available in Perthshire help tremendously with his menu planning and fish is landed only an hour away in the small fishing towns on the Fife coast. Having previously worked with the Allen family as Head Chef at The Airds Hotel, Port Appin, Steven has again joined up with them at Kinloch House.

Kinloch House

{ *Located in the heart of glorious Perthshire, famous for its stunningly beautiful countryside with lochs, rivers and trees, Kinloch House is the ideal base from which to explore the area while staying in a family-run Scottish country house providing a warm, welcoming and friendly environment.*

Dating from 1840 the charming house offers bedrooms and public rooms individually appointed with fine fabrics and furnishings and a stunning entrance hall with log fire, oak-panelled staircase and first floor portrait gallery while the elegant dining room serves quality food using the finest local ingredients. The indoor swimming pool and treatment room offer the opportunity to indulge at the end of the day.

ROAST LANGOUSTINE & RED MULLET WITH AUBERGINE PUREE & VEGETABLE RELISH
BY STEVEN MACCALLUM

This dish is fairly simple to produce but is visually stunning with clean, fresh flavours.

Serves 4
Preparation time: 1½ hours
Cooking time: 5 minutes

Special equipment:
Food processor.

Planning ahead:
N/A

INGREDIENTS

langoustine and red mullet:

12	large langoustine
4	small red mullet fillets

aubergine purée:

1	aubergine
1	clove garlic, chopped
juice of 1 lemon	
1	pinch salt
50ml	rapeseed oil

vegetable relish:

1	carrot
1	red pepper
1	shallot
1 tbsp	capers
6	green olives, pitted
1 tbsp	sherry vinegar

to serve:
rapeseed oil, as required
small soft herb leaves, as required
lemon vinaigrette, as required

METHOD

langoustine and red mullet:

Remove the heads and shells from the langoustines. Cut the red mullet fillets into three.

aubergine purée:

Preheat the oven to 250°C. Place the whole aubergine on a baking tray and bake in the oven for approximately 45 minutes until soft. While still hot remove the skin and lightly press the flesh into a sieve to remove excess juice. Place in a food processor with the other ingredients and blend till smooth, then pass through a fine sieve.

vegetable relish:

Finely chop all the ingredients and mix with the vinegar.

to serve:

Season and pan roast the langoustines and red mullet in the oil. Place on plates with spoonfuls of purée and small mounds of vegetable relish. Arrange the herb leaves around and dress with the vinaigrette.

HERB-CRUSTED LOIN OF PERTHSHIRE LAMB, SWEETBREADS, GOLDEN BEETROOT, CEP & POTATO GRATIN
BY STEVEN MACCALLUM

I chose this dish to highlight the wonderful lamb of Perthshire.

Serves 4
Preparation time: 2 hours
Cooking time: 20 minutes

Special equipment:
Food processor/blender.

Planning ahead:
The gratin can be made in advance then reheated as required.

INGREDIENTS

lamb:

1	loin of lamb
500g	sweetbreads

herb crust:

200g	white breadcrumbs
100g	butter
100g	Cheddar cheese
2 tbsp	chopped parsley
1 tbsp	chopped rosemary
½ tbsp	chopped tarragon

cep and potato gratin:

1	large onion
250g	butter
500g	Maris Piper potatoes
200g	ceps
salt and pepper	

golden beetroot:

1	large golden beetroot
20g	salt
100ml	white wine vinegar
water, to cover	
1	sprig thyme

lamb sauce:

lamb bones saved from the loin	
oil, as required	
2	sticks celery, chopped
1	onion, chopped
1	carrot, chopped
1	bulb garlic
200ml	Madeira
1 litre	lamb stock

to serve:

butter, as required
sliced ceps, sautéed
broad beans, cooked

METHOD

lamb:

Remove the bone (reserve for the sauce) and trim the lamb loin. Blanch the sweetbreads in boiling water, cool and remove the skin. Set aside.

herb crust:

Place all the ingredients in a food processor and blend till it all binds together. Place the mixture between sheets of greaseproof paper and roll out till 3mm thick, then place in the fridge to chill.

cep and potato gratin:

Preheat the oven to 200°C. Thinly slice the onion and cook in the butter until soft. Thinly slice the potatoes and ceps and layer with the onion and butter mixture in a baking tray, then season. Bake in the oven for 45 minutes or until the potatoes are cooked.

golden beetroot:

Place the beetroot in a saucepan with the other ingredients and boil until tender. Keep the beetroot covered and top up with water when required. Peel and dice the beetroot.

lamb sauce:

Chop the lamb bones, brown in a little oil and drain into a colander. Brown off the vegetables in the same pan and drain. Deglaze the pan with the Madeira, place the bones and vegetables back into the pan and top up with the stock. Simmer for 1 hour and then pass through a sieve and reduce the sauce by half.

to serve:

Preheat the oven to 220°C. Season and brown off the lamb loin and then place into the oven for 6 minutes. Remove from the oven, place the strip of herb crust on top of the lamb and brown under the grill. Leave to rest in a warm place. Sauté the sweetbreads in butter. Heat the gratin and beetroot. Serve the lamb on a plate with the beetroot, gratin, sweetbreads, ceps, broad beans and lamb sauce.

RASPBERRY & HAZELNUT TART WITH ICED VANILLA YOGHURT

BY STEVEN MACCALLUM

This dish was chosen as it makes use of the berries for which this area is famous.

Serves 4
Preparation time: 30 minutes
Cooking time: 30-40 minutes

Special equipment:
Ice-cream machine.

Planning ahead:
The iced yoghurt can be made in advance.

INGREDIENTS

pastry:

125g	butter
225g	plain flour
25g	caster sugar
1	egg

hazelnut filling:

170g	caster sugar
170g	butter
3	eggs
170g	ground hazelnuts
4 tbsp	raspberry jam
hazelnuts, as required	
raspberries, as required	

iced vanilla yoghurt:

90g	glucose
140g	caster sugar
140ml	water
1	vanilla pod
juice of 1 lemon	
500g	Greek yoghurt

to serve:

fresh raspberries

METHOD

pastry:
Rub the butter with the flour and sugar until the mixture resembles breadcrumbs.

Mix in the egg and form the mixture into a ball, wrap in cling film and chill for 20 minutes. Roll out the pastry and line a 30cm tart case.

hazelnut filling:
Preheat the oven to 180°C. Beat the sugar and butter till light then add the eggs and ground hazelnuts. Spoon four tablespoons of raspberry jam into the tart case and spread out evenly. Spoon in the hazelnut filling and level out. Scatter hazelnuts and raspberries on the top and bake in the oven for 30-40 minutes until golden brown.

iced vanilla yoghurt:
Boil the glucose, sugar, water and vanilla pod together. Remove from the heat and add the lemon juice and yoghurt. Chill and churn in an ice-cream machine.

to serve:
Cut a slice of tart and serve with a scoop of iced vanilla yoghurt and garnish with the fresh raspberries.

Wales

History and royal connections in the land of song

Wales is a country of outstanding natural beauty, with mountain peaks, brooding forests and national parks, some of the most beautiful beaches in the British Isles, broad rivers and lakes. Remarkable castles, abbeys, ruined mansions, great country houses and towns and cities with exceptional architecture provide huge variety. The Principality guards its Celtic heritage jealously and nowhere is this seen better than at the famous Eisteddfod in Llangollen, the male voice choirs that are still such a part of the life of the country, poetry and the fervour of the national sport of Rugby Union. Welsh food, invariably organic, including lamb, beef and Caerphilly cheese, has an excellent reputation and is highly sought after. Other Welsh traditions include laverbread, consisting of boiled seaweed, Welsh Rarebit – melted cheese on toast and Welsh Cakes, also known as Griddle Scones. The Welsh language remains a fundamental part of the nationhood and is taught in schools as a living language. All the road signs and public information notices in the Principality are bi-lingual.

Shane Hughes

Shane has spent his career training in some of the top restaurants and hotels in the UK – The Connaught, Whatley Manor and the Juniper – and with chefs such as John Burton Race. He has since developed his own style at Ynyshir Hall and has become an avid forager of the local countryside – you will often find him in the hills collecting mushrooms and wild garlic or at the salt marshes gathering samphire.

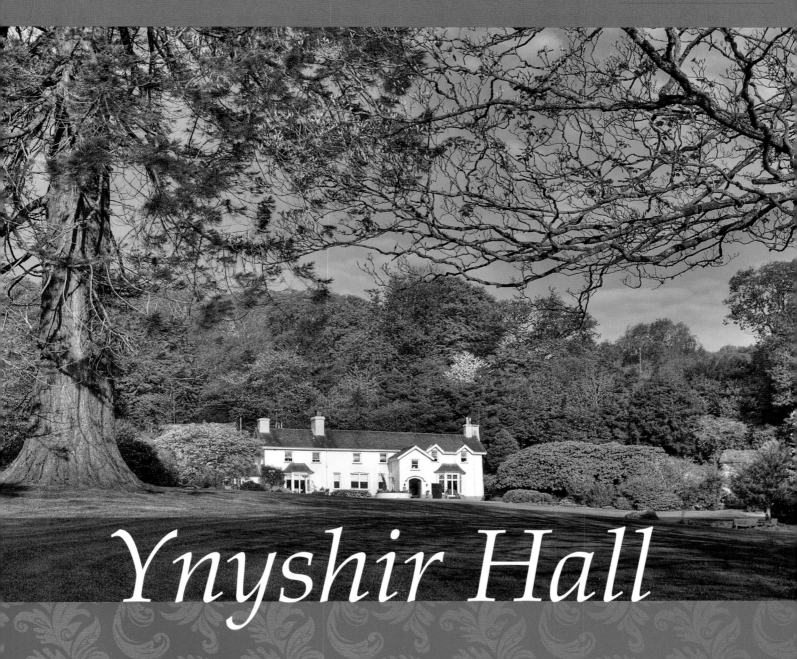

Ynyshir Hall

{ *This imposing white manor house used to belong to Queen Victoria who left her imprint on the décor and gardens and loved this part of the kingdom because of the abundance of birds flying in from the nearby estuary and beaches.*

Located in Machynlleth, ancient capital of Wales, the house is now run by Joan Reen and her husband, the painter Rob Reen. They have made it their own without losing sight of the influence of Her Royal Highness Queen Victoria, whose favourite trees still stand where she planted them. And now it is your turn to enjoy a royal welcome...

TORTELLINI OF SPICED BLACK BEEF SHIN, BORTH BAY LOBSTER & MUSHROOM SAUCE

BY SHANE HUGHES

Surf and turf with a twist.

Serves 8
Preparation time: 1 hour
Cooking time: Allow at least 4 hours.

Special equipment:
Planetary mixer.

Planning ahead:
Prepare at least 1 day in advance.

INGREDIENTS

braised beef shin:

2	onions
3	carrots
4	sticks celery
2	leeks
5	cloves garlic
1	shin of beef
olive oil, as required	
2 litres	chicken stock
1	bottle medium sweet white wine
4 tbsp	curry paste
4 tbsp	tomato purée
4	bay leaves
5	sprigs of thyme
7	tomatoes, seeds removed
4	chillies chopped
10	cardamom pods
½	bunch coriander

lobster:

2	medium-sized lobsters, approximately 700g each

mushroom sauce:

5	shallots, sliced
3	cloves garlic, crushed
4	sprigs of thyme
2	bay leaves
500g	mushroom/trimmings
50ml	olive oil
½	bottle Madeira
1.5 litres	chicken stock
400ml	double cream
25ml	truffle oil
salt and pepper	
lemon juice, as required	

pasta:

8	egg yolks
250g	'00' pasta flour
10g	olive oil
50ml	water
saffron (optional)	

METHOD

braised beef shin:

Roughly chop the onions, carrots, celery, leeks and garlic. Sear off the shin in a hot pan with olive oil until there is lots of colour, add the vegetables and continue to colour until golden brown. Pour the white wine over and reduce to a quarter, add the curry paste and tomato purée, then cook for 2 more minutes.

Finally add the remaining ingredients except the coriander and bring to a simmer, cover the pan tightly with foil or use a tight-fitting lid and braise in the oven at 175°C for 2 hours, then remove and leave to cool in the stock.

When cool, remove from the stock and pick through the beef, discarding any gristle or fat. The beef should then be flaked into a bowl and bound with a little of the reduced cooking liquor and some chopped coriander, then chilled ready for the tortellini.

lobster:

Cook your lobster depending on its size – a medium-sized lobster = 6 minutes cooking on a gentle boil. After you remove the lobster from the water, place it on a tray and immediately cover it with cling film to trap in the steam and heat, then refrigerate until cold.

mushroom sauce:

Sauté the shallots, garlic, thyme, bay leaves and mushroom trimmings in the olive oil, with no colour, until soft. Pour in the Madeira and reduce to a quarter, add the stock and simmer for 45 minutes then pass through a sieve. Reduce the stock to a sauce consistency then add the cream and truffle oil. Boil until the cream thickens and season to taste with salt, pepper and lemon juice.

pasta:

Mix the egg yolks and flour together in a small planetary mixer, pour in the olive oil and water and wait for the mix to bind then remove and knead for a few minutes. Rest for 1 hour covered with a damp cloth before rolling and shaping.

For the tortellini simply work the beef mixture into balls and wrap with thin sheets of pasta, ensuring there are no holes – the shape is not important. A little saffron in the cooking water will give the tortellini a lovely bright yellow colour. Boil for approximately 5 minutes.

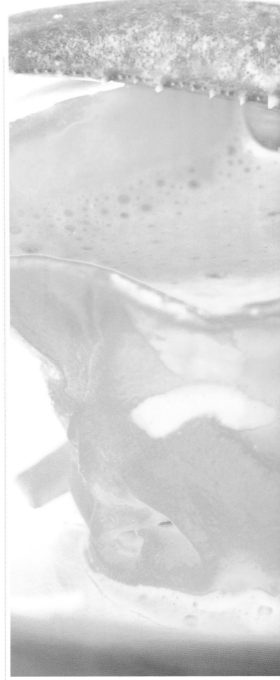

to serve:

Serve the tortellini straightaway with the lobster, mushroom sauce and some vegetables of your choice.

Chef's tip:

You can use any mushroom trimmings for the mushroom sauce as they all contain great flavour, but wild mushrooms are best.

Serves 8
Preparation time: 4 hours
Cooking time: 10 minutes

Special equipment:
N/A

Planning ahead:
The shallot crisps can be made a few hours
in advance.

INGREDIENTS

onion cream:

300g	onions, finely chopped
5g	garlic purée
30g	butter, unsalted
5g	salt
1g	pepper
125ml	double cream
lemon juice, as required	

lightly curried potatoes:

300g	shallots
5g	turmeric
10g	mild curry powder
3	cloves garlic, crushed
10g	salt
1g	black pepper
75g	sweet chilli sauce
1	bay leaf
5g	thyme
1.25 litres	chicken stock
1	star anise
3	cardamon pods
20	new potatoes, peeled

shallot crisps:

4	banana shallots
flour, as required	
oil, for deep frying	
salt, to taste	
sugar, to taste	

cod and scallops:

500g	fillet of cod
8	scallops
olive oil, as required for sautéing	

COD & SCALLOPS, LIGHTLY CURRIED NEW POTATOES, ONION CREAM & SHALLOT CRISPS
BY SHANE HUGHES

This lightly spiced dish contains the flavours of kedgeree without the rice.

METHOD

onion cream:
Put all of the ingredients except the cream into a small pan. Cover the pan with cling film (approximately 20 layers) and then tie string around the cling film – this is to pressure cook the onions. Cook on a gentle heat for about 40 minutes.

Remove the cling film and continue cooking to dry out the onions, add the cream and boil for 2 minutes then blend until smooth, season with a touch of lemon juice and chill until required.

lightly curried potatoes:
Slice up the shallots and put in a pan with all the ingredients except the potatoes, bring to the boil and leave to cool, then cook the potatoes in the stock at a gentle heat until just soft to the touch. Leave to cool in the stock and store.

shallot crisps:
Slice the shallots into rings with a sharp knife, separate them and pat them dry on tissue. Roll them in a bowl of flour, shake them off and deep fry at 140°C then sprinkle with salt and sugar. Leave somewhere warm for a few hours to crisp up.

cod and scallops:
Sauté the cod first in hot olive oil until light golden brown and ensure that you let it rest before serving for an even texture to the fish. Sauté the scallop in hot olive oil until light golden brown, and serve immediately with the cod, potatoes, onion cream and shallot crisps.

Chef's tip:
Buy the highest quality fish that is available to you, and ensure it is clean and dry.

HOT CHOCOLATE GALLETTE, CLEMENTINE SORBET & NATURAL YOGHURT
BY SHANE HUGHES

A rich and silky variation of chocolate fondant, wonderful when paired with the tart sorbet.

Serves 8
Preparation time: 30 minutes.
Cooking time: A few minutes.

Special equipment:
Sorbet machine.

Planning ahead:
The gallette can be made in advance.

INGREDIENTS

hot chocolate gallette:

150g	dark chocolate
175g	butter
5	eggs
175g	caster sugar
75g	strong flour
150g	cornflour
300g	crunchy nut cornflakes
3	eggs, for coating

clementine sorbet:

2	litres clementine orange juice
zest of 2 oranges	
150g	caster sugar
100ml	Cointreau
400ml	light stock syrup

to serve:

natural yoghurt

METHOD

hot chocolate gallette:

Melt the chocolate and butter together. Whisk the 5 eggs and sugar together until the mixture reaches a sabayon. Fold the chocolate and butter into the sabayon then sieve in the flour and mix completely. Chill and continue stirring on and off for 3 hours until it becomes glossy. Put into a piping bag and partially freeze. Pipe thin sausage shapes onto the cornflour on a tray then refreeze. Grind up the crunchy nut cornflakes, roll the chocolate shapes through the whisked eggs one by one and then through the ground cornflakes. Repeat this action to ensure a good coating, work fast and freeze straightaway.

clementine sorbet:

Reduce 1 litre of the juice in a pan with the zest, sugar and alcohol until it becomes a light coloured syrup. Churn all of the ingredients together in a sorbet machine following the manufacturer's instructions until smooth. Add extra alcohol to taste.

to serve:

Deep fry the gallette at 180°C until golden brown, drain on tissue and serve with the sorbet and yoghurt.

Ireland

{ *'A hundred thousand welcomes' is the English translation of an old Gaeilge greeting, "Cead Mile Failte". This welcome embodies what Ireland represents to the visitor.*

A small island which can offer the greatest hospitality and welcome anyone can experience. This small isle on the fringe of Western Europe is home to 4.2 million people, but it has a heritage and history which pre-dates the Ancient Pyramids of Egypt. The lush green of the fields and hills, the historic gems, ancient monuments and undiscovered historic castles will long remain in the memory of those who come here. However, what Ireland is best known for is the people who live here. The image of a friendly nation that goes out of its way to greet and help is not a myth; it exists and permeates every facet of Irish life. Much of Irish life revolves around the many pubs and restaurants, where the welcome is always warm. In terms of food, the Irish tend to keep it simple, with dishes such as lamb, Irish Stew, homemade cheeses, fresh fish, fish and chips (chippers) and many more. There is a heart and soul to this little island which once experienced is hard to forget.

Fred Cordonnier

As a third generation descendant of a line of bakers and pastry chefs, Fred takes his cooking philosophy from his French gourmet heritage. After his apprenticeship he took his first job as pastry commis in a Michelin-starred restaurant on the French Riviera and then onto London.

It was when Fred went to work under Bruno Loubet that he took an interest in working in the other side of the kitchen. From there Fred went to the two Michelin-starred Le Manoir aux Quat'Saisons under Raymond Blanc, gaining more experience in both kitchen and pastry.

Fred arrived in Ireland and worked in Longueville House and the K Club before moving to Restaurant Patrick Guilbaud, the only two Michelin-starred/5 AA rosette restaurant in Ireland, where he held the position of Head Chef for 10 years. Following that he worked for U2 at the Clarence Hotel before opening a small restaurant in partnership with the owner of the Brown Bear pub in Two Mile House, Co Kildare. The restaurant was named Newcomer of the Year in 2010 and won many great reviews. Now he is Executive Chef for Ballyfin.

Fred places an emphasis on the very finest ingredients and says "the star is not the chef but the produce and must be treated respectfully." He sources as much produce as possible from local artisan suppliers and is delighted to have the walled garden with its herbs, salads and vegetables at Ballyfin as a resource.

Ballyfin

{ *Set at the foot of the Slieve Bloom Mountains in the centre of Ireland, Ballyfin is a place of history and romance, of tranquillity and great natural beauty.*

The house has long been admired as the most lavish Regency mansion in Ireland, and after eight years of restoration, Ballyfin reopened in May 2011 as a small country house hotel like no other. It offers the very best of Irish hospitality in the most beautiful surroundings imaginable. With only 15 rooms for the 600-acre estate, it is the perfect place for a break from the stresses of the modern world and provides discretion and privacy like few other destinations. Come and enjoy life in one of the greatest country houses in Ireland.

CRUBEEN, CHEEK, BELLY, EARS, CARROTS, WATERCRESS, ONION
BY FRED CORDONNIER

This dish is my take on the traditional dishes from Cork; they used to serve them in the English market in Cork city.

Serves 4
Preparation time: 2 hours
Cooking time: See individual recipes

Special equipment:
Food blender, sharp mandoline, deep fryer.

Planning ahead:
Most of this recipe needs to be prepared a day in advance. Ask your butcher to cut the pig trotters long and only from the back leg – the front ones are tougher as they use them to dig the ground for food. Also make sure there is no nail remaining and burn any hair left with a blowtorch.

INGREDIENTS

crubeen croquette:

8	pig trotters
1	onion 'pique' ie. with a bay leaf secured to it with 4 cloves
2	medium carrots
1	stick celery
1	tomato
2	cloves garlic
½ tbsp	black pepper

pigs' ears:

4	pig ears, cleaned and any hair burned with a blowtorch
2	eggs, beaten
150g	fine dry breadcrumbs

to finish the croquettes:

2 tbsp	brunoise each of carrot, shallot, celery, leek and flat leaf parsley
2 tbsp	Dijon mustard
75ml	dry white wine
	sea salt
	freshly ground white pepper
200g	flour
4	eggs, beaten
200g	fine dry breadcrumbs

pork cheek:

1	carrot
1	celery stick
1	small onion
1	shallot
50ml	vegetable oil
25g	unsalted butter
1	sprig thyme
1	sprig rosemary
3	cloves garlic
	salt, to taste
7	juniper berries
½ tsp	fennel seed
¼ tsp	cumin seed
3	star anise
1	bay leaf
2	tomatoes
½ tbsp	tomato paste
300ml	white chicken stock
4	pork cheeks

pork belly:

1 x 500g	pork belly
2	large carrots, peeled and halved
½	garlic bulb
2	celery sticks, halved
3	small onions, peeled and quartered
2	shallots. peeled and halved
10g	salt
6	black peppercorns
1	bay leaf
1	small bunch thyme
	vegetable oil
50ml	balsamic vinegar

carrot purée:

25g	unsalted butter
300g	small carrots, peeled and finely chopped
2	sprigs tarragon
2	star anise
200ml	white chicken stock
100ml	double cream
	juice of 2 lemons
4g	caster sugar

pickled carrots:

300ml	fresh carrot juice
50g	caster sugar
20g	coriander seeds
1	sprig fresh tarragon
1	sprig fresh thyme
10	black peppercorns
100ml	water
100ml	white wine vinegar
100ml	white wine
250ml	olive oil
3	star anise
4	medium carrots of different colours with tops on, peeled
16	baby carrots with tops on, peeled

carrot gel:

300g	medium carrots. peeled and finely diced
3	star anise
200ml	fresh carrot juice
	sea salt
3g	agar agar

watercress purée:

5 litres	water
	rock salt, as required
1kg	watercress, picked
1 tsp	freshly grated horseradish
	butter, as required

baby onion shell:

20	baby onions
	vegetable oil
1	clove garlic
100ml	veal stock
1	sprig thyme

METHOD

crubeen croquette:

Place all the ingredients in a large pot on a medium heat, bring to a simmer and cook on a low heat for 3-4 hours until the meat falls off the bones. When cool enough to handle pick off all the meat, skin and everything else, only discarding the bones.

pigs' ears:

When there is 1 hour 30 minutes' cooking time left for the trotters add the ears in the same stock. When cooked delicately remove the ears, place on a cling-filmed tray side by side and cover with more cling film. Place another tray on top and add a weight to press the ears till cold and set. Using a sharp knife cut the ears into thin julienne, toss them in the eggs then into the breadcrumbs.

to finish the croquettes:

Mix all the picked trotter meat with the vegetables, parsley, mustard, wine and seasoning. Place on a sheet of cling film and roll into a tight sausage of 3cm diameter. Place in the fridge to set. Once set cut into little barrels 4cm high, roll in the flour, then the eggs and lastly the breadcrumbs and set aside.

pork cheek:

Peel and dice the carrots, celery, onion and shallot but keep separate. Heat up the oil and butter in a large casserole, add the carrot and slowly caramelise then add the thyme and rosemary. After 4-5 minutes add the celery and carry on cooking. After 3-4 minutes add the onion, shallot, garlic and salt and cook for a further 8 minutes. Add all the spices and bay leaf and cook for a further 2-3 minutes. Add the tomatoes and tomato paste and cook for another 2 minutes, then add the stock. Bring the casserole to a simmer, add the pork cheeks and top up with water if necessary. Place a lid on top and bake for 2-2½ hours at 170°C. Remove the cheeks from the liquid and keep warm. Pass the cooking liquor through a fine sieve in a pan and reduce to about 200ml, then add the cheeks to it.

pork belly:

Place the pork belly in a large pan and cover with cold water. Bring up to the boil then pour out the water, add more cold water then all the vegetables, salt, peppercorns, bay leaf and thyme. Bring to a slow simmer and skim off all the time. Place a weight on the pork to keep it submerged and gently simmer for 2-2½ hours. Once cooked place the belly skin-side down on a tray lined with cling film, then place the cling film over the top and add a light weight to compress the belly. Place in the fridge for at least 5 hours. With a sharp knife cut into cubes 2cm all round. In a pan heat up some vegetable oil and when very hot add the pork belly cubes, season and cook on each side until golden brown. Remove the fat from the pan, deglaze with the vinegar and reduce until sticky.

carrot purée:

Melt the butter in a saucepan over a low heat then sweat the carrots in it for a few minutes. Cover with a lid and cook for 4-5 minutes. Add the rest of the ingredients and cook until the carrots are soft, 6-8 minutes. Remove the star anise and put everything in the blender. Blend to a smooth purée. Warm through very gently when ready to serve.

pickled carrots:

Pass the carrot juice through a fine sieve into a pan, add the pickling ingredients (everything but the carrots), correct the seasoning and bring to a slow simmer. Slice the medium carrots lengthways on a mandoline as thinly as you can. Put the baby carrots in the pickling liquor for 3-4 minutes then add the carrot slices. Cook for 1-2 minutes, remove from the heat and leave the carrots to cool in the liquor.

carrot gel:

Place the carrots and star anise in a small pan, cover with the juice and season. Cook until soft. Remove the star anise and blend the mixture to a smooth purée in the blender. Weigh 300g and add the agar agar. Place in a small pan, bring to the boil and cook for 1 minute, mixing constantly. Let it set over ice. Once set place in the blender at full speed; to get to the right constituency you may need to add a little boiling water — the gel should be smooth and form a well in the blender.

watercress purée:

Heavily season the water and bring to a fast rolling boil, add the watercress and cook for a couple of minutes. Strain and place in the blender. Blend to a smooth purée, add the horseradish then pour over ice to cool it down very fast to keep it bright green. Warm up gently with a little butter before serving.

baby onion shell:

Cut the onions in half from top to bottom, leaving the skin and roots. In a large pan heat up a drizzle of oil, once almost smoking place the onions in face down with the garlic. Let them caramelise to a nice brown, then remove the fat and add the stock and thyme. Bring back to the boil, cover with a lid, remove from the heat and let the onions cool down in the stock. Once cold break down into little shells, discarding the skin and centre parts.

to serve:

Cook the croquette and pigs' ears in the fryer at 190°C until golden. Slowly warm up the cheeks in their cooking liquor. Sear and deglaze the pork belly. Gently warm up the purées and onion shells. Decorate the plate with carrot gel and pickled carrots as pictured.

SQUAB PIGEON, FOIE GRAS, BLACK FIG, PUMPKIN, PARSNIP, ROSCOFF ONION, CELERY

BY FRED CORDONNIER

I love cooking big 'plumpy' squab,with the last fruit of the summer and the first autumn vegetables – and foie gras, of course.

Serves 4

| Preparation time: | 1 hour plus longer if you are deboning the squab yourself |
| Cooking time: | Approximately 1 hour 10 minutes altogether |

Special equipment:
Vac pac machine and bags, water bath (optional – if none use a good thermometer and a large pot), food blender, piping bag, meat slicer.

Planning ahead:
Order your squab in advance as the nice plumpy one are hard to get – you need them to be 500g plus. You may ask your butcher to debone the pigeon into halves with the leg bone still in place but no thigh bone and vac pac them side by side for you.

INGREDIENTS

squab pigeon:

4 x 500g+ squab pigeons	
6	cloves garlic, crushed
1	large sprig thyme

foie gras mousse:

250g	foie gras extra, diced
150g	single cream
2	eggs
sea salt	
Madeira, to taste	

black fig purée:

125g	black figs
75ml	red port
75ml	red wine
50g	sugar
juice of 1 lemon	
¼	cinnamon stick

pumpkin purée:

20g	unsalted butter
250g	pumpkin, peeled and cut into small cubes, seeds and 1 wedge reserved
2g	finely chopped sage
sea salt	
20g	honey
½ tbsp	lemon juice
35ml	double cream

pumpkin seeds:

seeds removed from the pumpkin
pumpkin seed oil
sea salt

pumpkin 'ribbons':

1	wedge reserved from the pumpkin
pumpkin seed oil, as required	
lemon juice, as required	
sea salt, as required	

girolle mushrooms:

200g	very small girolle mushrooms
sea salt	
30g	unsalted butter
1 tbsp	finely chopped confit shallots
1	good drop Madeira
2 tbsp	finely chopped chives

parsnip:

2	small new season parsnips
vegetable oil, as required	
20g	honey
1	clove garlic
1	sprig rosemary
veal stock, as required	

Roscoff onion:

4	small Roscoff onions left whole but with no skin
vegetable oil, as required	
1	clove garlic
1	sprig thyme
veal stock	

pan-fried foie gras:

4 x 50g pieces of foie gras extra	
sea salt, to taste	
Xeres vinegar, as required	

to serve:

butter, as required

METHOD

squab pigeon:

Debone the squab leaving the leg bone only and place in a vac pac bag with the garlic and thyme side by side, seal thinly and place in the water bath at 60.5°C for 15 minutes, then submerge in ice water and put away until needed.

foie gras mousse:

In the food blender mix the foie gras, cream and eggs together, add seasoning and a little drop of Madeira. Pour into a container – the mix must be 2-3cm deep. Cover with cling film and steam at 85°C for 15-20 minutes – it should be wobbly like a crème brûlée. Once cool place in a piping bag ready to pipe onto the plates.

black fig purée:

Place all the ingredients in a pan on a medium heat, bring to a simmer then reduce until the liquid is almost evaporated. Remove the cinnamon stick and place the mixture in the blender and purée until smooth. This purée should be sweet and sharp – you may need to add more sugar or lemon juice depending on the ripeness of the figs.

pumpkin purée:

Heat a pan on a low heat then melt the butter. Add all the other ingredients except the cream. Cover with a lid to sweat the vegetables and cook for 10 minutes on a low heat, stirring now and again so that the vegetables do not brown. Add the cream and bring to the boil. Pour into the blender but keep some of the cooking liquid back. Purée until smooth, adding more liquid if necessary.

pumpkin seeds:

Wash the pumpkin seeds with cold water and pat dry with a kitchen towel. Fry the seeds in a pan with the oil until golden brown. Drain on kitchen paper and season.

pumpkin 'ribbons':

Place the wedge of pumpkin onto the meat slicer and slice it as thin as possible. Lay out the slices on a tray and drizzle with oil, seasoning and a few drops of lemon juice. After a couple of minutes roll up these ribbons into shape.

girolle mushrooms:

Trim any roots and scrape any dirt from the mushrooms. Wash and dry them quickly. Place a small frying pan on a medium heat. Once hot add the mushrooms and a little salt. Let all the water from the mushrooms evaporate then add the butter and shallots. Cook for a couple of minutes, add the splash of Madeira and remove from the pan once the Madeira is almost evaporated. Correct the seasoning and add the chives.

parsnip:

Preheat the oven to 190°C. Peel the parsnips and cut them in half lengthways. Place a pan on a medium heat with a drop of oil, place the parsnips in on the cut side and colour until dark golden brown. Remove the oil and add the honey, garlic and rosemary and let it all caramelise, then add enough veal stock to come half way up the parsnips. Bring up to the boil, cover and finish in the oven for 5-7 minutes until cooked through.

Roscoff onion:

Preheat the oven to 190°C. Cut off one-third of the top part of the onions. Place a small pan with a little oil on a medium heat Once hot place the onions in cut-side down and roast them until very dark. Remove the oil, add the garlic, thyme and enough stock to come half way up the onion. Bring to a simmer, cover with a lid and cook in the oven for 15-20 minutes depending on the size of the onions.

pan-fried foie gras:

When ready to serve season the foie gras and sear in a hot pan until nicely caramelised on one side, remove any excess fat then turn the foie gras onto the other side and deglaze with the vinegar. Keep warm.

to serve:

In a pan place a couple of spoons of butter and heat it up until melted, foamy and it starts to 'sing'. Place the squab skin-side down and cook on the skin side only until the skin is very crispy – don't hesitate to add a little more butter if needed and also to control the temperature of the butter as it should be nutty all the way through the cooking process. Once a drop of blood appears on top of the breasts turn them over for 30 seconds, remove from the pan and leave to rest for a few minutes. It is essential to cook the legs a little longer or they won't be cooked through – you will have to twist the breasts onto the legs in order not to overcook them. While the pigeon are resting cook the foie gras and heat up the rest of the garnishes. Place attractively on a large plate as pictured.

Serves 4
Preparation time: 1 hour 30 minutes
Cooking time: 7 hours for the meringue,
   3 hours for the jelly

Special equipment:
Sugar thermometer, kitchen aid (mixer), small square frame, Pacojet, food blender, squeezy bottle, stick blender (optional), iSi siphon and two gas cylinders, silpat, piping bag and large plain nozzle.

Planning ahead:
Make the meringue at least 24 hours before you want to use it.

INGREDIENTS

meringue:

200g	caster sugar
80g	water
120g	egg whites

Chantilly cream:

1	vanilla pod
250g	whipping cream

strawberry jelly:

500g	strawberries
50-70g	caster sugar, depending on the ripeness of the strawberries
100g	water
	juice and zest of 1 orange
1	vanilla pod
3	sheets gelatine

sorbet:

50g	water
	juice of 1 lemon
50g	glucose
500g	strawberry purée

strawberry gel:

250g	strawberry purée
2.5g	agar agar
	syrup, as required

strawberry foam:

500g	strawberry purée
1	pinch citric acid
40g	pro cold espuma from 'Sosa'

strawberry tuile:

75g	strawberry purée
75g	fondant
150g	isomalt sugar

to serve:

small fresh strawberries tossed in a little lemon juice and sugar, as required
small strawberry flowers, as required
small strawberry leaves, as required

BALLYFIN 'MESS'
BY FRED CORDONNIER

Inspired by the classic Eton Mess, I changed the name as Ballyfin also used to be a private school. And we love our garden strawberries!

METHOD

meringue:

Make a syrup by mixing the sugar with the water in a small pan, then cook on a medium heat until it reaches 118°C on a sugar thermometer. Have the egg whites ready in the mixer bowl and once the thermometer has reached 118°C turn the machine to high speed and pour the hot syrup slowly into the egg whites – pour it near the edge of the bowl otherwise the syrup will fly everywhere. Whisk until cold then thinly spread the meringue onto parchment paper. Place in the oven at 50°C for 7 hours or until dry. Break up the meringue into small, squarish pieces.

Chantilly cream:

Split the vanilla pod lengthwise and with a sharp knife scrape the vanilla seeds into the cream. Let this infuse in the fridge for a couple of hours then slowly whisk until it becomes medium peaks.

strawberry jelly:

Place all the ingredients except the gelatine into a bowl, Place over a bain marie on a low heat for 3 hours. Strain the juice – you should have 300ml. Add the gelatine, mix well and pour into the frame. Let it set then cut into cubes 1cm all round.

sorbet:

Boil the water, juice and glucose and add to the purée. Place in the Pacojet beaker and freeze until hard all the way through. Churn with the Pacojet just before you are about to serve the dish.

strawberry gel:

Mix the purée and agar agar together in a pan and bring to the boil over a medium heat, whisking all the time for 1 minute. Remove from the pan into a container and let it set. Once set place the gel into the food blender with a little spoon of syrup and blitz at full speed; you may have to add a little more syrup to ensure the gel is at the right consistency as it should form a well in the blender. Place into a squeezy bottle.

strawberry foam:

Mix all the ingredients with a stick blender or whisk, place in a siphon bottle, charge with the two gas cylinders and shake well.

strawberry tuile:

Cook all the ingredients in a pan to 80°C (check on a sugar thermometer), spread on a silpat and dry overnight in a warm place. Once dry break up into pieces the same size and shape as the meringue.

to serve:

On a long oval plate pipe the Chantilly cream into a long line (15 cm) using the large plain nozzle. On top place pieces of meringue and a few strawberries in-between some piece of tuile, Place a few cube of jelly around, pipe some gel at the last moment, and add a few dots of foam and the sorbet. Add a few flowers and leaves. See the picture – don't worry too much, it's supposed to be a mess!

Chef's tip:

Don't eat all the strawberries or you won't finish the dessert!

Martijn Kajuiter

Martijn grew up in the countryside in the northern part of Holland. His passion for good food began at an early age, as his parents owned a restaurant and they were both wonderful cooks. Martijn has worked with Dutch master chefs Wynand Vogel, Gert Jan Hageman and Henk Savelberg. In 1995 he moved to London where he worked at L' Ortolan, then The Waterside, followed by La Tante Claire and The Restaurant at The Hyde Park. He returned to The Netherlands to work at Les Quatre Canetons as Head Chef. In 2000 the Restaurant De Kas opened and Martijn became Head Chef – in six years it became one of Holland's most exciting and successful restaurants. In October 2007 Martijn decided that a new challenge awaited him and joined The Cliff House Hotel. In May 2008 the hotel opened its doors and within 18 months Martijn was awarded a Michelin star.

The chefs work with a maximum amount of produce grown on Irish land, some in their own nursery, and fished from the Irish seas for both The House Restaurant and The Bar Restaurant.

Cliff House Hotel

{ *Overlooking Ardmore Bay, the Cliff House Hotel boasts truly extraordinary architecture: the hotel, which is literally built on to the side of the cliff, seems to spring forth from the cliffs.*

The terrace, the House Restaurant, the Spa and each guest room – most with a private balcony – on this relaxing islet enjoy exceptional views of the bay. With its direct access to the sea, the hotel offers numerous outdoor activities such as ocean kayaking, surfing, diving, walking, fishing and rock climbing but also visits to historical sites like St Declan's Well situated nearby on the famous Cliff Walk – the pathway starts at the side of the hotel and is the ideal starting point for walks accompanied by the sounds of the waves after a delicious dinner in the restaurant or before breakfast in the morning.

ARDMORE ORGANIC CARROTS 2011, CASHEL
BLUE, HAZELNUTS, GARDEN SHOOTS
BY MARTIJN KAJUITER

Ardmore – the small village where the Cliff House Hotel is located – has a strong reputation for growing root vegetables. As an acknowledgement I created this dish, which reflects my belief that the most simple ingredient can be the centre of attention by preparing this dish multiple ways, giving it several textures, structures and temperatures. The result is a very satisfying and pretty dish packed with flavour and depth which gives a true feel of the surroundings.

Serves 4
Preparation time: 2 hours
Cooking time: 30 minutes

Special equipment:
Pacojet, vacuum bag, steam oven, siphon, dehydrator.

Planning ahead:
The carrot sorbet needs to be made 24 hours in advance. The carrot espuma needs 4-6 hours in the fridge. All other elements can be made a little while in advance.

INGREDIENTS

carrot sorbet:

1 litre	fresh carrot juice
1	anise cube
2 tbsp	olive oil
2	leaves gelatine
salt	
60g	glycerine

carrot purée:

500g	organic carrots
1 tbsp	olive oil
½ tsp	fennel seeds
peel of ⅛ orange	
sea salt and white pepper	

carrot drop:

100g	carrot purée (see above)
1g	glucolactate (spherification agent)
zest of ½ orange	
Sezchuan pepper and sea salt	
2.5g	algin powder
500ml	water

carrot mousse:

1	leaf gelatine
150ml	single cream
50ml	soft Ardsallagh goat's cheese
250g	carrot purée (see above)
salt/pink pepper	

carrot espuma:

2	leaves gelatine
400ml	fresh carrot juice
½g	saffron powder
0.1g	cardamom powder
60g	egg whites
salt	

purple carrot confit:

2	purple carrots
50ml	cumin oil
salt, thyme, pepper	

purple carrot pickle:

1	purple carrot
50ml	red wine vinegar
caster sugar, to taste	
twigs fresh tarragon	
sea salt and pepper	

carrot cylinder:

| 40g | isomalt |
| 100g | carrot purée (see above) |

baby carrot sweet and sour:

16	baby carrots
1	banana shallot
250ml	water
75ml	white wine vinegar
¼	lemon
rosemary/bayleaf	
10g	caster sugar
5g	salt

carrot vinaigrette:

200ml	fresh carrot juice
40ml	orange juice
1 tsp	olive oil
1	leaf gelatine
20ml	white wine vinegar
60ml	hazelnut oil
sea salt/white pepper	

Cashel Blue dome:

150g	Cashel Blue
½ tbsp	hazelnut oil
100ml	single cream
salt and pepper	
7.2g	kappa
500ml	carrot juice

balsamic tapioca:

100ml	water
200ml	balsamic vinegar
25g	Tapioca pearls, small
olive oil	
salt	

olive oil crumbs:

80g	olive oil or your favourite oil
25g	tapioca maltodextrin
3g	salt (only if using olive oil)

garnish:

mustard leaves
Barbara cress or watercress
beetroot cress
mizuna
Cashel Blue cubes
toasted nuts

METHOD

carrot sorbet:
Mix the carrot juice with the anise cube, oil and gelatine and let it reduce on a medium heat until 700ml is left. Chill, season to taste, add the glycerine and freeze in a Pacojet cup for 24 hours. Churn in the Pacojet for immediate use.

carrot purée:
Peel the carrots and slice in even chunks, then mix with the olive oil, fennel seeds, orange peel and seasoning. Put in a vacuum bag, seal very tight and cook in a steam oven on 100°C until tender. Purée in a blender until smooth, pass through a fine sieve and cool ready for further use.

carrot drop:
Mix the carrot purée with the glucolactate. Add the peel, season with the pepper and salt. Cover and cool until needed. Make an algin bath by mixing the algin powder with lukewarm water until the powder is dissolved, then cool the algin until needed.

carrot mousse:
Soak the gelatine. Measure off 50ml cream and heat, dissolve the gelatine in this, add the goat's cheese plus the remaining cream and whisk up until thick, mix through the carrot purée and season to taste. Put the mousse in a piping bag and cool until needed.

carrot espuma:
Soak the gelatine. Heat through 100ml of carrot juice and add the saffron and cardamom powder, then dissolve in the gelatine and add the remaining carrot juice. Cool, add the egg whites and season. Pass through a fine sieve and pour into a siphon, charge with 2 cream chargers and leave in the fridge to set (minimum 4-6 hours).

purple carrot confit:
Peel the carrots thinly and slice on an angle of 45 degrees in slices of 0.4cm. Mix the slices with the cumin oil, season with the thyme, salt and pepper, vacuum pack and cook on 85°C until tender. Cool until needed.

purple carrot pickle:
Peel the carrot thinly. Warm the red wine vinegar with the sugar, tarragon, some cracked pepper and a touch of salt, then put in a vacuum bag. With a Rex peeler, peel the carrot lengthwise into long stripes and put in the bag. Vacuum and infuse the carrots for a minimum of 30 minutes before use.

carrot cylinder:
In a thermoblender mix the isomalt and carrot purée on 85°C for 5 minutes, then spread thinly in a square mould on a Teflon sheet. Dry this in a dehydrator for 24 hours at 55-60°C. Shape the squares into cylinders by rolling them around a small pin.

baby carrot sweet and sour:
Peel the baby carrots, peel the shallots and chop into thin rings, bring the water and vinegar to a simmer and add the lemon, rosemary, bayleaf, sugar, salt and carrots. Bring to a simmer again, then turn off the heat and allow to cool down.

carrot vinaigrette:
Reduce the carrot and orange juices with the olive oil and gelatine until half the amount. Add the vinegar and hazelnut oil, and season to taste. Cool and set aside until needed.

Cashel Blue dome:
Warm the Cashel Blue cheese and add the hazelnut oil, push through a sieve and mix until smooth. Whip the cream and add to the cheese mixture. Add salt and pepper to taste. Pipe into a half-sphere mould and freeze.

Prepare the coating by dissolving the kappa into the carrot juice, add a pinch of salt and bring to a soft boil, then let it cool to 70°C. Carefully dip the frozen Cashel Blue dome in the kappa and remove directly, put on a small oiled tray and leave to defrost.

balsamic tapioca:
Bring the water and balsamic to the boil, add the tapioca pearls and simmer until cooked. Add a drop of olive oil and salt, then cool until needed.

olive oil crumbs:
Whisk together the oil, maltodextrin and salt (if using) in a bowl until individual crumbs begin to appear. Heat the crumbs in a saucepan until they start to take on a round shape and are crunchy on the outside. Reserve in a sealed container until needed.

to serve:
Assemble the dish as pictured.

ANNES GROVE PIGEON, RED CABBAGE, SHEEP SNOUT APPLE, SWISS CHARD
BY MARTIJN KAJUITER

Every year we look forward to the opening of the game season as then we get a exclusive stream of pigeons, snipe, teal and woodcock from this particular area. I like to cook all parts of the pigeon in a way that is tailor made in terms of extracting the maximum flavour. I have opted for a classic combination of apple and red cabbage with this dish, but prepared differently so that a complete scale of complementary flavours is created. It is a light and intense dish that eats very pleasantly.

Serves 4
Preparation time: 2 hours
Cooking time: 30 minutes

Special equipment:
Vacuum bags, water bath, thermoblender, kitchen aid

Planning ahead:
The confit pigeon legs take 8 hours and the apple balls should be prepared at least 4 hours in advance. The purée, meringues, pate and gel can all be prepared in advance.

INGREDIENTS

pigeon:

2	pigeons
2 tbsp	rapeseed oil
1	bay leaf
2	juniper berries, crushed
1	star anise
sea salt	
black pepper	
50ml	duck fat
½	clove garlic
1	sprig thyme
1	sprig rosemary

apple balls:

50g	apple vinegar
3g	clorophyll (natural green colourant)
2g	sugar
sea salt and pink pepper	
2	apples

apple purée:

25ml	per 100g apple vinegar
apple waste from the apple balls (min 100g)	
xanthan gum	
sugar	
salt	

red cabbage meringue:

125ml	red cabbage juice
80g	sugar
35g	Ovoneve 'egg-white powder'
salt	
juniper powder	

red cabbage 'pate':

1	leaf gelatine
350ml	red cabbage juice
2.5g	agar agar
zest of ¼ mandarin	
1	pinch star anise powder
salt	

red cabbage 'fluid gel':

100ml	red cabbage juice
10ml	lemon thyme oil
sea salt and pepper	
xanthan gum	

braised red cabbage:

½	apple, grated
125ml	mulled red wine
250g	red cabbage, finely sliced
1 tbsp	butter
salt	
sugar	

to serve:

butter, melted	
1	sprig thyme
Swiss chard	
bay leaf oil	

METHOD

pigeon:

Debone the pigeons. Trim the breast fillets and remove the skin. Marinate with the rapeseed oil, bay leaf, juniper berries, star anise, salt and black pepper. Vac pack the breasts individually, place in a waterbath and cook at 58°C for 15 minutes.

To make confit of pigeon salt the legs and vacuum pack with the duck fat, garlic, thyme and rosemary at 86°C for 8 hours.

apple balls:

Mix the apple vinegar with the chlorophyll, sugar, salt and pepper. Peel the apples, reserving the waste, and using a melon baller scoop out even round balls and drop them in the vinegar mixture. Put in a vacuum bag and seal very tight and leave for a minimum of 4 hours before use.

apple purée:
Set a thermoblender on 100°C and add the vinegar. While mixing and heating add the

chunks of apple that were left. When all the apple is added blend on high speed and add a touch of xanthan gum, plus seasoning (sugar and salt), then pass the purée through a sieve. Put in a small squeezy bottle and cool until needed.

red cabbage meringue:

In the kitchen aid whisk all the ingredients together until stiff peaks of meringue form. Put in a piping bag with a smooth nozzle and pipe small dots on baking paper. Dry the meringues in a still oven of 90°C for approximately 3 hours.

red cabbage 'pate':

Soak the gelatine. Bring the cabbage juice to a soft boil (not on high heat) and add the agar

agar, salt, mandarin zest and a pinch of star anise powder. Soft boil for 1 minute and add the gelatine, mix well and pour into a suitable container. Cool and when set cut out small buttons with your smallest round dough cutter.

red cabbage 'fluid gel':

Mix the cabbage juice with the oil and seasoning. While constantly stirring add small pinches of xanthan gum until a smooth transparent gel appears, taste and put in a small squeezy bottle until needed.

braised red cabbage:

Put the finely sliced red cabbage and the apple in a suitable pan and add the mulled wine. Put

on a low heat and stir frequently. When the cabbage starts to tenderise add the remaining ingredients and cook the cabbage through until very soft. Season to taste.

to serve:

Heat the confit of pigeon through in its own jus and place on the plate. Sear the pigeon breasts both sides in melted butter with a sprig of thyme and also add to the plate. Heat the braised cabbage and apple balls and arrange the other ingredients around the plate. Cut Swiss chard leaves with a dough cutter and brush with bay leaf oil as a final garnish for the dish.

Chef's tip

From the carcass make a jus with 50% chicken stock and 50% veal jus. The pigeon livers can be used to make a parfait: in a thermoblender cook and mix pigeon and duck livers with pigeon jus on 80°C for 4 minutes, add seasoning, vinegar and a gelatine leaf. Pass through a fine sieve and fill round moulds with the parfait mixure. Freeze and before use coat them in a fresh apple juice kappa.

IRISH COFFEE KILBEGGAN WHISKEY & TOASTED BARLEY ICE CREAM
BY MARTIJN KAJUITER

It is hard to find a person who does not know what Irish Coffee is! It is a must for anyone visiting Ireland to try one. In the winter months when there is a low supply of any Irish fruits we serve this dessert, entirely built up around this Irish evergreen only it comes with my twist!

Serves 4
Preparation time: 4 hours
Cooking time: 30 minutes

Special equipment:
Kitchen aid, vacuum pack, steam oven, ice-cream machine.

Planning ahead:
The ice cream, coffee oil crumbs and coffee ganache can be made in advance. The oblie pastry curl needs time to cool down and crisp up.

INGREDIENTS

coffee sponge:

8	eggs
100g	egg yolks
175g	icing sugar
1 tbsp	Nescafé Gold Blend
75g	butter
175g	almond powder
75g	plain white flour
250g	egg whites
50g	caster sugar

whiskey vegetal:

500g	caster sugar
140ml	water
100ml	whiskey
fresh nutmeg	
24.5g	vegetal (binding agent available online or from specialist shops)

coffee mousse base:

8	egg yolks
100g	caster sugar
65g	plain white flour
½ tbsp	Nescafé Gold Blend
500ml	strong coffee

mousse:

5	leaves gelatine
400g	single cream
800g	base (see above)

vanilla cream:

9	leaves gelatine
750ml	cream
500ml	vanilla sauce

toasted barley/whiskey ice cream:

150g	barley
12	egg yolks
280g	caster sugar
600ml	full-fat milk

400ml	single cream
100ml	whiskey

coffee oil crumbs:

22g	coffee oil (available from specialist shops)
40g	tapioca maltodextrin (available online)
0.2g	salt

oblie pastry:

100g	butter
100g	icing sugar
100g	egg whites
100g	plain white flour

coffee ganache:

750ml	single cream
250g	glucose
250g	caster sugar
2 tbsp	Nescafé Gold Blend
6	leaves gelatine
675g	Samona 70% Chocolate
250g	salted butter

whiskey jelly cubes:

1	leaf gelatine
100ml	whiskey
10g	caster sugar

cream jelly cubes:

1	leaf gelatine
100ml	single cream
10g	caster sugar

garnish:

silver leaf
espresso foam

METHOD

coffee sponge:
Mix the eggs, yolks, icing sugar and Nescafé Gold Blend and whip up in the kitchen aid until stiff peaks form. Melt the butter and add at the last moment. Mix the almond powder and flour and fold carefully through the mix. Whisk up the egg whites and sugar until soft peaks form. Fold through the basic mix until smooth. Spread out thinly and evenly on baking paper and put on a tray. Bake in the oven at 160°C for 8-10 minutes until cooked, then remove. Line a tray 25 x 25cm with cling film and carefully put one sheet of the sponge cut to the same size on the bottom.

whiskey vegetal:
Dissolve the sugar in a small amount of water and cook on a high heat until it starts to caramelise. Mix the water and whiskey and grate ⅛ nutmeg into the liquid, pour the liquid carefully on the dark brown caramel and bring back to a simmer until all the sugar crystals are dissolved, then add the vegetal and, stirring constantly, bring to a soft boil. Let the mixture cool a bit then pour on the tray with the sponge and cool completely. When the vegetal is set, add a second layer of sponge.

coffee mousse base:
Mix the egg yolks, sugar, flour and Nescafé Gold Blend until it becomes a smooth paste. Bring the coffee to the boil and pour on the egg mix. Cook this coffee pastry cream on a medium heat, stirring continuously until the mix has cooked out the flour and becomes thick. Pass through a fine sieve and cool.

mousse:
Soak the gelatine in cold water. Whisk up 350ml cream until stiff. Heat the remaining cream

and dissolve the gelatine. Add this to the 800g coffee base and mix well. Fold in the whipped cream and mix until smooth. Put the mix on top of the tray with the sponge and level out, making sure that there are no air pockets. Put the tray in the fridge to set.

vanilla cream:
Soak the gelatine in cold water. Whip 650ml cream. Heat 100ml cream through and dissolve the gelatine, add to the vanilla sauce and on ice bring it to set, then fold in the remaining cream. Pour this on top of the coffee mousse in the tray and spread out evenly. Cover with cling film and put in the fridge to set for at least 12 hours.

When the coffee tart is set, cut out rounds of 6cm and put on a tray. Freeze this so that the ganache can be poured over it later.

toasted barley and whiskey ice cream:
In a dry pan toast the raw barley until it starts to colour. Mix the egg yolks, sugar, milk and cream and put in a vacuum bag. Add the toasted barley and vacuum seal the mix. Cook the mix

in a steam oven at 85°C for 15 minutes. Shake well when cooked and chill back. Pour through a sieve into an ice cream machine and start churning. Warm the whiskey through and add to the churning ice cream. When the ice cream is fully churned, put it in a suitable container and keep in the freezer on -12 until needed.

coffee oil crumbs:
Mix the coffee oil with the malto and salt. Shape into small balls and heat through in a non-stick pan. Set aside until needed.

oblie pastry:
Melt the butter and add the icing sugar, mix well, then mix with the egg whites and stir through the flour in one go so no lumps are in the mix. Leave the base to cool for 1 hour, then spread on a silpat sheet and bake the pastry on 160°C until golden brown. Shape into a curly shape and let it set to crisp.

coffee ganache:
Bring the cream with the glucose and sugar to a soft boil. Add 2 tbsp of Nescafé gold blend. Soak

the gelatine in cold water and add to the warm base. Add the chocolate and butter to the cream mix. Stir until it becomes shiny and all the butter and chocolate have dissolved. Let the mix cool a bit then cover the round coffee tarts with the ganache and set in the fridge until needed.

whiskey jelly cubes:
Soak the gelatine. Heat the whiskey with the sugar, dissolve into the gelatine and let it set in a small tray. Cut into cubes before serving.

cream jelly cubes:
Soak the gelatine. Heat the cream with the sugar, dissolve into the gelatine and let it set in a small tray. Cut into cubes before serving.

to serve:
Position the Irish Coffee Tart in the centre of the plate and finish with a leaf of silver. From there make a line with some of the coffee oil crumbs and along that line set out the jelly cubes. On the end of that line put the oblie pastry curl and scoop a quenelle of ice cream. Add the espresso foam and serve immediately.

Marlfield House

Marlfield House is a beautifully restored Regency period house set on 36 acres of fine gardens and woodland and close to miles of golden beaches. The Bowe family opened its doors to guests over 30 years ago and it has continued as a highly acclaimed country house and restaurant ever since. Rooms are filled with beautiful antiques, paintings and vases of flowers from the garden. All overlook the gardens and grounds, and the six grand state rooms open on to the lake and wildfowl reserve. The extensive gardens include a croquet lawn, tennis court, woodland walks, a lake and a rose, vegetable and herb garden which provides much of the produce for the kitchen. Marlfield's conservatory restaurant with frescoed walls is highly acclaimed as one of Ireland's most charming dining rooms serving classical food using home-grown and local produce.

Marlfield House

{ *If you're coming from Dublin, on your way to this part of Ireland, you will pass through the magical countryside of Wicklow nestled between sea and hills and presenting some of the country's most stunning landscapes.*

Otherwise you can take the ferry from France or England to Rosslare, which is very close to your final destination. It is in this region, unspoilt and yet easily accessible, that the Bowe family chose to create their gem of a hotel, a model of conviviality that combines Irish elegance — you will love dining under the glass roof of the Victorian conservatory — and the sweet surprise of Celtic life like the delightfully copious breakfasts. Here life is about enjoying yourself: don't we call the Irish "the Latin people of the North"?

STEAMED MUSSELS WITH WILD GARLIC, SPRING ONIONS, FENNEL & CURRY

BY MARLFIELD HOUSE

Serves 4
Preparation time: 20 minutes
Cooking time: 20 minutes

INGREDIENTS

2kg	fresh mussels, scrubbed and de-bearded
	unsalted butter
1	bay leaf
1	sprig of fresh thyme
100ml	dry white wine
1	onion, finely diced
1	leek, finely diced
1	celery stick, finely diced
1	head fennel, finely sliced
200g	broad beans
100g	baby spinach
100g	wild garlic, shredded
2	spring onions, finely sliced
1 tsp	curry powder
300ml	double cream
	sea salt and freshly ground pepper

garnish:

250g	pasta (preferably fresh)
4	sprigs of dill
4	sprigs of tarragon
4	sprigs of chervil, snipped

METHOD

In a large saucepan, melt a knob of butter, add the onion and sweat until softened, add the bay leaf, thyme and a little ground pepper. Then add the mussels and white wine, cover and cook for 3-4 minutes, shaking the pan once or twice. Uncover the pan and strain reserving the juices. Discard any mussels that have not opened. Remove the mussels from their shell.

In a separate saucepan, melt a knob of butter and sauté the leek, celery and fennel until softened, add the teaspoon of curry powder and continue to cook for another minute. Add the reserved cooking juices from the mussels and reduce by half, then add the double cream and simmer for 5 minutes.

Finally add the wild garlic, broad beans, baby spinach, spring onions, mussels and pasta, season to taste.

to serve:
Divide the mussels between four warmed plates, garnish with fresh herbs.

ROAST PARTRIDGE WITH SMOKED GARLIC & ROSEMARY, POTATO & PANCETTA TERRINE, BUTTERED SAVOY CABBAGE WITH CHESTNUTS
BY MARLFIELD HOUSE

Serves 4
Preparation time: 30 minutes
Cooking time: 40 minutes
(for the partridge),
1-1½ hours (for the terrine)

INGREDIENTS

partridge:

4	partridges (or other game bird or poultry)
olive oil	
1	bulb smoked garlic, separated into cloves, skin on
200ml	white wine
2	sprigs rosemary
250ml	chicken stock
salt and pepper	

potato and pancetta terrine:

1 kg	potatoes
1	garlic clove
200g	butter, melted
12	long slices of pancetta
salt and pepper	

buttered savoy cabbage and chestnuts:

1	small Savoy cabbage, finely shredded
1	large carrot, peeled and thinly sliced
butter	
1	onion, sliced
2	spring onions
8	whole chestnuts, sliced

METHOD

partridge:

Preheat the oven to 160°C. Season the partridges with salt and pepper. Heat 2 tablespoons of olive oil in a large frying pan, add the garlic and then brown the partridges on all sides. Roast for approximately 20-25 minutes.

Remove the partridges and garlic cloves from the pan, deglaze the pan with the white wine and add the rosemary, reduce the liquid by one half, add the chicken stock, simmer for 10 minutes and season to taste. When the sauce is smooth and thickened, strain and keep warm.

potato and pancetta terrine:
Preheat the oven to 160°C.

Peel the garlic clove and use to rub the inside of a terrine mould (alternatively use a 23cm round baking pan) and butter the bottom and sides.

Peel the potatoes and slice into thin rounds. Season and pour over the melted butter, mix thoroughly. Carefully layer the potatoes to the top of the terrine mould (baking pan), placing the pancetta strips in three alternative layers, evenly distributed through the potatoes.

Cover with kitchen foil, set in a bain-marie and bake for about 1-1½ hours, until the potatoes are tender. Turn out of the mould, slice and serve.

buttered Savoy cabbage and chestnuts:
Blanch the cabbage in salted, boiling water for 1 minute until tender. Drain.

Melt a knob of butter in a large saucepan and add the sliced onion and carrot, sauté until softened, add the savoy cabbage, sauté for a further minute then add the spring onions and chestnuts and serve.

to serve:
Place a slice of terrine on each plate. Remove the legs and breast meat from the partridges and arrange on plates, add cabbage and sauce.

Serves 4
Preparation time: 20 minutes
Cooking time: 45 minutes

INGREDIENTS

pudding:

100g	fresh white breadcrumbs
5 tbsp	caster sugar
450ml	milk
2 tbsp	butter
3	eggs, separated
1	vanilla pod seeds (alternatively a few drops of vanilla essence)
1	lemon, zest only
3 tbsp	raspberry jam (or other sharp flavoured jam)

poached rhubarb:

4	stalks of rhubarb, peeled and chopped
1	vanilla pod
250g	caster sugar
300ml	water
2	oranges, juiced
2	lemons, juiced

QUEEN OF PUDDINGS WITH VANILLA & CITRUS POACHED RHUBARB

BY MARLFIELD HOUSE

METHOD

Preheat the oven to 190°C.

pudding:

In a bowl mix the breadcrumbs with 2 tablespoons of caster sugar.

Combine the milk and butter in a saucepan and bring to the boil, stirring until the butter has melted and pour over the breadcrumbs. Beat in the egg yolks, vanilla and lemon zest.

Grease 4 small (or alternatively one 1 litre) pie dishes lightly with butter and divide the breadcrumb mix, levelling them off, and bake for approximately 30 minutes, until the pudding is set and golden on top. Remove the pudding and leave to cool slightly.

Reduce the oven temperature to 170°C.

In a clean bowl whisk the egg whites until they form soft peaks, gradually add the remaining 3 tablespoons of caster sugar, continually whisking until they become stiff and glossy.

Take the raspberry jam and spread evenly over the puddings, then top with the meringue drawing it up in peaks.

Place the pudding in the oven and bake for 8-12 minutes until the meringue is set and golden in colour.

poached rhubarb:

To poach the rhubarb, slowly dissolve the caster sugar in the water, juice of lemons and oranges and vanilla pod. Place the rhubarb in the syrup and gently poach for 3-5 minutes being careful not to overcook. (should be softened but still hold a bite).

to serve:

Serve the pudding immediately with the poached rhubarb and syrup.

Heiko Riebandt

Heiko Riebandt is the Head Chef at Sheen Falls Lodge, Ireland's most luxurious 5-star hotel. Heiko, together with his team of Irish and International chefs, manages all of the culinary demands at the hotel, including fine dining at the award-winning La Cascade Restaurant, refreshments at The Sun Lounge and Private Dining.

Heiko joined Sheen Falls Lodge in May 2007 when he was given the position of Executive Sous Chef. He was soon promoted to Executive Head Chef due to his creative and ambitious menus as well as his leadership skills to motivate and work alongside the team.

Before moving to Ireland Heiko amassed 16 years' experience abroad in deluxe hotels and Michelin-starred restaurants including the Grand Hotel Kronenhof (Switzerland) and Wald Und Shlosshotel Friedrichsruhe (Germany).

Heiko brings his experience of European culture to inspire the menu itself. He uses the best of fresh local ingredients and classical recipes, and then adds his own modern interpretation to create something new. Fresh ingredients are prepared with respect and used to create dishes that are international but always acknowledging their Irish roots.

Sheen Falls Lodge

{ *The bustling town of Kenmare with its colourful streets is one of the spots in Ireland that the Irish themselves like best.*

Surrounded by purple heather-coloured mountains and cascading blue waters into Kenmare Bay, the backdrop to the quaint town is breathtaking. Sheen Falls Lodge is not only perfectly placed for exploring the southwest of Ireland, the world famous Ring of Beara, Ring of Kerry and the famous Killarney Lakes, it is also the favourite address for those in the know with its piano-jazz ambience, its collection of old Irish whiskeys, its selection of fine wines as one of Ireland's largest wine cellars and the fabulous dishes prepared with the salmon caught in the nearby river. All of this combined with outstanding Irish hospitality and Celtic legends creates the magic that seems to float over this land.

Serves 4
Preparation time: 1 hour plus overnight to
                      freeze the sorbet
Cooking time: 15 minutes

Special equipment:
4 small ring moulds, ice-cream machine
(optional), stick blender.

Planning ahead:
The sorbet can be made in advance.

INGREDIENTS

lobster:

2	lobsters, approximately 500g each
salt	
15ml	cumin
3	camomile tea bags
4	fresh basil leaves
4	coriander seeds

tomato chartreuse:

5	tomatoes
dried camomile flowers	
4	fresh basil leaves
4	coriander seeds

lime chilli sorbet:

15g	sea salt
1	garlic clove
3	hot green chillis
20g	palm sugar
5	shallots
30ml	Thai fish sauce
60ml	lime juice
3	coriander sprigs

tempura batter:

65g	strong flour
65g	corn starch
1	egg yolk
125ml	ice-cold water

to serve:

100g	samphire

LOBSTER VARIATION
BY HEIKO RIEBANDT

East meets West at the Co Kerry Shores. Fresh local lobster prepared three ways inspired by different cultures.

METHOD

lobster:

Cook the lobster in lightly salted boiling water seasoned with the cumin and camomile tea bags. The cooking time is about 1 minute per 100g. When cooked, take the lobster out of the boiling water and refresh in ice water. Separate the claws from the lobster and cook the claws for an additional 1-2 minutes, depending on size.

Cut away the two biggest medallions of the tail and put aside to grill later. Break out the rest of the lobster from the tail and claws. Leave the claws on one side for deep frying in the tempura batter.

Cut the rest of the lobster into small dice and season with some sliced basil and fresh ground coriander. Keep the prepared lobster in the fridge.

tomato chartreuse:

Cut a cross in the tomato skin and blanch the tomatoes in boiling water for about 20 seconds. Take out and refresh in ice water. Peel, cut into quarters and take out the heart with the seeds; put the 'fillets' onto a dry towel.

Lightly oil four small ring moulds. Cut the tomatoes to the desired length and line the rings tightly. Cut tomato rings for the top and bottom. Press rings out for the bottom and top. Fill the lined moulds with the lobster mix and close the top with a tomato ring.

To smoke, take a lidded bamboo basket and a suitable old pot (make sure the basket does not touch the bottom of the pot and that the lid seals tight). Heat the pot, add sawdust and some dried camomile flowers. Place the tomato chartreuse into the basket and cover the basket with a lid. Let the tomato chartreuse smoke for about 5-7 minutes depending on the heat and how much smoke the sawdust produces.

lime chilli sorbet:

Put all the ingredients into a blender and purée; strain through a sieve. Ideally use an ice-cream machine to churn the sorbet. Alternatively put the liquid into the freezer overnight and stir from time to time with a whisk.

tempura batter:

Mix all the ingredients with a stick blender and season. Use ice-cold water for the best results. Lightly flour the lobster claws and coat with the batter. Deep fry at 160°C till nice and crisp. Drain on kitchen paper.

to serve:

Blanch the samphire in boiling water for 10 seconds and refresh in ice water. For best results, smoke the chartreuse about 4-5 minutes before the claws go into the oil. At the same time grill the lobster medallions. Plate the chartreuse first – the metal ring will help to keep it warm. Plate the rest of the items, remove the metal ring and lastly add the sorbet.

TRILOGY OF VEAL
BY HEIKO RIEBANDT

Milk-fed veal is a delicacy which I love to prepare and enjoy when available. Some things in life just have to be enjoyed at the right moment.

Serves 4

Preparation time:	3 hours plus overnight
Cooking time:	30 minutes

Special equipment:
2 cream chargers for iSi bottle, stick blender, food processor, (optional), spaghetti slicer.

Planning ahead:
The sweetbreads need to soak in milk overnight in the fridge.

INGREDIENTS

veal steaks:

4	veal fillet medallions 160-180g each
salt and pepper	
oil, as required	

veal sweetbreads:

150g	veal sweetbreads
milk, as required	
80ml	white wine vinegar
1	onion
3	cloves
1	bay leaf
flour, as required	
butter, as required	
salt and pepper	

veal kidneys:

150g	veal kidneys

sauce:

50g	shallots, chopped
50g	unsalted butter
75ml	aged balsamic vinegar
200ml	veal stock
50g	gherkins
salt and pepper	

white truffle froth:

2	shallots
100ml	Riesling (white wine)
1	bay leaf
5	white peppercorns
2	juniper berries
1	sprig fresh thyme
200ml	chicken stock
75ml	whipping cream
25ml	skimmed milk
salt and pepper	
truffle oil, to taste	

vegetable garnish:

250g	baby spinach
whipping cream, as required	
salt and pepper	
nutmeg, to taste	
4	baby turnips
4	baby carrots
100g	morel mushrooms
butter, as required	
shallots, finely diced, as required	

potato espuma:

200g	potatoes suitable for mash
salt	
100ml	boiling water from the cooked potatoes
125ml	whipping cream
35ml	extra virgin olive oil
salt, to taste	
nutmeg, to taste	

potato towers:

4	large hard boiling potatoes

to serve:

1	sprig fresh sage
3	sprigs fresh thyme

METHOD

veal steaks:

Season the veal steaks with salt and pepper. Sear the steaks on all sides in a hot pan with some oil. Cook in a preheated oven at 150°C for 10-13 minutes (medium). Take out and let the steaks rest for about 15 minutes.

veal sweetbreads:

Soak the sweetbreads for about 30 minutes in cold water. Strain and put in a bowl and cover with milk. Cover and leave overnight in the fridge.

The following day, rinse the sweetbreads and soak again for 30 minutes in cold water.

Take a small pot, add 1 litre of water and vinegar. Do not season the water with salt as it will make the sweetbreads tough.

Peel the onion. Press the cloves through the bay leaf and into the whole onion. Add it to the water and bring to the boil. Add the sweetbreads and turn the heat down. Simmer for about 15-20 minutes. When the sweetbreads feel like a medium hard-boiled egg they are ready. Leave to cool down in the water. Take out and cut into pieces. Dust with flour and pan-fry in butter. Season with salt and pepper just before serving.

veal kidneys:

Clean the kidneys, cut the fat out and a bit of the shiny inside. Pan fry in a hot pan making sure that they are not cooked through. Do not season at this stage. Drain in a sieve to bleed out (for a minimum of 10-15 minutes) and discard the liquid. To serve, place into the hot sauce (see below) to reheat.

sauce:

Sweat the shallots in the butter, add the balsamic and let it reduce. Add the veal stock and reduce again. To serve, add the gherkins and season with salt and pepper. The butter and liquid should be emulsified. If the butter splits, whisk some diced cold butter into the sauce to thicken it again.

white truffle froth:

Peel and slice the shallots. Place the shallots, white wine and the herbs/spices in a pot and let it slowly reduce till only the shallots are left. Add the stock and let it reduce to half, then add the cream and milk and reduce again till three-quarters of the liquid is left. Season with salt and pepper and add the truffle oil. Strain through a sieve and blend it with a stick blender till smooth. Taste the froth and adjust the seasoning if needed.

vegetable garnish:

Blanch the spinach quickly in boiling water. Cool it down in ice water. Take the spinach out and press all the water out. Add some cream and blend with a stick blender or in a food processor. Freeze the spinach slightly as this make it easier to create a nice smooth mousse/cream. Reheat and season with salt and nutmeg. Cook the turnips and carrots and glaze in butter; season with salt. Sauté the morels in some butter with finely diced shallots and season with salt and pepper.

potato espuma:

Peel the potatoes and boil them in lightly salted water. Strain and keep 100g of the cooking liquid. Let the potatoes cool down to 60°C, purée with a stick blender and the cooking liquid. Slowly add the cream and then the olive oil. Blend till smooth. Season with salt and nutmeg and strain through a fine sieve. Reheat and fill a pre-heated iSi bottle. Close the bottle tight and add two cream chargers. Use to fill the potato towers (see below).

potato towers:

Peel the potatoes and with a spaghetti slicer make long spaghetti. Roll them tight around a suitable greased round metal mould. Deep fry slowly at 160°C till golden. Take out of the hot oil and let the towers cool down a bit before carefully removing them from the mould.

to serve:

Take a pan and melt some butter; add a few leaves of fresh sage and a couple of sprigs of fresh thyme. Place the veal fillets in the pan and spoon the melted butter constantly over the meat (for approximately 2 minutes), making sure the butter does not get burned. Serve immediately along with all the other elements.

Serves 4
Preparation time: 90 minutes plus overnight
Cooking time: 8-12 minutes

Special equipment:
4 dessert rings – 8-10cm diameter. Ice-cream machine (optional).

Planning ahead:
The ice cream can be made in advance. The tuile will keep for 3 days and the meringues for 5 days.

INGREDIENTS

warm chocolate mousse:

250g	dark chocolate
50g	butter
8	large eggs
150g	caster sugar
50g	cocoa powder
butter and sugar for the rings	

rose water ice cream:

325ml	semi-skimmed milk
325ml	whipping cream
225ml	caster sugar
¾	vanilla pod
30ml	rose water
325ml	sour cream

krokant tuile:

27g	unsalted butter
50g	sugar
25g	golden syrup
25g	strong flour
zest of ¼ lemon	
zest of ¼ orange	
zest of ¼ lime	

vanilla meringue:

25g	egg whites
25g	caster sugar
25g	icing sugar
¼	vanilla pod
4	pieces gold leaf

WARM MOUSSE AUX CHOCOLATE
BY HEIKO RIEBANDT

We created this dessert with romance and couples in mind. Chocolate and roses have always been associated with love and this is our tribute.

METHOD

warm chocolate mousse:

Butter and sugar the four dessert rings and put on a baking tray lined with greaseproof paper. Preheat the oven to 190°C.

Melt the chocolate and the butter in a bowl over warm water. Whisk the eggs with the sugar in a bowl over hot water until warm. Be careful not to make scrambled eggs. Whisk the eggs until lukewarm; the volume should go up to three times the size. Add the cocoa powder to the lukewarm egg; do not over mix or the egg mix will collapse. Add the melted chocolate and fold in gently. Immediately fill the dessert rings before the mix starts to set. Don't overfill the rings as it will rise to about double the volume.

Cook in the oven for about 8-12 minutes depending on the size of the ring. The middle should still be soft when you cut into the mousse.

rose water ice cream:

Bring the milk, cream, sugar and vanilla pod to the boil. Leave to cool down and to allow the flavours to infuse. Add the rose water and sour cream. Use an ice-cream machine to churn the ice cream. Alternatively pour into a flat dish and put in a freezer. Whisk from time to time to prevent ice crystals forming and freeze overnight.

krokant tuile:

Preheat the oven to 180°C.

Mix all the ingredients together and allow to rest for 4 hours in the fridge. Take the mix out and let it get slightly warm so that you can spread thin layers out with a spatula onto greaseproof paper.

Bake in the oven till a brown honey colour - approximately 5 minutes. Take out and leave to cool slightly. Take the warm tuile and place them into four bowls to get a round shape and let them cool down completely.

vanilla meringue:

Preheat the oven to 80°C.

Whisk the egg whites till slightly stiff then add the rest of the ingredients apart from the gold leaf. Beat till stiff peaks form. Pipe walnut-size rosettes onto greaseproof paper and bake for 90 minutes in the oven.

When cool, brush with the gold leaf. Use a soft brush or the gold leaf will stick to your fingers.

to serve:

Assemble all the elements on a plate as pictured.

CONVERSIONS

Conversion Chart Weight (Solids)

¼ oz	7 g
½ oz	10 g
¾ oz	20 g
1 oz	25 g
1½ oz	40 g
2 oz	50 g
2½ oz	60 g
3 oz	75 g
3½ oz (1 cup)	100 g
4 oz (¼lb)	110 g
4½ oz	125 g
5½ oz	150 g
6 oz	175 g
7 oz (2 cups)	200 g
8 oz (½lb)	225 g
9 oz	250 g
10 oz	275 g
10½ oz (3 cups)	300 g
11 oz	310 g
11½ oz	325 g
12 oz (¾lb)	350 g
13 oz	375 g
14 oz (4 cups)	400 g
15 oz	425 g
1 lb	450 g
18 oz	500 g (½ kg)
1¼ lb	600 g
1½ lb	700 g
1 lb 10 oz	750 g
2 lb	900 g
2¼ lb	1 kg
2½ lb	1.1 kg
2 lb 12 oz	1.2 kg
3 lb	1.3 kg
3 lb 5 oz	1.5 kg
3½ lb	1.6 kg
4 lb	1.8 kg
4 lb 8oz	2 kg
5 lb	2.25 kg
5 lb 8 oz	2.5 kg
6 lb 8 oz	3 kg

Volume (Liquids)

1 teaspoon (tsp)	5 ml
1 dessertspoon	10 ml
1 tablespoon (tbsp)	15 ml or ½fl oz
1 fl oz	30 ml
1 ½fl oz	40 ml
2 fl oz	50 ml
2 ½fl oz	60 ml
3 fl oz	75 ml
3 ½fl oz	100 ml
4 fl oz	125 ml
5 fl oz	150 ml or ¼ pint (pt)
5 ½fl oz	160 ml
6 fl oz	175 ml
7 fl oz	200 ml
8 fl oz	225 ml
9 fl oz	250ml (¼litre)
10 fl oz	300 ml or ½ pint
11 fl oz	325 ml
12 fl oz	350 ml
13 fl oz	370 ml
14 fl oz	400 ml
15 fl oz	425 ml or ¾ pint
16 fl oz	450 ml
18 fl oz	500 ml (½ litre)
19 fl oz	550 ml
20 fl oz	600 ml or 1 pint
1¼ pints	700 ml
1½ pints	850 ml
1¾ pints	1 litre
2 pints	1.2 litres
2½ pints	1.5 litres
3 pints	1.8 litres
3½ pints	2 litres
1 qt	950 ml
2 qt	1 litre
3 qt	2 litres
4 qt	3 litres
5 qt	4 litres

Oven Temperatures

Celsius *	Farenheit	Gas	Description
110°C	225°F	Gas Mark ¼	Cool
120°C	250°F	Gas Mark ½	Cool
130°C	275°F	Gas Mark 1	Very low
150°C	300°F	Gas Mark 2	Very low
160°C	325°F	Gas Mark 3	Low
180°C	350°F	Gas Mark 4	Moderate
190°C	375°F	Gas Mark 5	Moderate, Hot
200°C	400°F	Gas Mark 6	Hot
220°C	425°F	Gas Mark 7	Hot
230°C	450°F	Gas Mark 8	Very hot
240°C	475°F	Gas Mark 9	Very hot

Length

¼ inch (")	5 mm
½ inch	1 cm
¾ inch	2 cm
1 inch	2½ cm
1¼ inches	3 cm
1½ inches	4 cm
2 inches	5 cm
3 inches	7½ cm
4 inches	10 cm
6 inches	15 cm
7 inches	18 cm
8 inches	20 cm
10 inches	24 cm
11 inches	28 cm
12 inches	30 cm

* For fan assisted ovens, reduce temperatures by 10°C

Temperature conversion

$C = 5/9 (F-32)$

$F = 9/5 C + 32$

GLOSSARY

à l'Anglaise: Typically English cooking style eg. boiled vegetables, deep-fried breadcrumbed fish, custard made with fresh eggs.

Bain Marie: A container filled with hot water to cook or to hold at a temperature.

Beignet: A type of fritter.

Blanch: To transfer food to ice water to stop the cooking process; 'blanch the vegetables'.

Blind Bake: To partially or completely cook a pastry case by lining it with parchment paper and uncooked rice or beans which are removed before filling.

Bloom: To expand molecules or herbs in water or oil, often used with gelatine as it absorbs liquid; 'bloom the gelatine'.

Braise: To brown and then cook in liquid; 'braise the beef until tender'.

Brunoise: To cut into a very small dice approximately 2 x 2 x 2mm; 'Carrots, Brunoise'.

Carpaccio: A dish of raw meat or fish, thinly sliced or pounded thin.

Caramelise: To convert sugar to caramel; 'caramelise the sauce'.

Cartouche: A circle of paper that is placed onto a sauce or gravy to stop a skin forming.

Caul: Thin membrane of fat covering the intestines of a pig, cow or sheep.

Chinoise: A conical sieve with an extra fine mesh.

Cook Out: To finish cooking.

Coulis: A thick sauce made of puréed fruit or vegetables.

Créme Anglaise: A rich vanilla-flavoured sauce that can be served hot or cold with cake, fruit or another dessert.

Crepinette: A small, slightly flattened sausage.

Compote: Food stewed or cooked in syrup.

Confit: Food immersed in a substance for flavour and preservation.

Consommé: A clear soup or bouillion boiled down so as to be very rich.

Court Bouillon: A flavoured liquid for poaching or quickly cooking foods.

Croquant: French for crispy or crunchy.

Deglaze: To use a liquid to remove cooked-on residue from a pan.

Dehydrator: An appliance to dry food by removing water.

Dice: To cut into small cubes; 'dice the onions'.

Drum Sieve: A kitchen utensil, shaped somewhat like a snare drum, that acts as a strainer, grater or food mill.

Egg Wash: Beaten eggs, used to brush pastry, sometimes with the addition of water, milk or other liquid.

Emulsify: To combine two liquids together which don't mix easily; 'emulsify the water and oil'.

Farce: To stuff; 'farce the chicken with the mix'.

Feuilletine: A rough, crunchy textured praline.

Fold: To combine ingredients using a 'cutting' motion.

Fondant:

1. A paste made by mixing boiled sugar and water.

2. A smooth creamy mixture, often used as an accompaniment or filling.

Fricassée: A stewed dish typically made with poultry or vegetables.

Ganache: A glaze, icing or filling.

Glace: Thick, syrup-like reduction of stock.

Glaze: To thinly coat with a mixture; 'glaze the pastry with the mixture'.

Heavy-bottomed Pan: A pan similar to a skillet, often made from cast iron.

Ice Bath: A container holding ice and water used to lower the temperature of something or to keep it cold.

Julienne: To cut into thin strips; 'Carrots, Julienne'.

Jus: A sauce made by diluting the pan juices of a roast with liquid then boiling until it thickens.

Lardons: A small strip or cube of pork fat used in cooking to flavour foods.

Mandoline: Kitchen utensil used for slicing and cutting, especially into julienne (long and thin) strips.

Marinate/Macerate: To soak a meat, fish or vegetables in a seasoned liquid mixture to absorb the flavours of the marinade or to tenderise. When fruits are soaked in liquid it is referred to as Macerate; 'Marinate the steak in the stock', 'Macerate the strawberries in water and sugar'.

Matignon: To dice very finely or mince.

Mirepoix: A combination of chopped carrots, celery and onions used to add flavour and aroma to stocks, sauces, soups and other foods.

Mount: To stir in pieces of cold, unsalted butter into a sauce.

Noisette:

1. A small round piece of meat.

2. French liqueur made from hazelnuts.

3. Butter cooked to a light hazelnut colour.

Pacojet: A food processor which purées fruit frozen to produce an ice cream or sorbet.

Pain D'épices: A type of spiced bread or biscuit.

Panna Cotta: An Italian dish using cream and milk.

Parfait: A dish of layers, often sweet.

Pass/Pass Off: To put through a sieve.

Poach: To cook in boiling or simmering liquid; 'poach the fish'.

Purée: To blend or strain cooked food until a thick consistency; 'blend until a purée'.

Quenelle: To shape with two spoons into small round or oval dumplings; 'a quenelle of ice cream'.

Ramekin: A small individual circular, porcelain, glass or earthenware oven-proof dish.

Reduce: To simmer or boil a liquid until much of it evaporates, making it more concentrated; 'reduce the sauce'.

Render: To heat pieces of meat to produce fat that can be heated for cooking; 'render the bacon'.

Reserve: To keep to one side; 'reserve until serving'.

Rosette: A rose-like shape.

Sabayon: Ingredients beaten together to make a 'custard'.

Sachet: Square of cheesecloth used to contain herbs and tied with butcher's twine.

Saddle: A cut of meat consisting of part of the backbone and both loins.

Sauté: To fry briefly over high heat; 'sauté the onions'.

Score: To cut shallow slits at regular intervals on the surface, 'score the meat'.

Sear: To brown quickly over very high heat, 'sear the meat'.

Silpat: A popular silicone mat used in baking to provide a non-stick surface without fat.

Soufflé: A light, fluffy baked dish made with egg yolks and beaten egg.

Sous Vide: A method of cooking ingredients in a plastic pouch.

Sugar Syrup: Combination of sugar and water. A 30% sugar syrup would be 30% water and 70% sugar.

Sweat: To cook slowly over a low heat; 'sweat the onions'.

Temper: To bring a food to the desired consistency, texture or temperature, 'temper over a low heat'.

Toast: To brown using a dry heat source such as an oven or toaster. Seeds, nuts, grains or spices may be toasted in an oven or a skillet, with or without oil, with a low heat, stirring or tossing often until browned, taking care not to burn.

Tuile: A thin, crisp cookie that is placed over a rounded object to mould into shape.

Vacuum Pack: A method of storing food in a plastic airless vacuum to either cook or store.

Velouté: A white sauce made with stock instead of milk.

Verjus: Juice from unripened green grapes that have been processed without fermentation, therefore alcohol free.

Water Bath: See Bain Marie.

Whip: To mix ingredients quickly and vigorously to incorporate air to make them light; 'whip the egg whites'.

DIRECTORY OF PROPERTIES

■ RELAIS & CHATEAUX PROPERTIES ■ GRANDS CHEFS RELAIS & CHATEAUX

Airds Hotel

Port Appin, Argyll PA38 4DF – United Kingdom
Tel.: + 44 (0)1631 730236
Fax: + 44 (0)1631 730535
airds@relaischateaux.com
www.airds-hotel.com
Owners: Shaun and Jenny McKivragan
Maître de Maison: Robert McKay

Amberley Castle

Amberley, BN18 9LT Arundel (West Sussex) –
United Kingdom
Tel.: + 44 (0)1798 831992
Fax: + 44 (0)1798 831998
amberley@relaischateaux.com
www.amberleycastle.co.uk
Owner: Andrew Davis
Maître de Maison: Oliver Smith

Ballyfin

Ballyfin Demesne, Ballyfin, County Laois
Ireland
Tel: +353 (0)5787 55866
Fax: +353 (0)5787 55883
info@ballyfin.com
www.ballyfin.com
Owner: Fred and Kay Krehbiel
Maître de Maison: Frederic Poivre

The Bath Priory Hotel

The Bath Priory Hotel, Weston Road, Bath BA1
2XT (Somerset) – United Kingdom
Tel.: + 44 (0)1225 331922
Fax: + 44 (0)1225 448276
priory@relaischateaux.com
www.thebathpriory.co.uk
Owners: Andrew and Christina Brownsword
Maitre de Maison: Sue Williams

Buckland Manor

Buckland Manor, Buckland near Broadway WR12
7LY (Worcestershire) – United Kingdom
Tel.: + 44 (0)1386 852626
Fax: + 44 (0)1386 853557
buckland@relaischateaux.com
www.bucklandmanor.co.uk
Maître de Maison: Nigel Power

Chewton Glen

Christchurch Road, New Milton BH25 6QS
(Hampshire) – United Kingdom
Tel.: + 44 (0)1425 275341
Fax: + 44 (0)1425 272310
chewton@relaischateaux.com
www.chewtonglen.com
Maître de Maison: Andrew Stembridge

Cliff House Hotel

Cliff House Hotel, Ardmore, Co. Waterford
(Waterford) – Ireland
Tel.: +353 (0)24 87800
Fax: +353 (0)24 87820
cliffhouse@relaischateaux.com
www.thecliffhousehotel.com
Owner: Barry O'Callaghan
Maître de Maison: Adriaan Bartels

The Connaught

The Connaught, Carlos Place, Mayfair, London
W1K 2AL – United Kingdom
Tel. : + 44 (0)20 7 107 8889
Fax: + 44 (0)20 7 495 3262
connaught@relaischateaux.com
www.the-connaught-co.uk
Maître de Maison: Nathalie Seiler
Grand Chef Relais & Châteaux: Hélène Darroze

Farlam Hall

Brampton CA8 2NG (Cumbria) – United Kingdom
Tel.: + 44 (0)1697 746234
Fax: + 44 (0)1697 746683
farlam@relaischateaux.com
www.farlamhall.co.uk
Owners and Maîtres de Maison: Quinion and
Stevenson Families

The Fat Duck

High Street, Bray SL6 2AQ (Berkshire) –
United Kingdom
Tel.: + 44 (0)1628 580333
fatduck@relaischateaux.com
www.fatduck.co.uk
Maître de Maison and Grand Chef Relais &
Châteaux: Heston Blumenthal

Gidleigh Park

Chagford TQ13 8HH (Devon) – United Kingdom
Tel.: + 44 (0)1647 432367
Fax: + 44 (0)1647 432574
gidleigh@relaischateaux.com
www.gidleigh.com
Owners: Andrew and Christina Brownsword
Maître de Maison: Sue Williams
Grand Chef Relais & Châteaux: Michael Caines MBE

Gilpin Lodge Country House & Spa

Crook Road, Near Windermere LA23 3NE
(Cumbria) – United Kingdom
Tel.: + 44 (0)1539 488818
Fax: + 44 (0)1539 488058
gilpin@relaischateaux.com
www.gilpinlodge.co.uk
Owners and Maîtres de Maison: Cunliffe Family

Glenapp Castle

Ballantrae KA26 ONZ (Ayrshire) – United
Kingdom
Tel.: + 44 (0)1465 831212
Fax: + 44 (0)1465 831000
glenapp@relaischateaux.com
www.glenappcastle.com
Owners: Graham and Fay Cowan
Maîtres de Maison: Graham and Fay Cowan,
John Orr

Gravetye Manor

Vowels Lane, Near East Grinstead RH19 4LJ
(West Sussex) - United Kingdom
Tel.: + 44 (0)1342 810567
Fax: + 44 (0)1342 810080
gravetye@relaischateaux.com
www.gravetyemanor.co.uk
Owners: Andrew N. Russell and Mark T. Raffan
Maître de Maison: Andrew Russell

Greywalls Hotel and Chez Roux Restaurant

Muirfield, Gullane, East Lothian, Scotland EH31
2EG – United Kingdom
Tel: +44 (0) 1620 842144
Fax: + 44 (0) 1620 842241
enquiries@greywalls.co.uk
www.greywalls.co.uk
Owner: Mr and Mrs Weaver
Maitre de Maison: Duncan Fraser

For reservations and information, please call 00 800 2000 00 02

Hambleton Hall

Hambleton, Oakham – Rutland LE15 8TH –
United Kingdom
Tel.: + 44 (0)1572 756991
Fax: + 44 (0)1572 724721
hambleton@relaischateaux.com
www.hambletonhall.com
Owners: Tim and Stefa Hart
Maître de Maison: Chris Hurst

Inverlochy Castle

Torlundy-Fort William, Scotland PH33 6SN –
United Kingdom
Tel.: + 44 (0)1397 702177
Fax: + 44 (0)1397 702953
inverlochy@relaischateaux.com
www.inverlochycastlehotel.com
Maître de Maison: Calum Milne

The Isle of Eriska Hotel, Spa & Golf

Benderloch, By Oban, Argyll, Scotland, PA37 1SD
– United Kingdom
Tel: +44 (0)1631 720371
Fax: +44 (0)1631 720531
office@eriska-hotel.co.uk
www.eriska-hotel.co.uk
Owner: Buchanan-Smith family
Maître de Maison: Beppo Buchanan-Smith

Kinloch House

Blairgowrie PH10 6SG (Perthshire) – United
Kingdom
Tel.: + 44 (0)1250 884237
Fax: + 44 (0)1250 884333
kinloch@relaischateaux.com
www.kinlochhouse.com
Owners: Allen Family
Maître de Maison: Graeme Allen

Le Gavroche

43 Upper Brook Street, London W1K 7QR –
United Kingdom
Tel.: + 44 (0)20 7 499 1826
Fax: + 44 (0)20 7 491 4387
gavroche@relaischateaux.com
www.le-gavroche.co.uk
Owners: Michel Roux Jr. and Albert Roux
Maître de Maison: Emmanuel Landré
Grand Chef Relais & Châteaux: Michel Roux Jr.

Le Manoir Aux Quat'Saisons

Church Road, Great Milton, Oxford OX44 7PD
(Oxfordshire) – United Kingdom
Tel.: + 44 (0)1844 278881
Fax: + 44 (0)1844 278847
4saisons@relaischateaux.com
www.manoir.com
Owner: Raymond Blanc
Maître de Maison: Tom Lewis
Grands Chefs Relais & Châteaux: Raymond Blanc
and Gary Jones

Lime Wood Hotel and Restaurant

Beaulieu Road Lyndhurst
New Forest Hampshire
Lyndhurst SO43 7FZ (Hampshire)
United Kingdom
Tel.: +44 2380 287 177
Fax.: +44 2380 287 199
limewood@relaischateaux.com
www.limewoodhotel.co.uk
Maître de Maison: Justin Pinchbeck

Longueville Manor

Longueville Road, St Saviour JE2 7WF (Jersey) –
United Kingdom
Tel.: + 44 (0)1534 725501
Fax: +44 (0)1534 731613
longueville@relaischateaux.com
www.longuevillemanor.com
Owner: Malcolm Lewis
Maître de Maison: Pedro Bento

Lower Slaughter Manor

Lower Slaughter GL54 2HP (Gloucestershire) –
United Kingdom
Tel.: + 44 (0)1451 820456
Fax: + 44 (0)1451 822150
slaughter@relaischateaux.com
www.lowerslaughter.co.uk
Maître de Maison: Andrew Thomason

Lucknam Park

Bath, Colerne, Chippenham, SN14 8AZ
(Wiltshire) - United Kingdom
Tel.: + 44 (0)1225 742777
Fax: + 44 (0)1225 743536
lucknam@relaischateaux.com
www.lucknampark.co.uk
Maître de Maison: Harry Murray MBE

Mallory Court

Harbury Lane, Bishops Tachbrook, Leamington
Spa CV33 9QB (Warwickshire) – United Kingdom
Tel.: + 44 (0)1926 330214
Fax: + 44 (0)1926 451714
mallory@relaischateaux.com
www.mallory.co.uk
Owner: Sir Peter Rigby
Maître de Maison: Mark E. Chambers

Marlfield House

Courtown Road R742, Gorey Co. Wexford –
Ireland
Tel.: + 353 (0)53 9421124
Fax: + 353 (0)53 9421572
marlfield@relaischateaux.com
www.marlfieldhouse.com
Owners: Ray and Mary Bowe
Maîtres de Maison: Margaret and Laura Bowe

Restaurant Andrew Fairlie

The Gleneagles Hotel, Auchterarder, Perthshire,
Scotland PH3 1NF – United Kingdom
Tel: +44 (0)1764 694267
Fax: +44 (0)1764 694163
reservations@andrewfairlie.co.uk
www.andrewfairlie.com
Owner: Andrew Fairlie
Maître de Maison: Ben Dantzic

The Royal Crescent Hotel

16 Royal Crescent, Bath BA1 2LS –
United Kingdom
Tel.: + 44 (0)1225 823333
Fax: + 44 (0)1225 339401
crescent@relaischateaux.com
www.royalcrescent.co.uk
Maître de Maison: Sharon Love

Sharrow Bay Country House

Lake Ullswater, Howtown, Penrith CA10 2LZ
(Lake District) – United Kingdom
Tel.: + 44 (0)1768 486301
Fax: + 44 (0)1768 486349
sharrow@relaischateaux.com
www.sharrowbay.co.uk
Maître de Maison: Andrew King

Sheen Falls Lodge

Kenmare Co. Kerry (Kerry) – Ireland
Tel.: + 353 (0)64 6641600
Fax: + 353 (0)64 6641386
sheenfalls@relaischateaux.com
www.sheenfallslodge.ie
Owner: Bent Hoyer
Maître de Maison: Alan Campbell

Summer Lodge Country House & Spa

9 Fore Street, Evershot DT2 0JR (Dorset) -
United Kingdom
Tel.: + 44 (0)1935 482000
Fax: + 44 (0)1935 482040
summer@relaischateaux.com
www.summerlodgehotel.co.uk
Owner: Beatrice Tollman
Maître de Maison: Charles Lotter

The Vineyard at Stockcross

Newbury RG20 8JU (Berkshire) –
United Kingdom
Tel.: + 44 (0)1635 528770
Fax: + 44 (0)1635 528398
vineyard@relaischateaux.com
www.the-vineyard.co.uk
Owner: Sir Peter Michael
Maître de Maison: Andrew McKenzie
Grand Chef Relais & Châteaux: John Campbell

The Waterside Inn

Ferry Road, Bray SL6 2AT (Berkshire) –
United Kingdom
Tel.: + 44 (0)1628 620691
Fax: + 44 (0)1628 784710
waterside@relaischateaux.com
www.waterside-inn.co.uk
Owners: Michel Roux and Alain Roux
Maître de Maison: Diego Masciaga
Grands Chefs Relais & Châteaux:
Michel and Alain Roux

Whatley Manor

Easton Grey, Malmesbury SN16 ORB (Wiltshire)
– United Kingdom
Tel.: + 44 (0)1666 822888
Fax: + 44 (0)1666 826120
whatley@relaischateaux.com
www.whatleymanor.com
Owners: Alix Landolt and Christian Landolt
Maître de Maison: Peter Egli

Ynyshir Hall

Eglwysfach, Machynlleth SY20 8TA (Powys –
Mid-Wales) – United Kingdom
Tel.: + 44 (0)1654 781209
Fax: + 44 (0)1654 781366
ynyshir@relaischateaux.com
www.ynyshirhall.co.uk
Maître de Maison: Joan Reen

RECITES: ALPHABETICAL INDEX OF RECIPES

■ RELAIS & CHATEAUX

■ GRANDS CHEFS RELAIS & CHATEAUX

Airds Hotel

P266   Wild Mushroom Risotto with Wilted Spinach & Parmesan

P268   Roasted Highland Venison with Red Cabbage, Beetroot & a Berry Vinegar Reduction

P270   Prune & Armagnac Soufflé

Amberley Castle

P128   Salad of Beetroot, Fennel, Goat's Curd, Black Olive Reduction, Powder & Pickled Beetroot Sorbet

P130   Roast Loin of Rabbit, Polenta, Black Pudding, Spinach & Root Vegetable Sauce

P132   The Banoffee Pie

Ballyfin

P334   Crubeen, Cheek, Belly, Ears, Carrots, Watercress, Onion

P338   Squab Pigeon, Foie Gras, Black Fig, Pumpkin, Parsnip, Roscoff Onion, Celery

P340   Ballyfin 'Mess'

The Bath Priory Hotel

P192   Plate of Roast & Confit Rabbit, Crispy Ham Hock, Pease Pudding, Mustard Jus Roti

P194   Brixham Turbot Roasted on the Bone, Potato Purée, Red Wine Jus

P196   Coconut Rice Pudding Beignet, Spiced Poached Pineapple, Mango Sorbet

Buckland Manor

P210   Pressing of Pigeon & Foie Gras, Ruby Wine Jelly, Pain d'Epices Crumb & Balsamic Gel

P212   Herb-Crusted Loin of Cotswold Lamb, Braised Shoulder, Honey-Roasted Sweetbreads, Smoked Aubergine Purée & Black Olives

P214   Dark Chocolate Cannelloni, Passion Fruit Curd & Cocoa Ice Cream

Chewton Glen Hotel & Spa

P110   Dressed Dorset Crab, Apple & Celeriac Remoulade, Rye Crisp

P112   Tronçon of Halibut with Capers & Preserved Amalfi Lemons

P114   Tahitian Vanilla & Orange Panna Cotta, Seasonal Berries

Cliff House Hotel

P344   Ardmore Organic Carrots 2011, Cashel Blue, Hazelnuts, Garden Shoots

P348   Annes Grove Pigeon, Red Cabbage, Sheep Snout Apple, Swiss Chard

P350   Irish Coffee Kilbeggan Whiskey & Toasted Barley Ice Cream

The Connaught

P20   Caviar, Fine de Claire Oyster & Bay Scallops with Apple & Cauliflower Emulsion

P22   Milk-fed Lamb from the Pyrenees, Roasted Saddle 'En Rognonnade', Grilled Chuletillas & 'Cailette' of 'Pieds de Paquet', Fondant Japanese Aubergine, Roasting Jus Infused with Cardamom & Confit Citrus from Menton

P24   Pistachio Biscuit, Pink Grapefruit, Greek Yoghurt Sorbet

Farlam Hall

P240   Spinach & Tomato Mousse

P242   Grilled Fillet of Sea Bass with a Sun-blushed Tomato & Basil Risotto

P244   Lemon Mousse with Blueberries, Raspberries & a Raspberry Coulis

The Fat Duck

P64   Snail Porridge, Jabugo Ham

P66   Saddle of Venison, Celeriac & Sauce Poivrade, Civet of Venison with Pearl Barley, Venison & Frankincense Tea

P70   The BFG! (Black Forest Gateau)

Gidleigh Park

P86   River Dart Wild Salmon, Oscietra Caviar, Salmon Jelly, Cucumber, Honey & Soy Vinaigrette, Wasabi & Greek Yoghurt Vinaigrette

P88   Scallops with Celeriac Purée & Soy & Truffle Vinaigrette

P90   Pan-fried Duck Foie Gras with Braised Chicory with Orange & Raisins

P92   Roast Pheasant with Lentils, & Pumpkin & Cumin Purée

P94   Caramel & Cardamom Parfait, Nougatine Milk Chocolate Mousse

Gilpin Lodge Country House

P248   Twice-baked Stichelton Cheese Soufflé, Waldorf Salad, Red Wine Reduction

P250   Pan-fried Fillet of Organic Sea Trout, Fennel, Carrot & Orange Purée, Star Anise Nage

P252   Poached Rhubarb, Pistachio & White Chocolate Powder

Glenapp Castle

P282   Wild Halibut with Chervil Root, Capers, Cockles, Parma Ham & Yellow Mustard Seed

P284   Loin of Hare with Red Cabbage, Brussels Sprouts, Purple Sprouting Broccoli & Sea Purslane

P286   Liquid Dark Chocolate Tart with Peanuts & a Granny Smith Apple Sorbet

Gravetye Manor

P136   Risotto of Native Lobster, Butter Poached Lobster, Crisp Frogs' Legs & Saffron Aioli

P138   Seared Fillet of English Red Mullet, King Prawn & Squid Ink Ravioli, Soft Shell Crab Tempura, Chorizo Oil

P140   Garden Blackberry Soufflé, Elderflower Sorbet & Poached Blackberries

INDEX OF RECIPES

INDEX OF RECIPES

INDEX OF RECIPES

BUCKINGHAM
BOOK PUBLISHING LTD

Other titles available...

Whether it's a compilation of the very best chef talent or a dedicated cookbook of a chef's favourite recipes, discover our highly acclaimed cookbooks featuring some of the world's top chefs.

85 Inspirational Chefs £40

Relais & Châteaux chefs in North America, Mexico and The Carribbean reveal the recipes to their most desirable of dishes.

Chefs at Home £20

A compilation of the most-loved dishes chefs like to cook at home, using their favourite ingredients for quick bite and family recipes.

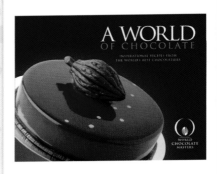

A World of Chocolate £25

A selection of recipes from chocolatiers and pâtissiers around the globe to celebrate the world's favourite ingredient.

Handmade Homemade £20

Celebrating the abundance of fresh produce available on Jersey, *Handmade Homemade* holds a wide collection of recipes that are synonymous with the island.

Creative Chocolate £25

John Slattery, master patissier and chocolatier, shares his secrets for making stunning cakes and chocolate creations for celebrations or everyday.

32 Inspirational Chefs £30

Recipes from Relais & Châteaux in South Africa, Namibia, Tanzania, Mauritius and The Seychelles. Includes traditional dishes, regional fare and home-cooking favourites.

(Prices do not include postage and packaging)

For more information and to view other books in our collection visit...

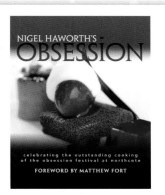

Nigel Haworth's Obsession £35

Michelin-starred Lancashire chef Nigel Haworth celebrates over 11 years of his Obsession festival with this compilation cookbook.

At Home £25

All 63 chefs who have cooked at Nigel Haworth's Obsession festival present their favourite recipes to cook at home. Why not try them too?

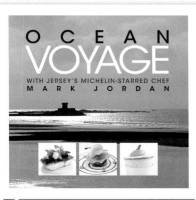

Mark Jordan's Ocean Voyage £30

Michelin-starred Jersey-based chef Mark Jordan shares his most mouthwatering recipes, as served in the Atlantic Hotel's Ocean Restaurant.

A Taste of Summer £20

Enjoy the taste of summer with Brian Turner – including a range of dishes perfect for barbecues, desserts and even the odd rain shower!

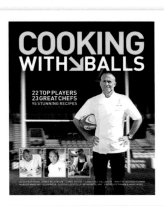

Cooking with Balls £25

Twenty-two of the game's top players leave the line out and step up to the hotplate with 22 of the country's top chefs. Ninety-five recipes all worth a try!

Palm Sized Plan £25

Matt Lovell, top sports nutritionist, outlines easy-to-follow recipes for healthy eating and living, based on palm-sized portions.

(Prices do not include postage and packaging)

www.chefmagazine.co.uk

ELEVATE TALENT

www.all-clad.co.uk